ROBERT LOUIS STEVENSON was born in Edinburgh in 1850 into a distinguished family of engineers and inventors. He gave up his apprenticeship in his father's business at the age of twenty to study law, a profession he hoped would cover for his real ambition to be a writer. Though Stevenson qualified for the Bar in 1875, he never practised, having by that time begun to write poems, essays and articles for publication. In 1876 he made a trip through France by canoe and wrote of it in his first book, *An Inland Voyage* (1878); a later tour in the Cévennes was described in *Travels with a Donkey* (1879). During this period he met Fanny Osbourne, an American ten years his senior who was estranged from her husband. When she secured a divorce in 1879, Stevenson made the long and difficult journey to California in order to marry her. This journey, and their subsequent honeymoon in the Napa Valley, provided the material for two more books, *Across the Plains* (1892) and *The Silverado Squatters* (1883). He returned to Europe with his wife and stepson Lloyd Osbourne in 1880 and began writing *Treasure Island*, which was published in 1883. Its success was a turning-point for Stevenson, whose popularity increased with the publication in 1886 of both *The Strange Case of Dr Jekyll and Mr Hyde* and *Kidnapped*. Stevenson's frail health necessitated a life of travel in search of a congenial climate. He lived in France, the South of England, Switzerland and America before settling with an extended family group, Fanny, Lloyd, Fanny's daughter and grandson, and Stevenson's widowed mother, Margaret, on the South Pacific island of Samoa. Here he wrote *The Master of Ballantrae* (1889), *Catriona* (1893) and the stories collected in *Island Nights' Entertainments* (1893). Two other novels, *St Ives* and *Weir of*

Continued on next page

Hermiston, were unfinished when Stevenson died suddenly of a cerebral haemorrhage on 3 December 1894, aged forty-four.

CLAIRE HARMAN was born in 1957 and read English at university. She was Co-ordinating Editor of *PN Review* in the early 1980s, and is now a freelance writer. Her first book, a biography of the novelist Sylvia Townsend Warner, won the John Llewelyn Rhys prize in 1990.

ROBERT LOUIS STEVENSON

Essays and Poems

Edited by
CLAIRE HARMAN

J. M. Dent Ltd
London
Charles E. Tuttle Co., Inc.
Rutland, Vermont
EVERYMAN'S LIBRARY

Selection and introduction © Claire Harman 1992

This title first published in Everyman in 1992

Typeset at The Spartan Press Ltd,
Lymington, Hants
Printed in Great Britain by
The Guernsey Press Co. Ltd,
Guernsey, C.I.

for J. M. Dent Ltd
Orion Publishing Group
Orion House
5 Upper St Martin's Lane
London
WC2H 9EA

and

Charles E. Tuttle Co., Inc.
28 South Main Street
Rutland, Vermont 05701
USA

British Library Cataloguing-in-Publication Data for this
title is available upon request.

ISBN 0 460 87224 9

Everyman's Library
Reg. U.S. Patent Office

CONTENTS

Contents

POEMS

i. from *A Child's Garden of Verses*

ii. from *Underwoods*

iii. from *Songs of Travel*

iv. from *Ballads*

INTRODUCTION

Robert Louis Stevenson was a writer even before he could write. His first book, a 'History of Moses', was dictated to his mother in 1856, when he was six years old, and 'The Book of Joseph' followed, by the same agency, a year later. All through his childhood he composed stories, wrote accounts of his travels, and made up plays for his toy theatre, 'wallowing in the raw stuff of story-books' (p. 54). When he was only fifteen, Stevenson wrote a short history of the Pentland Rising, a seventeenth-century religious dispute, which was privately printed by his father, and by the time he reached maturity, he had a string of half-made novels and plays in progress. 'Men are born with various manias,' Stevenson wrote in 'My First Book'. 'From my earliest childhood it was mine to make a plaything of imaginary series of events' (p. 209).

Stevenson was born and brought up in Edinburgh's New Town, into a family of distinguished engineers and inventors on one side, and churchmen on the other. He was an only child, with a weak chest and delicate constitution; long days spent ill in bed were wiled away by reading, playing, and living in the dreamy state of private fantasy famously evoked in 'The Land of Counterpane' and other poems from *A Child's Garden of Verses*. As the titles of his earliest works suggest, Louis (the name used by his family) had a pious upbringing; both his parents were devout members of the Church of Scotland and his nurse, Alison Cunningham – or 'Cummy', as she was known –, was a strict Presbyterian. Cummy, who deplored the theatre, and even playing cards, as being inherently wicked, would censor any story in the weekly papers which she felt was turning into a 'regular novel';[1] however, she had remarkable rhetorical powers when it came to describing hell-fire and damnation, and little Louis's imagination – which was made of highly combustible material –

---

[1] Quoted in Daiches, *Robert Louis Stevenson and his World* (Thames & Hudson, 1973), p. 12.

was constantly fired up. Under Cummy's influence, as he wrote later, 'I was sentimental, snivelling, goody, morbidly religious';[2] but he was also an avid reader of Presbyterian Covenanting writers, the style of which he said influenced his own writing profoundly.

It seems remarkable, with hindsight, that Thomas and Margaret Stevenson ever believed Louis would settle into the family engineering business, which had to its credit the Bell Rock and Skerryvore lighthouses, the first 'wave dynamometer', and numerous harbours and bridges. In its early stages, Louis's literary activity seemed to his parents more a general manifestation of intelligence and originality than a threat to his future career; he was encouraged, even indulged, because they expected him to fit into the family pattern. But letters home to his mother, written from Wick, where Louis, aged seventeen, was observing the new harbour works as his father's apprentice, should have shown them which way things were going:

> The thunder at the wall when it first struck – the rush along ever growing higher – the great jet of snow-white spray some forty feet above you – and the 'noise of many waters', the roar, the hiss, the 'shrieking' among the shingle as it fell head over heels at your feet. I watched if it threw the big stones at the wall; but it never moved them.[3]

This is not the language of a young technocrat. During the next three years, while Stevenson was a student of Natural Philosophy at Edinburgh University, the technocrat side of him dwindled to an imperceptible speck: he had formed a private determination to be an author and self-consciously developed his personality along what he considered the appropriate lines, frequenting the least respectable Edinburgh drinking-dens and becoming 'a dead hand with a harridan'.[4] He gave up engineerng in 1871, his swan-song was a paper 'On a New Form of Intermittent Light for Lighthouses', an exemplary bit of leg-work which won him a silver medal from the Royal Scottish Society of Arts. But his experiences at Wick harbour were written up more characteristically in an article for *The Portfolio* called 'On the Enjoyment of Unpleasant Places' (1874).

Stevenson's parents were very wary of his ambitions to be a writer, and only allowed him to give up engineering on condition that he study for the law as a means of livelihood. No doubt they hoped that by the time he qualified Louis would have come to

---

[2]Quoted in Rankin, *Dead Man's Chest* (Faber, 1987), p. 19.
[3]RLS to Mrs Thomas Stevenson, *Letters*, ed. Colvin (1906 edition), Vol. I, p. 23.
[4]Quoted in Rankin, op. cit. p. 58.

see sense, but in fact Louis gave up the law too, as soon as he was admitted to the Scottish Bar in 1875. Another, and much worse, break with his family came in 1873, when, under interrogation by his father, Stevenson admitted that he was an atheist. 'The thunderbolt has fallen with a vengeance now',[5] Stevenson wrote to his closest friend, Charles Baxter; indeed it is hard to imagine how he could have rocked the boat more. A period of great unhappiness and difficulty at home followed, and Louis began to make prolonged trips away, which were to propel him into literary society and into print.

It was on one of these trips, at the house of a cousin in Suffolk, that Stevenson met Fanny Sitwell, an attractive and intelligent married woman who became his 'Madonna' and confidante. She encouraged his literary ambitions rather than his suit, and through her circle of friends, dominated by the influential art critic Sidney Colvin, Stevenson made the important friendships and connections which were to sustain him as a writer through years of exile on account of his health. During this period he met and made friends with Colvin, Edmund Gosse, J. A. Symonds, W. E. Henley and Leslie Stephen, then editor of the *Cornhill Magazine*, which published many of Stevenson's essays. Stevenson was by all accounts a brilliant talker and delightful company; he was keen to live up to his new friends' expectations of him, and experimented widely with different styles in both poetry and prose in a sort of self-regulated apprenticeship. 'I practised to acquire [proficiency], as men learn to whittle, in a wager with myself,' he wrote in an essay 'A College Magazine', recalling this period of his life:

> Whenever I read a book or passage that particularly pleased me, in which a thing was said or an effect rendered with propriety, in which there was either some conspicuous force or some happy distinction in the style, I must sit down at once and set myself to ape that quality. I was unsuccessful, and I knew it; and tried again, and was again unsuccessful and always unsuccessful; but at least in these vain bouts, I got some practice in rhythm, in harmony, in construction and the co-ordination of parts. I have thus played the sedulous ape to Hazlitt, to Lamb, to Wordsworth, to Sir Thomas Browne, to Defoe, to Hawthorne, to Montaigne, to Baudelaire and to Obermann. [. . .] That, like it or not, is the way to learn to write[.][6]

Much in this passage is characteristic of Stevenson's prose; its cards-on-the-table honesty (or the assumption of such), its elegant

[5]*Letters*, Vol. I, p. 40.
[6]'A College Magazine', *Memoirs and Portraits* (1887).

cadences – those of beautifully tailored *talk*; its clarity, and humorous, almost flippant, stoicism. Stevenson was, by any standards, a great stylist, but was always quick to de-bunk the idea that it was easily come by. 'You make no allowance for the slowness with which a man finds and tries to learn his tools,' Stevenson wrote to one of his critics, William Archer, in 1885. In many ways Stevenson never gave up his apprenticeship, and never settled down into predictability or even consistency; 'My theory is that literature must always be most at home in treating movement and change,' he wrote, again to Archer, 'hence I look for them.'[7] It is a nice irony that he was able to coin such a phrase as 'playing the sedulous ape' to express the extent of his debt to other writers. As an epigram it is so effective and original that it has passed into the common stock of language.

The influence of his favourite writers, particularly that of Lamb and Carlyle, hangs over some of Stevenson's early essays, but many of these early works remained unfinished or unpublished. His letters of the period are full of plans for books and stories which came to nothing. Stevenson seemed to be waiting to write a 'great work', specifically a great novel in the familiar Victorian three-volume form: 'I remember I used to look, in those days, upon every three-volume novel with a sort of veneration, as a feat – not possibly of literature – but at least of physical and moral endurance and the courage of Ajax' (p. 210). In fact, Stevenson was part of the movement which supplanted that model, a prototype *fin-de-siècle* 'man of letters', maturing into an age blessed with a multiplicity of literary magazines and periodicals, many of which had a very wide readership. By the time his first book, *An Inland Voyage*, was published in 1878, Stevenson was already well-known as a writer of short stories and quirky, amusing essays, and serial publication was the *sine qua non* of his existence.

An Inland Voyage and Stevenson's next book, *Travels with a Donkey in the Cévennes* (1879) were both humorous write-ups (or send-ups) of experiences undergone, in part at least, to provide himself with grist for the mill. They are bright, charming and very deliberately constructed, unlike the essays of the same period, which form a counterpoint of Stevenson's real preoccupations, fears and discoveries. 'Ordered South' was written in Mentone, where Stevenson was convalescing from a

[7]*Letters*, Vol. I, p. 367.

physical collapse brought about by the rift with his parents. Alone, ill and troubled, he found the essay form could be turned to a new purpose; to re-build himself after the ideological break with his past. In 'Ordered South', and the essays in similar vein which eventually made up his collection *Virginibus Puerisque*, we see Stevenson setting out his own system of belief with a desperate urgency and ardour. It is essentially kind ('violently kind' at times, to use his own description of love), humane, rational, hopeful. With a sort of sublime bloody-mindedness which, like his urgency, is a youthful attribute, he examines his own foibles and feelings, beginning at the beginning in 'Ordered South' with an anatomical account of how we perceive things physically. Stevenson was taking nothing on trust, and the results were often surprising. In 'Child's Play' he concludes that children's imaginations are defective, in 'Beggars' he pins down some painful social truths, in 'The Foreigner at Home' he describes the English (in beautifully-turned examples of their own language) as an alien race. Much of this is humorous, all of it in earnest. Stevenson was a born moralist, and his constant ill-health had impressed on him from an early age the wisdom of living life to the full. What he is urging the reader of his essays to do is look at the familiar with new eyes, and come alive.

These ideas are beautifully and very forcibly expressed in his essay on Walt Whitman, whose poetry had had a profound effect on Stevenson when he first read it as a student. On the face of it, it might seem an unlikely enthusiasm; Whitman was still treated with caution or derision by the reading public at this time, the main stumbling block being his lack of 'literary tact', to use Stevenson's discreet phrase, the very quality that Stevenson himself possessed to the point of surfeit. But what Stevenson admires (almost venerates) in Whitman is the poet's dedication to life and his ambitious, uncompromising use of his art:

> Life is a business we are all apt to mismanage [wrote Stevenson], either living recklessly from day to day, or suffering ourselves to be gulled out of our moments by the inanities of custom. [. . .] It is the duty of the poet to induce [. . .] moments of clear sight. He is the declared enemy of all living by reflex action, of all that is done betwixt sleep and waking, of all the pleasureless pleasurings and imaginary duties in which we coin away our hearts and fritter invaluable years (p. 135).

Although the whole of Stevenson's life was spent in the vicinity of death's door, he avoided references to his illness in his work.

'Ordered South' is an exception, but even here he assumes the slightly flippant tone which always helped him get out of having to appear heroic. The camouflage was so successful that he acquired something of a reputation as a dilettante, and at least one reviewer, William Archer, openly questioned the basis of Stevenson's philosophy of 'aggressive optimism', '[which] is just as distinctly a pose as Wertherism, or Byronism, or Heineism, or Musset-ism, and is in the long run quite as offensive'.[8] A spirited correspondence followed, in which Stevenson wrote to Archer:

> To me, the medicine bottles on my chimney and the blood on my handkerchief are accidents; they do not colour my view of life, as you would know, I think, if you had experience of sickness; they do not exist in my prospect; I would as soon drag them under the eye of my readers as I would mention a pimple I might chance to have (saving your presence) on my posteriors.[9]

This is disingenuous, for Stevenson's illness shaped and refined his remarkable stoicism, awareness of death was the vital factor in his philosophy of 'aggressive optimism', and he was to a great extent at the mercy of circumstance.

An overriding preoccupation was the need to make money, at first, to establish his independence from his parents, and repay their patience and trust, later on, to support his wife and her family. Stevenson married his American lover Fanny Osbourne in 1880, as soon as her divorce was finalised. She had two surviving children from her first marriage, for whom Stevenson was now responsible, and after the death of his father in 1887, he took on the care of his mother as well. This large group of dependents was a considerable financial burden for a young man in his thirties embarked on a literary career, and he strove to make as much money as possible to provide for the future he was certain not to share. In his 'Letter to a Young Gentleman who Proposes to Embrace the Career of Art', Stevenson states baldly that the writer must strive to please his paymasters: 'To live by pleasure is not a high calling; it involves patronage, however veiled, it numbers the artist, however ambitious, along with dancing girls and billiard makers' (p. 205). This view of the artist as prostitute is typical self-deprecation on Stevenson's part, who saves his most extravagant criticism for himself, and dispenses it with the

---

[8] William Archer, 'Robert Louis Stevenson: His Style and Thought'; see *Robert Louis Stevenson: The Critical Heritage* (Routledge, 1981), p. 168.

[9] *Letters*, Vol. I, p. 373.

'lightness of touch' which William Archer found suspect. But by this method, Stevenson was able to indulge his instinct as a lay moralist, without the taint of moralising. He took, as it were, the moral low ground. He also gained an audience, and lucrative deals from magazine publishers, such as the American firm Scribners, who paid him £720 for a series of twelve essays to run one a month from October 1887, with a view to collecting them in book form later on. 'I am like to be a millionaire if this goes on, and be publicly hanged at the social revolution,'[10] Stevenson wrote to Archer, but of course no such arrangement could be the water-tight business deal he recommended to the 'Young Gentleman' of his essay, and, given free rein by Scribners as regards subject-matter, he produced twelve essays which were too diverse to make into a book.

A surprising friendship, given the nature of the two men's æsthetics, sprung up between Stevenson and Henry James some years prior to this, when Stevenson was living in Bournemouth with Fanny. Stevenson had been following the public debate between Henry James and Walter Besant, founder of the Society of Authors, about 'the art of fiction', the very existence of which Stevenson called into question. His essay, 'A Humble Remonstrance', which is directed mostly against James's contention that art should 'compete with life', shows his powers of analysis and argument at their best. He says that the novel is never a 'transcript of life', but a significant simplification of some aspect of it; the very difference of fiction from reality is both 'the method and the meaning of the work' (p. 183). Like all Stevenson's best essays, 'A Humble Remonstrance' is strewn with aphorisms, and contains passages of great rhetoric, such as his distinction between life and art:

Life is monstrous, infinite, illogical, abrupt and poignant; a work of art, in comparison, is neat, finite, self-contained, rational, flowing and emasculate. Life imposes by brute energy, like inarticulate thunder; art catches the ear, among the far louder noises of experience, like an air artificially made by a discreet musician (p. 182).

In this essay, Stevenson develops a theory of composition out of the ideas he put forward in 'Ordered South' and 'Walt Whitman', that 'many elements' go to make 'one [. . .] moment of intense perception' (p. 7). He deconstructs James's idea of the art of

[10]*Letters*, Vol. II, p. 71.

fiction with relish but no antagonism, unlike his sly satirising of the French realists in 'Child's Play'. James, who had not taken to Stevenson on their first meeting, was deeply impressed by 'A Humble Remonstrance', and began a correspondence and an admiring friendship which lasted until Stevenson's death ten years later. When Stevenson's health prompted him to settle on the island of Samoa in the South Seas in the late 1880s, James was one of the few friends not to deplore the removal or criticise out of hand Stevenson's subsequent involvement in Polynesian politics.

There are two poems addressed to Henry James in Stevenson's *Underwoods*, a volume of poetry which slipped into publication in 1887. In a letter to James, Stevenson described his work in progress as follows: 'I am on the start with three volumes, that one of tales [*The Merry Men*], a second one of essays [*Memories and Portraits*], and one – ahem – of verse.'[11] The order and the cough are both deliberately revealing, for *Underwoods* was very close to Stevenson's heart. The first section, in English, contains many poems addressed to friends; it is highly personal and pervasively melancholy in tone. The second section is written in a form of Lallans (Lowland dialect), and consists of bracing lyrics and narratives. In a prefatory note, Stevenson laments the fact that Scots is a dying language, and also takes this as an excuse for the impurities and inconsistencies in his own use of it: 'if it be not pure, alas! what matters it?'[12]

Stevenson wrote poetry all his adult life, but the three collections published in his lifetime were distinctly different. *A Child's Garden of Verses* was written specifically for a young audience and *Ballads* (1893), a collection of three long and two short narrative poems, reflects in form and subject matter Stevenson's desire to write about, and partly *for*, the South Seas in ways which are natural to him, that is, in Scots ways. When Stevenson had said, in his preface to *Underwoods*, 'I would love to have my hour as a native Maker',[13] he had not meant this sort of native. But whereas his poetry was not particularly well-received at home, his ballads were eagerly requested by the Polynesian royalty. *A Child's Garden of Verses*, from which I have included a relatively small selection because of its wide availability, was begun in 1883 in the wake of *Treasure Island*,

[11] *Letters*, Vol. II, p. 48.
[12] RLS, *Complete Poems* (Scribners, 1908), p. 88.
[13] ibid., p. 88.

and continued under extraordinary circumstances while Stevenson was very ill at his home in Hyères, in the south of France. Bed-ridden, with his right arm bound close because of haemorrhaging, and the room darkened on account of an attack of opthalmia, Stevenson asked for paper to be pinned to a board, and wrote out, with his left hand, his famous poems about his childhood. In some respects, this seems a bizarre parody of 'The Land of Counterpane', in others, a continuation and a triumph of imagination over circumstances.

Looking over this selection of Stevenson's prose and verse, every reader will be struck by his unstoppable wittiness. His aphorisms are the very stuff of quotation-books: Marriage is 'a field of battle, not a bed of roses' and 'a sort of friendship recognised by the police' ('Virginibus Puerisque'); and 'Every one lives by selling something' ('Beggars'). Stevenson would have made a formidable barrister, or preacher. As a child, he used to play at being a minister, and though he rejected conventional morality in adult life, Stevenson adhered to his own moral code with a religious fervour. The prayers he wrote for use in his large household at Vailima to fit in with the local custom of gathering together at the end of the day, show the earnest side of this code, stripped of the wit with which he decorated much the same messages in his essays. The prayer 'Sunday' was written on Sunday 2 December 1894, the night before Stevenson's death at the early age of forty-four. Its air of premonition is spurious, for it was anxiety about his cousin Graham Balfour, not himself, that caused Stevenson to reflect on a 'day [. . .] marked for sorrow'. His attitude in the last months of his life is better represented in a letter of September 1894 to his old friend Charles Baxter where he says, 'I have been so long waiting for death, I have unwrapped my thoughts from about life so long, that I have not a filament left to hold by: [. . .] Literally no man has more wholly outlived life than I. And still it is good fun.'[14]

Claire Harman
August 1992

[14]*Letters*, Vol. II, p. 355.

DATES OF FIRST PUBLICATION OF ESSAYS

(with first publication in book form)

'Ordered South': *Macmillan's Magazine*, 30 (May 1874); *Virginibus Puerisque* 1881 [hereafter *VP*].

'The Foreigner at Home': *Cornhill Magazine*, 45 (May 1882); *Memories and Portraits* 1887 [hereafter *M&P*].

'Beggars': *Scribner's Magazine*, 3 (March 1888); *Across the Plains* 1892 [hereafter *AP*].

'Some Portraits by Raeburn': *VP*.

'The Philosophy of Umbrellas': *The Edinburgh University Magazine* (Jan–April 1871); Edinburgh Edition of Stevenson's Works, 1896, vol. 21.

'The Character of Dogs': *The English Illustrated Magazine*, 5 (Feb 1884); *M&P*.

'Child's Play': *Cornhill Magazine*, 38 (Sept 1878); *VP*.

'A Penny Plain and Twopence Coloured': *The Magazine of Art* (April 1884); *M&P*.

'Virginibus Puerisque (I)': *Cornhill Magazine*, 34 (Aug 1876): *VP*.

'On Falling in Love': *Cornhill Magazine*, 35 (Feb 1877); *VP*.

'Some Aspects of Robert Burns': *Cornhill Magazine*, 40 (Oct 1879); *Familiar Studies of Men and Books*, 1882 [hereafter *FS*].

'Samuel Pepys': *Cornhill Magazine*, 44 (July 1881); *FS*.

'Walt Whitman': *FS*.

'Talk and Talkers (I): *Cornhill Magazine*, 45 (April 1882); *M&P*.

'Talk and Talkers (II): *Cornhill Magazine*, 46 (Aug 1882); *M&P*.

'Thomas Stevenson, Civil Engineer': *The Contemporary Review*, 51 (June 1887); *M&P*.

'A Humble Remonstrance': *Longman's Magazine*, 5 (Dec 1884); *M&P*.

'A Chapter on Dreams': *Scribner's Magazine*, 3 (Jan 1888); *AP*.

'Letter to a Young Gentleman who Proposes to Embrace the Career of Art': *Scribner's Magazine*, 4 (Sept 1888); *AP*.

'My First Book: *Treasure Island*': *The Idler*, 6 (Aug 1894); *My First Book*, ed. J. K. Jerome, 1894.

'The Genesis of *The Master of Ballantrae*': Edinburgh Edition of Stevenson's Works (1896), vol. 21.

BIBLIOGRAPHY

ESSAYS (including history and biography). *The Pentland Rising*, 1866; *The Charity Bazaar, an Allegorical Dialogue*, 1868; *An Appeal to the Clergy of the Church of Scotland*, 1875; *Picturesque Notes on Edinburgh*, 1878; *Virginibus Puerisque*, 1881; *Familiar Studies of Men and Books*, 1882; *The Silverado Squatters*, 1883; *Memories and Portraits*, 1887; *Memoir of Fleeming Jenkin*, 1888; *Father Damien*, 1890; *Across the Plains*, 1892; *A Footnote to History*, 1892; *Fables*, 1896; *Essays in the Art of Writing*, 1905; *Lay Morals*, 1911; *Records of a Family of Engineers*, 1912; *The Lantern-Bearers and other Essays*, edited by Jeremy Treglown, 1988.

TRAVEL. *An Inland Voyage*, 1878; *Travels with a Donkey in the Cévennes*, 1879; *The South Seas* (privately 1890), 1900; *Essays of Travel*, 1905; *The Amateur Emigrant*, 1895.

PLAYS (all in collaboration with W. E. Henley). *Deacon Brodie*, 1880; *Admiral Guinea*, 1884; *Beau Austin*, 1884; *Robert Macaire*, 1885. (All privately printed: published in one volume, 1892.)

SHORT STORIES. *New Arabian Nights*, 1882; *More New Arabian Nights* ('The Dynamiter'), 1885; *The Merry Men*, 1887; *Island Nights' Entertainments*, 1893; *Fables*, 1896.

NOVELS (including fiction other than short stories). *Treasure Island*, 1883; *Prince Otto*, 1885; *The Strange Case of Dr Jekyll and Mr Hyde*, 1886; *Kidnapped*, 1886; *The Black Arrow*, 1888; *The Master of Ballantrae*, 1889; *The Wrong Box* (in collaboration with Lloyd Osbourne), 1889; *The Wrecker* (with Lloyd Osbourne), 1892; *Catriona*, 1893; *The Ebb-Tide* (with Lloyd

Osbourne) 1894; *Weir of Hermiston*, 1896; *St Ives* (completed by Q), 1898.

POEMS. *A Child's Garden of Verses*, 1885; *Underwoods*, 1887; *Ballads*, 1890; *Songs of Travel*, 1896.

LETTERS. *Vailima Letters*, 1895; *Letters to his Family and Friends*, 1899; *Robert Louis Stevenson's Letters to Charles Baxter*, 1956.

EDITIONS. The *Edinburgh*, 1894–8, ed. S. Colvin, and in part revised by Stevenson himself; of subsequent editions the *Pentland* and the *Swanston* may be mentioned. The *Tusitala* edition of his works by Lloyd Osbourne, 1923, contains 5 volumes of letters. His *Collected Poems*, edited by J. A. Smith, appeared in 1950 and *The Collected Shorter Fiction*, edited by Peter Stoneley was published in 1991.

BIOGRAPHY AND CRITICISM. Graham Balfour: *The Life of Robert Louis Stevenson*, 1901; F. Swinnerton: *R. L. Stevenson: A Critical Study*, 1914; J. A. Steuart: *Robert Louis Stevenson, Man and Writer*, 1924; D. Daiches: *Robert Louis Stevenson: a Revaluation*, 1946; J. A. Smith (ed.): *Henry James and Robert Louis Stevenson: A Record of Friendship*, 1948; M. Elwin: *The Strange Case of Robert Louis Stevenson*, 1950; R. Kiely: *Robert Louis Stevenson and the Fiction of Adventure*, 1965; E. M. Eigner: *Robert Louis Stevenson and Romantic Tradition*, 1967; M. Myoshi: *The Divided Self*, 1967; J. Pope-Hennessy: *Robert Louis Stevenson*, 1974; J. Calder: *RLS: A Life Study*, 1980; J. Calder (ed.): *Stevenson and Victorian Scotland*, 1981; Paul Maixner (ed.): *Robert Louis Stevenson: The Critical Heritage*, 1981; Andrew Noble (ed.): *Robert Louis Stevenson*, 1983; Barry Menikoff: *Robert Louis Stevenson and the Beach of Falesa: A Study in Victorian Publishing*, 1984; Nicholas Rankin: *Dead Man's Chest: Travels after Robert Louis Stevenson*, 1987; Forbes Macgregor: *Robert Louis Stevenson*, 1989; Richard Holmes: *Footsteps*, 1985; Elaine Showalter: *Sexual Anarchy*, 1990.

BIBLIOGRAPHY: Col. W. F. Prideaux, C.S.I.: *Bibliography of Robert Louis Stevenson*, 1903, revised, 1917; G. L. Mackay: *A Stevenson Library: Catalogue of a Collection of Writings about Robert Louis Stevenson formed by Edwin J. Beinecke*, 6 vols., 1954–1961; A. D. Wainwright: *Robert Louis Stevenson, A Catalogue of the Henry E. Girstley Stevenson Collection of the*

Stevenson Section of the Morris L. Parrish Collection of Victorian Novelists and Items from Other Collections in the Department of Rare Books and Special Collections of the Princeton University Library, 1971; R. G. Swearingen: *The Prose Writings of Robert Louis Stevenson,* 1980; J. R. Hammond: *A Robert Louis Stevenson Companion: A Guide to the Novels,* 1984; Alanna Knight: *The Robert Louis Stevenson Treasury,* 1985.

Other Stevenson titles published in Everyman

Travels with a Donkey, An Inland Voyage, The Silverado Squatters
Introduced by Trevor Royle (1984, reissued 1992)

The Master of Ballantrae and Weir of Hermiston
Introduced by Claire Harman (1992)

The Strange Case of Dr Jekyll and Mr Hyde and Other Stories
Selected and introduced by Claire Harman (1992)

ESSAYS

ORDERED SOUTH

By a curious irony of fate, the places to which we are sent when health deserts us are often singularly beautiful. Often, too, they are places we have visited in former years, or seen briefly in passing by, and kept ever afterwards in pious memory; and we please ourselves with the fancy that we shall repeat many vivid and pleasurable sensations, and take up again the thread of our enjoyment in the same spirit as we let it fall. We shall now have an opportunity of finishing many pleasant excursions, interrupted of yore before our curiosity was fully satisfied. It may be that we have kept in mind, during all these years, the recollection of some valley into which we have just looked down for a moment before we lost sight of it in the disorder of the hills; it may be that we have lain awake at night, and agreeably tantalised ourselves with the thought of corners we had never turned, or summits we had all but climbed: we shall now be able, as we tell ourselves, to complete all these unfinished pleasures, and pass beyond the barriers that confined our recollections.

The promise is so great, and we are all so easily led away when hope and memory are both in one story, that I daresay the sick man is not very inconsolable when he receives sentence of banishment, and is inclined to regard his ill-health as not the least fortunate accident of his life. Nor is he immediately undeceived. The stir and speed of the journey, and the restlessness that goes to bed with him as he tries to sleep between two days of noisy progress, fever him, and stimulate his dull nerves into something of their old quickness and sensibility. And so he can enjoy the faint autumnal splendour of the landscape, as he sees hill and plain, vineyard and forest, clad in one wonderful glory of fairy gold, which the first great winds of winter will transmute, as in the fable, into withered leaves. And so too he can enjoy the admirable brevity and simplicity of such little glimpses of country and country ways as flash upon him through the windows of the train; little glimpses that have a character all their own; sights seen as a travelling swallow might see them from the wing, or Iris as she went abroad over the land on some Olympian errand. Here and there, indeed, a few children huzzah and wave their hands to the express; but for the most part it is an interruption too brief and isolated to attract much notice; the sheep do not cease from browsing; a girl sits balanced on the projecting tiller of a canal boat, so precariously that it seems as if a fly or the splash of a leaping fish would be enough to overthrow the dainty equilibrium, and yet all these hundreds of tons of coal and wood and iron have been precipitated roaring past her very ear, and there is not a start, not a tremor, not a turn of the averted head, to indicate that she has been even conscious of its passage. Herein, I think, lies the chief attraction of railway travel. The speed is so easy, and the train disturbs so little the scenes through which it takes us, that our heart becomes full of the placidity and stillness of the country; and while the body is borne forward in the flying chain of carriages, the thoughts alight, as the humour moves them, at unfrequented stations; they make haste up the poplar alley that leads toward the town; they are left behind with the signalman as, shading his eyes with his hand, he watches the long train sweep away into the golden distance.

Moreover, there is still before the invalid the shock of wonder and delight with which he will learn that he has passed the indefinable line that separates South from North. And this is an uncertain moment; for sometimes the consciousness is forced upon him early, on the occasion of some slight association, a colour, a flower, or a scent; and sometimes not until, one fine morning, he wakes up with the southern sunshine peeping through the *persiennes,* and the southern patois confusedly audible below the windows. Whether it come early or late, however, this pleasure will not end with the anticipation, as do so many others of the same family. It will leave him wider awake than it found him, and give a new significance to all he may see for many days to come. There is something in the mere name of the South that carries enthusiasm along with it. At the sound of the word, he pricks up his ears; he becomes as anxious to seek out beauties and to get by heart the permanent lines and character of the landscape, as if he had been told that it was all his own – an estate out of which he had been kept unjustly, and which he was now to receive in free and full possession. Even those who have never been there before feel as if they had been; and everybody goes comparing, and seeking for the familiar, and finding it with such ecstasies of recognition, that one would think they were coming home after a weary absence, instead of travelling hourly farther abroad.

It is only after he is fairly arrived and settled down in his chosen corner, that the invalid begins to understand the change that has befallen him. Everything about him is as he had remembered, or as he had anticipated. Here, at his feet, under his eyes, are the olive gardens and the blue sea. Nothing can change the eternal magnificence of form of the naked Alps behind Mentone; nothing, not even the crude curves of the railway, can utterly deform the suavity of contour of one bay after another along the whole reach of the Riviera. And of all this, he has only a cold head knowledge that is divorced from enjoyment. He recognises with his intelligence that this thing and that thing is beautiful, while in his heart of hearts he has to confess that it is not beautiful for him. It is in vain that he spurs his discouraged spirit; in vain that he chooses out points of view, and stands there, looking with all his eyes, and waiting for some return of the pleasure that he remembers in other days, as the sick folk may have awaited the coming of the angel at the pool of Bethesda. He is like an enthusiast leading about with him a stolid, indifferent tourist. There is some one by who is out of sympathy with the scene, and is not moved up to the measure of the occasion; and that some one is himself. The world is disenchanted for him. He seems to himself to touch things with muffled hands, and to see them through a veil. His life becomes a palsied fumbling after notes that are silent when he has found and struck them. He cannot recognise that this phlegmatic and unimpressionable body with which he now goes burthened, is the same that he knew heretofore so quick and delicate and alive.

He is tempted to lay the blame on the very softness and amenity of the climate, and to fancy that in the rigours of the winter at home, these dead emotions would revive and flourish. A longing for the brightness and silence of fallen snow seizes him at such times. He is homesick for the hale rough weather; for the tracery of the frost upon his window-panes at morning, the reluctant descent of the first flakes, and the white roofs relieved against the sombre sky. And yet the stuff of which these yearnings are made, is of the flimsiest: if but the thermometer fall a little below its ordinary Mediterranean level, or a wind come down from the snow-clad Alps behind, the spirit of his fancies changes upon the instant, and many a doleful vignette of the grim wintry streets at home returns to him, and begins to haunt his memory. The hopeless, huddled attitude of tramps in doorways; the flinching gait of barefoot children on the icy pavement; the sheen of the rainy streets towards afternoon; the meagre anatomy of the poor defined by the clinging of wet garments; the high canorous note of the North-easter on days when the very houses seem to stiffen with cold: these, and such as these, crowd back upon him, and mockingly substitute themselves for the fanciful winter scenes with which he had pleased himself a while before. He cannot be glad enough that he is where he is. If only the others could be there also; if only those tramps could lie down for a little in the sunshine, and those children warm their feet, this once, upon a kindlier earth; if only there were no cold anywhere, and no nakedness, and no hunger; if only it were as well with all men as it is with him!

For it is not altogether ill with the invalid after all. If it is only rarely that anything penetrates vividly into his numbed spirit, yet, when anything does, it brings with it a joy that is all the more poignant for its very rarity. There is something pathetic in these occasional returns of a glad activity of heart. In his lowest hours he will be stirred and awakened by many such; and they will spring perhaps from very trivial sources; as a friend once said to me, the 'spirit of delight' comes often on small wings. For the pleasure that we take in beautiful nature is essentially capricious. It comes sometimes when we least look for it; and sometimes, when we expect it most certainly, it leaves us to gape joylessly for days together, in the very homeland of the beautiful. We may have passed a place a thousand times and one; and on the thousand and second it will be transfigured, and stand forth in a certain splendour of reality from the dull circle of surroundings; so that we see it 'with a child's first pleasure', as Wordsworth saw the daffodils by the lake side. And if this falls out capriciously with the healthy, how much more so with the invalid. Some day he will find his first violet, and be lost in pleasant wonder, by what alchemy the cold earth of the clods, and the vapid air and rain, can be transmuted into colour so rich and odour so touchingly sweet. Or perhaps he may see a group of washerwomen relieved, on a spit of shingle, against the blue sea, or a meeting of flower-gatherers in the tempered daylight of an olive-garden; and something significant or monumental in the grouping, something in the harmony of faint colour that is always characteristic of the dress of these southern women, will come home to him unexpectedly, and awake in him that satisfaction with which we tell ourselves that we are the richer by one more beautiful experience. Or it may be something even slighter: as when the opulence of the sunshine, which somehow gets lost and fails to produce its effect on the large scale, is suddenly revealed to him by the chance isolation – as he changes the position of his sunshade – of a yard or two of roadway with its stones and weeds. And then, there is no end to the infinite variety of the olive-yards themselves. Even the colour is indeterminate and continually shifting: now you would say it was green, now grey, now blue; now tree stands above tree, like 'cloud on cloud', massed into filmy indistinctness; and now, at the wind's will, the whole sea of foliage is shaken and broken up with little momentary silverings and shadows. But every one sees the world in his own way. To some the glad moment may have arrived on other provocations; and their recollection may be most vivid of the stately gait of women carrying burthens on their heads; of tropical effects, with canes and naked rock and sunlight; of the relief of cypresses; of the troubled, busy-looking groups of sea-pines, that seem always as if they were being wielded and swept together by a whirlwind; of the air coming, laden with virginal perfumes, over the myrtles and the scented underwood; of the empurpled hills standing up, solemn and sharp, out of the green-gold air of the east at evening.

There go many elements, without doubt, to the making of one such moment of intense perception; and it is on the happy agreement of these many elements, on the harmonious vibration of many nerves, that the whole delight of the moment must depend. Who can forget how, when he has chanced upon some attitude of complete restfulness, after long uneasy rolling to and fro on grass or heather, the whole fashion of the landscape has been changed for him, as though the sun had just broken forth, or a great artist had only then completed, by some cunning touch, the composition of the picture? And not only a change of posture – a snatch of perfume, the sudden singing of a bird, the freshness of some pulse of air from an invisible sea, the light shadow of a travelling cloud, the merest nothing that sends a little shiver along the most infinitesimal nerve of a man's body – not one of the least of these but has a hand somehow in the general effect, and brings some refinement of its own into the character of the pleasure we feel.

And if the external conditions are thus varied and subtle, even more so are those within our own bodies. No man can find out the world, says Solomon, from beginning to end, because the world is in his heart; and so it is impossible for any of us to understand, from beginning to end, that agreement of harmonious circumstances that creates in us the highest pleasure of admiration, precisely because some of these circumstances are hidden from us for ever in the constitution of our own bodies. After we have reckoned up all that we can see or hear or feel, there still remains to be taken into account some sensibility more delicate than usual in the nerves affected, or some exquisite refinement in the architecture of the brain, which is indeed to the sense of the beautiful as the eye or the ear to the sense of hearing or sight. We admire splendid views and great pictures; and yet what is truly admirable is rather the mind within us, that gathers together these scattered details for its delight, and makes out of certain colours, certain distributions of graduated light and darkness, that intelligible whole which alone we call a picture or a view. Hazlitt, relating in one of his essays how he went on foot from one great man's house to another's in search of works of art, begins suddenly to triumph over these noble and wealthy owners, because he was more capable of enjoying their costly possessions than they were; because they had paid the money and he had received the pleasure. And the occasion is a fair one for self-complacency. While the one man was working to be able to buy the picture, the other was working to be able to enjoy the picture. An inherited aptitude will have been diligently improved in either case; only the one man has made for himself a fortune, and the other has made for himself a living spirit. It is a fair occasion for self-complacency, I repeat, when the event shows a man to have chosen the better part, and laid out his life more wisely, in the long run, than those who have credit for most wisdom. And yet even this is not a good unmixed; and like all other possessions, although in a less degree, the possession of a brain that has been thus improved and cultivated, and made into the prime organ of a man's enjoyment, brings with it certain inevitable cares and disappointments. The happiness of such an one comes to depend greatly upon those fine shades of sensation that heighten and harmonise the coarser elements of beauty. And thus a degree of nervous prostration, that to other men would be hardly disagreeable, is enough to overthrow for him the whole fabric of his life, to take, except at rare moments, the edge off his pleasures, and to meet him wherever he goes with failure, and the sense of want, and disenchantment of the world and life.

It is not in such numbness of spirit only that the life of the invalid resembles a premature old age. Those excursions that he had promised himself to finish, prove too long or too arduous for his feeble body; and the barrier-hills are as impassable as ever. Many a white town that sits far out on the promontory, many a comely fold of wood on the mountain side, beckons and allures his imagination day after day, and is yet as inaccessible to his feet as the clefts and gorges of the clouds. The sense of distance grows upon him wonderfully; and after some feverish efforts and the fretful uneasiness of the first few days, he falls contentedly in with the restrictions of his weakness. His narrow round becomes pleasant and familiar to him as the cell to a contented prisoner. Just as he has fallen already out of the mid race of active life, he now falls out of the little eddy that circulates in the shallow waters of the sanatorium. He sees the country people come and go about their everyday affairs, the foreigners stream out in goodly pleasure parties; the stir of man's activity is all about him, as he suns himself inertly in some sheltered corner; and he looks on with a patriarchal impersonality of interest, such as a man may feel when he pictures to himself the fortunes of his remote descendants, or the robust old age of the oak he has planted overnight.

In this falling aside, in this quietude and desertion of other men, there is no inharmonious prelude to the last quietude and desertion of the grave; in this dullness of the senses there is a gentle preparation for the final insensibility of death. And to him the idea of mortality comes in a shape less violent and harsh than is its wont, less as an abrupt catastrophe than as a thing of infinitesimal gradation, and the last step on a long decline of way. As we turn to and fro in bed, and every moment the movements grow feebler and smaller and the attitude more restful and easy, until sleep overtakes us at a stride and we move no more, so desire after desire leaves him; day by day his strength decreases, and the circle of his activity grows ever narrower; and he feels, if he is to be thus tenderly weaned from the passion of life, thus gradually inducted into the slumber of death, that when at last the end comes, it will come quietly and fitly. If anything is to reconcile poor spirits to the coming of the last enemy, surely it should be such a mild approach as this; not to hale us forth with violence, but to persuade us from a place we have no further pleasure in. It is not so much, indeed, death that approaches as life that withdraws and withers up from round about him. He has outlived his own usefulness, and almost his own enjoyment; and if there is to be no recovery; if never again will he be young and strong and passionate, if the actual present shall be to him always like a thing read in a book or remembered out of the far-away past; if, in fact, this be veritably nightfall, he will not wish greatly for the continuance of a twilight that only strains and disappoints the eyes, but steadfastly await the perfect darkness. He will pray for Medea: when she comes, let her either rejuvenate or slay.

And yet the ties that still attach him to the world are many and kindly. The sight of children has a significance for him such as it may have for the aged also, but not for others. If he has been used to feel humanely, and to look upon life somewhat more widely than from the narrow loophole of personal pleasure and advancement, it is strange how small a portion of his thoughts will be changed or embittered by this proximity of death. He knows that already, in English counties, the sower follows the ploughman up the face of the field, and the rooks follow the sower; and he knows also that he may not live to go home again and see the corn spring and ripen, and be cut down at last, and brought home with gladness. And yet the future of this harvest, the continuance of drought or the coming of rain unseasonably, touch him as sensibly as ever. For he has long been used to wait with interest the issue of events in which his own concern was nothing; and to be joyful in a plenty, and sorrowful for a famine, that did not increase or diminish, by one half loaf, the equable sufficiency of his own supply. Thus there remain unaltered all the disinterested hopes for mankind and a better future which have been the solace and inspiration of his life. These he has set beyond the reach of any fate that only menaces himself; and it makes small difference whether he die five thousand years, or five thousand and fifty years, before the good epoch for which he faithfully labours. He has not deceived himself; he has known from the beginning that he followed the pillar of fire and cloud, only to perish himself in the wilderness, and that it was reserved for others to enter joyfully into possession of the land. And so, as everything grows greyer and quieter about him, and slopes towards extinction, these unfaded visions accompany his sad decline, and follow him, with friendly voices and hopeful words, into the very vestibule of death. The desire of love or of fame scarcely moved him, in his days of health, more strongly than these generous aspirations move him now; and so life is carried forward beyond life, and a vista kept open for the eyes of hope, even when his hands grope already on the face of the impassable.

Lastly, he is bound tenderly to life by the thought of his friends; or shall we not say rather, that by their thought for him, by their unchangeable solicitude and love, he remains woven into the very stuff of life, beyond the power of bodily dissolution to undo? In a thousand ways will he survive and be perpetuated. Much of Etienne de la Boetie survived during all the years in which Montaigne continued to converse with him on the pages of the ever-delightful essays. Much of what was truly Goethe was dead already when he revisited places that knew him no more, and found no better consolation than the promise of his own verses, that soon he too would be at rest. Indeed, when we think of what it is that we most seek and cherish, and find most pride and pleasure in calling ours, it will sometimes seem to us as if our friends, at our decease, would suffer loss more truly than ourselves. As a monarch who should care more for the outlying colonies he knows on the map or through the report of his vicegerents, than for the trunk of his empire under his eyes at home, are we not more concerned about the shadowy life that we have in the hearts of others, and that portion in their thoughts and fancies which, in a certain far-away sense, belongs to us, than about the real knot of our identity – that central metropolis of self, of which alone we are immediately aware – or the diligent service of arteries and veins and infinitesimal activity of ganglia, which we know (as we know a proposition in Euclid) to be the source and substance of the whole? At the death of every one whom we love, some fair and honourable portion of our existence falls away, and we are dislodged from one of these dear provinces; and they are not, perhaps, the most fortunate who survive a long series of such impoverishments, till their life and influence narrow gradually into the meagre limit of their own spirits, and death, when he comes at last, can destroy them at one blow.

NOTE. To this essay I must in honesty append a word or two of qualification; for this is one of the points on which a slightly greater age teaches us a slightly different wisdom:

A youth delights in generalities, and keeps loose from particular obligations; he jogs on the footpath way, himself pursuing butterflies, but courteously lending his applause to the advance of the human species and the coming of the kingdom of justice and love. As he grows older, he begins to think more narrowly of man's action in the general, and perhaps more arrogantly of his own in the particular. He has not that same unspeakable trust in what he would have done had he been spared, seeing finally that that would have been little; but he has a far higher notion of the blank that he will make by dying. A young man feels himself one too many in the world; his is a painful situation: he has no calling; no obvious utility; no ties, but to his parents, and these he is sure to disregard. I do not think that a proper allowance has been made for this true cause of suffering in youth; but by the mere fact of a prolonged existence, we outgrow either the fact or else the feeling. Either we become so callously accustomed to our own useless figure in the world, or else – and this, thank God, in the majority of cases – we so collect about us the interest or the love of our fellows, so multiply our effective part in the affairs of life, that we need to entertain no longer the question of our right to be.

And so in the majority of cases, a man who fancies himself dying, will get cold comfort from the very youthful view expressed in this essay. He, as a living man, has some to help, some to love, some to correct; it may be, some to punish. These duties cling, not upon humanity, but upon the man himself. It is he, not another, who is one woman's son and a second woman's husband and a third woman's father. That life which began so small, has now grown, with a myriad filaments, into the lives of others. It is not indispensable; another will take the place and shoulder the discharged responsibility; but the better the man and the nobler his purposes, the more will he be tempted to regret the extinction of his powers and the deletion of his personality. To have lived a generation, is not only to have grown at home in that perplexing medium, but to have assumed innumerable duties. To die at such an age, has, for all but the entirely base, something of the air of a betrayal. A man does not only reflect upon what he might have done in a future that is never to be his; but beholding himself so early a deserter from the fight, he eats his heart for the good he might have done already. To have been so useless and now to lose all hope of being useful any more – there it is that death and memory assail him. And even if mankind shall go on, founding heroic cities, practising heroic virtues, rising steadily from strength to strength; even if his work shall be fulfilled, his friends consoled, his wife remarried by a better than he; how shall this alter, in one jot, his estimation of a career which was his only business in this world, which was so fitfully pursued, and which is now so ineffectively to end?

THE FOREIGNER AT HOME

This is no my ain house;
I ken by the biggin' o't.

Two recent books, one by Mr Grant White on England, one on France by the diabolically clever Mr Hillebrand, may well have set people thinking on the divisions of races and nations. Such thoughts should arise with particular congruity and force to inhabitants of that United Kingdom, peopled from so many different stocks, babbling so many different dialects, and offering in its extent such singular contrasts, from the busiest over-population to the unkindliest desert, from the Black Country to the Moor of Rannoch. It is not only when we cross the seas that we go abroad; there are foreign parts of England; and the race that has conquered so wide an empire has not yet managed to assimilate the islands whence she sprang. Ireland, Wales, and the Scottish mountains still cling, in part, to their old Gaelic speech. It was but the other day that English triumphed in Cornwall, and they still show in Mousehole, on St Michael's Bay, the house of the last Cornish-speaking woman. English itself, which will now frank the traveller through the most of North America, through the greater South Sea Islands, in India, along much of the coast of Africa, and in the ports of China and Japan, is still to be heard, in its home country, in half a hundred varying stages of transition. You may go all over the States, and – setting aside the actual intrusion and influence of foreigners, negro, French, or Chinese – you shall scarce meet with so marked a difference of accent as in the forty miles between Edinburgh and Glasgow, or of dialect as in the hundred miles between Edinburgh and Aberdeen. Book English has gone round the world, but at home we still preserve the racy idioms of our fathers, and every county, in some parts every dale, has its own quality of speech, vocal or verbal. In like manner, local custom and prejudice, even local religion and local law, linger on into the latter end of the nineteenth century – *imperia in imperio,* foreign things at home.

In spite of these promptings to reflection, ignorance of his neighbours is the character of the typical John Bull. His is a domineering nature, steady in fight, imperious to command, but neither curious nor quick about the life of others. In French colonies, and still more in the Dutch, I have read that there is an immediate and lively contact between the dominant and the dominated race, that a certain sympathy is begotten, or at the least a transfusion of prejudices, making life easier for both. But the Englishman sits apart, bursting with pride and ignorance. He figures among his vassals in the hour of peace with the same disdainful air that led him on to victory. A passing enthusiasm for some foreign art or fashion may deceive the world, it cannot impose upon his intimates. He may be amused by a foreigner as by a monkey, but he will never condescend to study him with any patience. Miss Bird, an authoress with whom I profess myself in love, declares all the viands of Japan to be uneatable – a staggering pretension. So, when the Prince of Wales's marriage was celebrated at Mentone by a dinner to the Mentonese, it was proposed to give them solid English fare – roast beef and plum pudding, and no tomfoolery. Here we have either pole of the Britannic folly. We will not eat the food of any foreigner; nor, when we have the chance, will we suffer him to eat of it himself. The same spirit inspired Miss Bird's American missionaries, who had come thousands of miles to change the faith of Japan, and openly professed their ignorance of the religions they were trying to supplant.

I quote an American in this connection without scruple. Uncle Sam is better than John Bull, but he is tarred with the English stick. For Mr Grant White the States are the New England States and nothing more. He wonders at the amount of drinking in London; let him try San Francisco. He wittily reproves English ignorance as to the status of women in America; but has he not himself forgotten Wyoming? The name Yankee, of which he is so tenacious, is used over the most of the great Union as a term of reproach. The Yankee States, of which he is so staunch a subject, are but a drop in the bucket. And we find in his book a vast virgin ignorance of the life and prospects of America; every view partial, parochial, not raised to the horizon; the moral feeling proper, at the largest, to a clique of States; and the whole scope and atmosphere not American, but merely Yankee. I will go far beyond him in reprobating the assumption and the incivility of my countryfolk to their cousins from beyond the sea; I grill in my blood over the silly rudeness of our newspaper articles; and I do not know where to look when I find myself in company with an American and see my countrymen unbending to him as to a performing dog. But in the case of Mr Grant White example were better than precept. Wyoming is, after all, more readily accessible to Mr White than Boston to the English, and the New England self-sufficiency no better justified than the Britannic.

It is so, perhaps, in all countries; perhaps in all, men are most ignorant of the foreigners at home. John Bull is ignorant of the States; he is probably ignorant of India; but considering his opportunities, he is far more ignorant of countries nearer his own door. There is one country, for instance – its frontier not so far from London, its people closely akin, its language the same in all essentials with the English – of which I will go bail he knows nothing. His ignorance of the sister kingdom cannot be described; it can only be illustrated by anecdote. I once travelled with a man of plausible manners and good intelligence, – a University man, as the phrase goes, – a man, besides, who had taken his degree in life and knew a thing or two about the age we live in. We were deep in talk, whirling between Peterborough and London; among other things, he began to describe some piece of legal injustice he had recently encountered, and I observed in my innocence that things were not so in Scotland. 'I beg your pardon,' said he, 'this is a matter of law.' He had never heard of the Scots law; nor did he choose to be informed. The law was the same for the whole country, he told me roundly; every child knew that. At last, to settle matters, I explained to him that I was a member of a Scottish legal body, and had stood the brunt of an examination in the very law in question. Thereupon he looked me for a moment full in the face and dropped the conversation. This is a monstrous instance, if you like, but it does not stand alone in the experience of Scots.

England and Scotland differ, indeed, in law, in history, in religion, in education, and in the very look of nature and men's faces, not always widely, but always trenchantly. Many particulars that struck Mr Grant White, a Yankee, struck me, a Scot, no less forcibly; he and I felt ourselves foreigners on many common provocations. A Scotchman may tramp the better part of Europe and the United States, and never again receive so vivid an impression of foreign travel and strange lands and manners as on his first excursion into England. The change from a hilly to a level country strikes him with delighted wonder. Along the flat horizon there arise the frequent venerable towers of churches. He sees at the end of airy vistas the revolution of the windmill sails. He may go where he pleases in the future; he may see Alps, and Pyramids, and lions; but it will be hard to beat the pleasure of that moment. There are, indeed, few merrier spectacles than that of many windmills bickering together in a fresh breeze over a woody country; their halting- alacrity of movement, their pleasant business, making bread all day with uncouth gesticulations, their air, gigantically human, as of a creature half alive, put a spirit of romance into the tamest landscape. When the Scotch child sees them first he falls immediately in love; and from that time forward windmills keep turning in his dreams. And so, in their degree, with every feature of the life and landscape. The warm, habitable age of towns and hamlets, the green, settled, ancient look of the country; the lush hedgerows, stiles, and privy pathways in the fields; the sluggish, brimming rivers; chalk and smock-frocks; chimes of bells and the rapid, pertly-sounding English speech – they are all new to the curiosity; they are all set to English airs in the child's story that he tells himself at night. The sharp edge of novelty wears off; the feeling is scotched, but I doubt whether it is ever killed. Rather it keeps returning, ever the more rarely and strangely, and even in scenes to which you have been long accustomed suddenly awakes and gives a relish to enjoyment or heightens the sense of isolation.

One thing especially continues unfamiliar to the Scotchman's eye – the domestic architecture, the look of streets and buildings; the quaint, venerable age of many, and the thin walls and warm colouring of all. We have, in Scotland, far fewer ancient buildings, above all in country places; and those that we have are all of hewn or harled masonry. Wood has been sparingly used in their construction; the window-frames are sunken in the wall, not flat to the front, as in England; the roofs are steeper-pitched; even a hill farm will have a massy, square, cold and permanent appearance. English houses, in comparison, have the look of cardboard toys, such as a puff might shatter. And to this the Scotchman never becomes used. His eye can never rest consciously on one of these brick houses – rickles of brick, as he might call them – or on one of these flat-chested streets, but he is instantly reminded where he is, and instantly travels back in fancy to his home. 'This is no my ain house; I ken by the biggin' o't.' And yet perhaps it is his own, bought with his own money, the key of it long polished in his pocket; but it has not yet been, and never will be, thoroughly adopted by his imagination; nor does he cease to remember that, in the whole length and breadth of his native country, there was no building even distantly resembling it.

But it is not alone in scenery and architecture that we count England foreign. The constitution of society, the very pillars of the empire, surprise and even pain us. The dull, neglected peasant, sunk in matter, insolent, gross and servile, makes a startling contrast with our own long-legged, long-headed, thoughtful, Bible-quoting ploughman. A week or two in such a place as Suffolk leaves the Scotchman gasping. It seems incredible that within the boundaries of his own island a class should have been thus forgotten. Even the educated and intelligent, who hold our own opinions and speak in our own words, yet seem to hold them with a difference or from another reason, and to speak on all things with less interest and conviction. The first shock of English society is like a cold plunge. It is possible that the Scot comes looking for too much, and to be sure his first experiment will be in the wrong direction. Yet surely his complaint is grounded; surely the speech of Englishmen is too often lacking in generous ardour, the better part of the man too often withheld from the social commerce, and the contact of mind with mind evaded as with terror. A Scotch peasant will talk more liberally out of his own experience. He will not put you by with conversational counters and small jests; he will give you the best of himself, like one interested in life and man's chief end. A Scotchman is vain, interested in himself and others, eager for sympathy, setting forth his thoughts and experience in the best light. The egotism of the Englishman is self-contained. He does not seek to proselytise. He takes no interest in Scotland or the Scotch, and, what is the unkindest cut of all, he does not care to justify his indifference. Give him the wages of going on and being an Englishman, that is all he asks; and in the meantime, while you continue to associate, he would rather not be reminded of your baser origin. Compared with the grand, tree-like self-sufficiency of his demeanour, the vanity and curiosity of the Scot seem uneasy, vulgar and immodest. That you should continually try to establish human and serious relations, that you should actually feel an interest in John Bull, and desire and invite a return of interest from him, may argue something more awake and lively in your mind, but it still puts you in the attitude of a suitor and a poor relation. Thus even the lowest class of the educated English towers over a Scotchman by the head and shoulders.

Different indeed is the atmosphere in which Scotch and English youth begin to look about them, come to themselves in life, and gather up those first apprehensions which are the material of future thought and, to a great extent, the rule of future conduct. I have been to school in both countries, and I found, in the boys of the North, something at once rougher and more tender, at once more reserve and more expansion, a greater habitual distance chequered by glimpses of a nearer intimacy, and on the whole wider extremes of temperament and sensibility. The boy of the South seems more wholesome, but less thoughtful; he gives himself to games as to a business, striving to excel, but is not readily transported by imagination; the type remains with me as cleaner in mind and body, more active, fonder of eating, endowed with a lesser and a less romantic sense of life and of the future, and more immersed in present circumstances. And certainly, for one thing, English boys are younger for their age. Sabbath observance makes a series of grim, and perhaps serviceable, pauses in the tenor of Scotch boyhood – days of great stillness and solitude for the rebellious mind, when in the dearth of books and play, and in the intervals of studying the Shorter Catechism, the intellect and senses prey upon and test each other. The typical English Sunday, with the huge midday dinner and the plethoric afternoon, leads perhaps to different results. About the very cradle of the Scot there goes a hum of metaphysical divinity; and the whole of two divergent systems is summed up, not merely speciously, in the two first questions of the rival catechisms, the English tritely inquiring, 'What is your name?' the Scottish striking at the very roots of life with, 'What is the chief end of man?' and answering nobly, if obscurely, 'To glorify God and to enjoy Him for ever.' I do not wish to make an idol of the Shorter Catechism; but the fact of such a question being asked opens to us Scotch a great field of speculation; and the fact that it is asked of all of us, from the peer to the ploughboy, binds us more nearly together. No Englishman of Byron's age, character and history, would have had patience for long theological discussions on the way to fight for Greece; but the daft Gordon blood and the Aberdonian schooldays kept their influence to the end. We have spoken of the material conditions; nor need much more be said of these: of the land lying everywhere more exposed, of the wind always louder and bleaker, of the black, roaring winters, of the gloom of high-lying, old stone cities, imminent on the windy seaboard; compared with the level streets, the warm colouring of the brick, the domestic quaintness of the architecture, among which English children begin to grow up and come to themselves in life. As the stage of the University approaches, the contrast becomes more express. The English lad goes to Oxford or Cambridge; there, in an ideal world of gardens, to lead a semi-scenic life, costumed, disciplined and drilled by proctors. Nor is this to be regarded merely as a stage of education; it is a piece of privilege besides, and a step that separates him further from the bulk of his compatriots. At an earlier age the Scottish lad begins his greatly different experience of crowded class-rooms, of a gaunt quadrangle, of a bell hourly booming over the traffic of the city to recall him from the public-house where he has been lunching, or the streets where he has been wandering fancy-free. His college life has little of restraint, and nothing of necessary gentility. He will find no quiet clique of the exclusive, studious and cultured; no rotten borough of the arts. All classes rub shoulders on the greasy benches. The raffish young gentleman in gloves must measure his scholarship with the plain, clownish laddie from the parish school. They separate, at the session's end, one to smoke cigars about a watering-place, the other to resume the labours of the field beside his peasant family. The first muster of a college class in Scotland is a scene of curious and painful interest; so many lads, fresh from the heather, hang round the stove in cloddish embarrassment, ruffled by the presence of their smarter comrades, and afraid of the sound of their own rustic voices. It was in these early days, I think, that Professor Blackie won the affection of his pupils, putting these uncouth, umbrageous students at their ease with ready human geniality. Thus, at least, we have a healthy democratic atmosphere to breathe in while at work; even when there is no cordiality there is always a juxtaposition of the different classes, and in the competition of study the intellectual power of each is plainly demonstrated to the other. Our tasks ended, we of the North go forth as freemen into the humming, lamplit city. At five o'clock you may see the last of us hiving from the college gates, in the glare of the shop windows, under the green glimmer of the winter sunset. The frost tingles in our blood; no proctor lies in wait to intercept us; till the bell sounds again, we are the masters of the world; and some portion of our lives is always Saturday, *la trêve de Dieu*.

Nor must we omit the sense of the nature of his country and his country's history gradually growing in the child's mind from story and from observation. A Scottish child hears much of shipwreck, outlying iron skerries, pitiless breakers, and great sea-lights;

much of heathery mountains, wild clans, and hunted Covenanters. Breaths come to him in song of the distant Cheviots and the ring of foraying hoofs. He glories in his hard-fisted forefathers, of the iron girdle and the handful of oatmeal, who rode so swiftly and lived so sparely on their raids. Poverty, ill-luck, enterprise, and constant resolution are the fibres of the legend of his country's history. The heroes and kings of Scotland have been tragically fated; the most marking incidents in Scottish history – Flodden, Darien, or the Forty-five – were still either failures or defeats; and the fall of Wallace and the repeated reverses of the Bruce combine with the very smallness of the country to teach rather a moral than a material criterion for life. Britain is altogether small, the mere taproot of her extended empire; Scotland, again, which alone the Scottish boy adopts in his imagination, is but a little part of that, and avowedly cold, sterile and unpopulous. It is not so for nothing. I once seemed to have perceived in an American boy a greater readiness of sympathy for lands that are great, and rich, and growing, like his own. It proved to be quite otherwise: a mere dumb piece of boyish romance, that I had lacked penetration to divine. But the error serves the purpose of my argument; for I am sure, at least, that the heart of young Scotland will be always touched more nearly by paucity of number and Spartan poverty of life.

So we may argue, and yet the difference is not explained. That Shorter Catechism which I took as being so typical of Scotland, was yet composed in the city of Westminster. The division of races is more sharply marked within the borders of Scotland itself than between the countries. Galloway and Buchan, Lothian and Lochaber, are like foreign parts; yet you may choose a man from any of them, and, ten to one, he shall prove to have the headmark of a Scot. A century and a half ago, the Highlander wore a different costume, spoke a different language, worshipped in another church, held different morals, and obeyed a different social constitution from his fellow-countrymen either of the south or north. Even the English, it is recorded, did not loathe the Highlander and the Highland costume as they were loathed by the remainder of the Scotch. Yet the Highlander felt himself a Scot. He would willingly raid into the Scotch lowlands; but his courage failed him at the border, and he regarded England as a perilous, unhomely land. When the Black Watch, after years of foreign service, returned to Scotland, veterans leaped out and kissed the earth at Port Patrick. They had been in Ireland, stationed among men of their own race and language, where they were well liked and treated with affection; but it was the soil of Galloway that they kissed at the extreme end of the hostile lowlands, among a people who did not understand their speech, and who had hated, harried, and hanged them since the dawn of history. Last, and perhaps most curious, the sons of chieftains were often educated on the continent of Europe. They went abroad speaking Gaelic; they returned speaking, not English, but the broad dialect of Scotland. Now, what idea had they in their minds when they thus, in thought, identified themselves with their ancestral enemies? What was the sense in which they were Scotch and not English, or Scotch and not Irish? Can a bare name be thus influential on the minds and affections of men, and a political aggregation blind them to the nature of facts? The story of the Austrian Empire would seem to answer, No; the far more galling business of Ireland clenches the negative from nearer home. Is it common education, common morals, a common language or a common faith, that join men into nations? There were practically none of these in the case we are considering.

The fact remains: in spite of the difference of blood and language, the Lowlander feels himself the sentimental countryman of the Highlander. When they meet abroad, they fall upon each other's necks in spirit; even at home there is a kind of clannish intimacy in their talk. But from his compatriot in the south the Lowlander stands consciously apart. He has had a different training; he obeys different laws; he makes his will in other terms, is otherwise divorced and married; his eyes are not at home in an English landscape or with English houses; his ear continues to remark the English speech; and even though his tongue acquire the Southern knack, he will still have a strong Scotch accent of the mind.

BEGGARS

I

In a pleasant, airy, up-hill country, it was my fortune when I was young to make the acquaintance of a certain beggar. I call him beggar, though he usually allowed his coat and his shoes (which were open-mouthed, indeed) to beg for him. He was the wreck of an athletic man, tall, gaunt, and bronzed; far gone in consumption, with that disquieting smile of the mortally stricken on his face; but still active afoot, still with the brisk military carriage, the ready military salute. Three ways led through this piece of country; and as I was inconstant in my choice, I believe he must often have awaited me in vain. But often enough, he caught me; often enough, from some place of ambush by the roadside, he would spring suddenly forth in the regulation attitude, and launching at once into his inconsequential talk, fall into step with me upon my farther course. 'A fine morning, sir, though perhaps a trifle inclining to rain. I hope I see you well, sir. Why, no, sir, I don't feel as hearty myself as I could wish, but I am keeping about my ordinary. I am pleased to meet you on the road, sir. I assure you I quite look forward to one of our little conversations.' He loved the sound of his own voice inordinately, and though (with something too off-hand to call servility) he would always hasten to agree with anything you said, yet he could never suffer you to say it to an end. By what transition he slid to his favourite subject I have no memory; but we had never been long together on the way before he was dealing, in a very military manner, with the English poets. 'Shelley was a fine poet, sir, though a trifle atheistical in his opinions. His Queen Mab, sir, is quite an atheistical work. Scott, sir, is not so poetical a writer. With the works of Shakespeare I am not so well acquainted, but he was a fine poet. Keats — John Keats, sir — he was a very fine poet.' With such references, such trivial criticism, such loving parade of his own knowledge, he would beguile the road, striding forward up-hill, his staff now clapped to the ribs of his deep, resonant chest, now swinging in the air with the remembered jauntiness of the private soldier; and all the while his toes looking out of his boots, and his shirt looking out of his elbows, and death looking out of his smile, and his big, crazy frame shaken by accesses of cough.

He would often go the whole way home with me: often to borrow a book, and that book always a poet. Off he would march, to continue his mendicant rounds, with the volume slipped into the pocket of his ragged coat; and although he would sometimes keep it quite a while, yet it came always back again at last, not much the worse for its travels into beggardom. And in this way, doubtless, his knowledge grew and his glib, random criticism took a wider range. But my library was not the first he had drawn upon: at our first encounter, he was already brimful of Shelley and the atheistical Queen Mab, and 'Keats – John Keats, sir.' And I have often wondered how he came by these acquirements; just as I often wondered how he fell to be a beggar. He had served through the Mutiny – of which (like so many people) he could tell practically nothing beyond the names of places, and that it was 'difficult work, sir,' and very hot, or that so-and-so was 'a very fine commander, sir.' He was far too smart a man to have remained a private; in the nature of things, he must have won his stripes. And yet here he was without a pension. When I touched on this problem, he would content himself with diffidently offering me advice. 'A man should be very careful when he is young, sir. If you'll excuse me saying so, a spirited young gentleman like yourself, sir, should be very careful. I was perhaps a trifle inclined to atheistical opinions myself.' For (perhaps with a deeper wisdom than we are inclined in these days to admit) he plainly bracketed agnosticism with beer and skittles.

Keats – John Keats, sir – and Shelley were his favourite bards. I cannot remember if I tried him with Rossetti; but I know his taste to a hair, and if ever I did, he must have doted on that author. What took him was a richness in the speech; he loved the exotic, the unexpected word; the moving cadence of a phrase; a vague sense of emotion (about nothing) in the very letters of the alphabet: the romance of language. His honest head was very nearly empty, his intellect like a child's; and when he read his favourite authors, he can almost never have understood what he was reading. Yet the taste was not only genuine, it was exclusive; I tried in vain to offer him novels; he would none of them, he cared for nothing but romantic language that he could not understand.

The case may be commoner than we suppose. I am reminded of a lad who was laid in the next cot to a friend of mine in a public hospital, and who was no sooner installed than he sent out (perhaps with his last pence) for a cheap Shakespeare. My friend pricked up his ears; fell at once in talk with his new neighbour, and was ready, when the book arrived, to make a singular discovery. For this lover of great literature understood not one sentence out of twelve, and his favourite part was that of which he understood the least – the inimitable, mouth-filling rodomontade of the ghost in *Hamlet*. It was a bright day in hospital when my friend expounded the sense of this beloved jargon: a task for which I am willing to believe my friend was very fit, though I can never regard it as an easy one. I know indeed a point or two, on which I would gladly question Mr Shakespeare, that lover of big words, could he revisit the glimpses of the moon, or could I myself climb backward to the spacious days of Elizabeth. But in the second case, I should most likely pretermit these questionings, and take my place instead in the pit at the Blackfriars, to hear the actor in his favourite part, playing up to Mr Burbage, and rolling out – as I seem to hear him – with a ponderous gusto –

Unhousel'd, disappointed, unanel'd.

What a pleasant chance, if we could go there in a party! and what a surprise for Mr Burbage, when the ghost received the honours of the evening!

As for my old soldier, like Mr Burbage and Mr Shakespeare, he is long since dead; and now lies buried, I suppose, and nameless and quite forgotten, in some poor city graveyard. – but not for me, you brave heart, have you been buried! For me, you are still afoot, tasting the sun and air, and striding southward. By the groves of Comiston and beside the Hermitage of Braid, by the Hunters' Tryst, and where the curlews and plovers cry around Fairmilehead, I see and hear you, stalwartly carrying your deadly sickness, cheerfully discoursing of uncomprehended poets.

II

The thought of the old soldier recalls that of another tramp, his counterpart. This was a little, lean, and fiery man, with the eyes of a dog and the face of a gipsy; whom I found one morning encamped with his wife and children and his grinder's wheel, beside the burn of Kinnaird. To this beloved dell I went, at that time, daily; and daily the knife-grinder and I (for as long as his tent continued pleasantly to interrupt my little wilderness) sat on two stones, and smoked, and plucked grass, and talked to the tune of the brown water. His children were mere whelps, they fought and bit among the fern like vermin. His wife was a mere squaw; I saw her gather brush and tend the kettle, but she never ventured to address her lord while I was present. The tent was a mere gipsy hovel, like a sty for pigs. But the grinder himself had the fine self-sufficiency and grave politeness of the hunter and the savage; he did me the honours of this dell, which had been mine but the day before, took me far into the secrets of his life, and used me (I am proud to remember) as a friend.

Like my old soldier, he was far gone in the national complaint. Unlike him, he had a vulgar taste in letters; scarce flying higher than the story papers; probably finding no difference, certainly seeking none, between Tannahill and Burns; his noblest thoughts, whether of poetry or music, adequately embodied in that somewhat obvious ditty,

> Will ye gang, lassie, gang
> To the braes o' Balquidder.

– which is indeed apt to echo in the ears of Scottish children, and to him, in view of his experience, must have found a special directness of address. But if he had no fine sense of poetry in letters, he felt with a deep joy the poetry of life. You should have heard him speak of what he loved; of the tent pitched beside the talking water; of the stars overhead at night; of the blest return of morning, the peep of day over the moors, the awaking birds among the birches; how he abhorred the long winter shut in cities; and with what delight, at the return of the spring, he once more pitched his camp in the living out-of-doors. But we were a pair of tramps; and to you, who are doubtless sedentary and a consistent first-class passenger in life, he would scarce have laid himself so open; – to you, he might have been content to tell his story of a ghost – that of a buccaneer with his pistols as he lived – whom he had once encountered in a seaside cave near Buckie; and that would have been enough, for that would have shown you the mettle of the man. Here was a piece of experience solidly and livingly built up in words, here was a story created, *teres atque rotundus*.

And to think of the old soldier, that lover of the literary bards! He had visited stranger spots than any seaside cave; encountered men more terrible than any spirit; done and dared and suffered in that incredible, unsung epic of the Mutiny War; played his part with the field force of Delhi, beleaguering and beleaguered; shared in that enduring, savage anger and contempt of death and decency that, for long months together, bedevil'd and inspired the army; was hurled to and fro in the battle-smoke of the assault; was there, perhaps, where Nicholson fell; was there when the attacking column, with hell upon every side, found the soldier's enemy – strong drink, and the lives of tens of thousands trembled in the scale, and the fate of the flag of England staggered. And of all this he had no more to say than 'hot work, sir,' or 'the army suffered a great deal, sir,' or 'I believe General Wilson, sir, was not very highly thought of in the papers.' His life was naught to him, the vivid pages of experience quite blank: in words his pleasure lay – melodious, agitated words – printed words, about that which he had never seen and was connatally incapable of comprehending. We have here two temperaments face to face; both untrained, unsophisticated, surprised (we may say) in the egg; both boldly charactered: – that of the artist, the lover and artificer of words; that of the maker, the seeër, the lover and forger of experience. If the one had a daughter and the other had a son, and these married, might not some illustrious writer count descent from the beggar-soldier and the needy knife-grinder?

III

Every one lives by selling something, whatever be his right to it. The burglar sells at the same time his own skill and courage and my silver plate (the whole at the most moderate figure) to a Jew receiver. The bandit sells the traveller an article of prime necessity: that traveller's life. And as for the old soldier, who stands for central mark to my capricious figures of eight, he dealt in a speciality; for he was the only beggar in the world who ever gave me pleasure for my money. He had learned a school of manners in the barracks and had the sense to cling to it, accosting strangers with a regimental freedom, thanking patrons with a merely regimental difference, sparing you at once the tragedy of his position and the embarrassment of yours. There was not one hint about him of the beggar's emphasis, the outburst of revolting gratitude, the rant and cant, the 'God bless you, Kind, Kind gentleman,' which insults the smallness of your alms by disproportionate vehemence, which is so notably false, which would be so unbearable if it were true. I am sometimes tempted to suppose this reading of the beggar's part, a survival of the old days when Shakespeare was intoned upon the stage and mourners keened beside the death-bed; to think that we cannot now accept these strong emotions unless they be uttered in the just note of life; nor (save in the pulpit) endure these gross conventions. They wound us, I am tempted to say, like mockery; the high voice of keening (as it yet lingers on) strikes in the face of sorrow like a buffet; and the rant and cant of the staled beggar stirs in us a shudder of disgust. But the fact disproves these amateur opinions. The beggar lives by his knowledge of the average man. He knows what he is about when he bandages his head, and hires and drugs a babe, and poisons life with *Poor Mary Ann* or *Long, long ago*; he knows what he is about when he loads the critical ear and sickens the nice conscience with intolerable thanks; they know what they are about, he and his crew, when they pervade the slums of cities, ghastly parodies of suffering, hateful parodies of gratitude. This trade can scarce be called an imposition; it has been so blown upon with exposures; it flaunts its fraudulence so nakedly. We pay them as we pay those who show us, in huge exaggeration, the monsters of our drinking-water; or those who daily predict the fall of Britain. We pay them for the pain they inflict, pay them, and wince, and hurry on. And truly there is nothing that can shake the conscience like a beggar's thanks; and that polity in which such protestations can be purchased for a shilling, seems no scene for an honest man.

Are there, then, we may be asked, no genuine beggars? And the answer is, Not one. My old soldier was a humbug like the rest; his ragged boots were, in the stage phrase, properties; whole boots were given him again and again, and always gladly accepted; and the next day, there he was on the road as usual, with toes exposed. His boots were his method; they were the man's trade; without his boots he would have starved; he did not live by charity, but by appealing to a gross taste in the public, which loves the limelight on the actor's face, and the toes out of the beggar's boots. There is a true poverty, which no one sees: a false and merely mimetic poverty, which usurps its place and dress, and lives and above all drinks, on the fruits of the usurpation. The true poverty does not go into the streets; the banker may rest assured, he has never put a penny in its hand. The self-respecting poor beg from each other; never from the rich. To live in the frock-coated ranks of life, to hear canting scenes of gratitude rehearsed for twopence, a man might suppose that giving was a thing gone out of fashion; yet it goes forward on a scale so great as to fill me with surprise. In the houses of the working class, all day long there will be a foot upon the stair; all day long there will be a knocking at the doors; beggars come, beggars go, without stint, hardly with intermission, from morning till night; and meanwhile, in the same city and but a few streets off, the castles of the rich stand unsummoned. Get the tale of any honest tramp, you will find it was always the poor who helped him; get the truth from any workman who has met misfortunes, it was always next door that he would go for help, or only with such exceptions as are said to prove a rule; look at the course of the mimetic beggar, it is through the poor quarters that he trails his passage, showing his bandages to every window, piercing even to the attics with his nasal song. Here is a remarkable state of things in our Christian commonwealths, that the poor only should be asked to give.

IV

There is a pleasant tale of some worthless, phrasing Frenchman, who was taxed with ingratitude: '*Il faut savoir garder l'indépendance du cœur,*' cried he. I own I feel with him. Gratitude without familiarity, gratitude otherwise than as a nameless element in a friendship, is a thing so near to hatred that I do not care to split the difference. Until I find a man who is pleased to receive obligations, I shall continue to question the tact of those who are eager to confer them. What an art it is, to give, even to our nearest friends! and what a test of manners, to receive! How, upon either side, we smuggle away the obligation, blushing for each other; how bluff and dull we make the giver; how hasty, how falsely cheerful, the receiver! And yet an act of such difficulty and distress between near friends, it is supposed we can perform to a total stranger and leave the man transfixed with grateful emotions. The last thing you can do to a man is to burthen him with an obligation, and it is what we propose to begin with! But let us not be deceived: unless he is totally degraded to his trade, anger jars in his inside, and he grates his teeth at our gratuity.

We should wipe two words from our vocabulary: gratitude and charity. In real life, help is given out of friendship, or it is not valued; it is received from the hand of friendship, or it is resented. We are all too proud to take a naked gift: we must seem to pay it, if in nothing else, then with the delights of our society. Here, then, is the pitiful fix of the rich man; here is that needle's eye in which he stuck already in the days of Christ, and still sticks to-day, firmer, if possible, than ever: that he has the money and lacks the love which should make his money acceptable. Here and now, just as of old in Palestine, he has the rich to dinner, it is with the rich that he takes his pleasure: and when his turn comes to be charitable, he looks in vain for a recipient. His friends are not poor, they do not want; the poor are not his friends, they will not take. To whom is he to give? Where to find — note this phrase — the Deserving Poor? Charity is (what they call) centralised; offices are hired; societies founded, with secretaries paid or unpaid: the hunt of the Deserving Poor goes merrily forward. I think it will take more than a merely human secretary to disinter that character. What! a class that is to be in want from no fault of its own, and yet greedily eager to receive from strangers; and to be quite respectable, and at the same time quite devoid of self-respect; and play the most delicate part of friendship, and yet never be seen; and wear the form of man, and yet fly in the face of all the laws of human nature: — and all this, in the hope of getting a belly-god Burgess through a needle's eye! O, let him stick, by all means: and let his polity tumble in the dust; and let his epitaph and all his literature (of which my own works begin to form no inconsiderable part) be abolished even from the history of man! For a fool of this monstrosity of dullness, there can be no salvation: and the fool who looked for the elixir of life was an angel of reason to the fool who looks for the Deserving Poor!

V

And yet there is one course which the unfortunate gentleman may take. He may subscribe to pay the taxes. There were the true charity, impartial and impersonal, cumbering none with obligation, helping all. There were a destination for loveless gifts; there were the way to reach the pocket of the deserving poor, and yet save the time of secretaries! But, alas! there is no colour of romance in such a course; and people nowhere demand the picturesque so much as in their virtues.

SOME PORTRAITS BY RAEBURN

Through the initiative of a prominent citizen, Edinburgh has been in possession, for some autumn weeks, of a gallery of paintings of singular merit and interest. They were exposed in the apartments of the Scotch Academy; and filled those who are accustomed to visit the annual spring exhibition, with astonishment and a sense of incongruity. Instead of the too common purple sunsets, and pea-green fields, and distances executed in putty and hog's lard, he beheld, looking down upon him from the walls of room after room, a whole army of wise, grave, humorous, capable, or beautiful countenances, painted simply and strongly by a man of genuine instinct. It was a complete act of the Human Drawing-Room Comedy. Lords and ladies, soldiers and doctors, hanging judges, and heretical divines, a whole generation of good society was resuscitated; and the Scotchman of to-day walked about among the Scotchmen of two generations ago. The moment was well chosen, neither too late nor too early. The people who sat for these pictures are not yet ancestors, they are still relations. They are not yet altogether a part of the dusty past, but occupy a middle distance within cry of our affections. The little child who looks wonderingly on his grandfather's watch in the picture, is now the veteran Sheriff *emeritus* of Perth. And I hear a story of a lady who returned the other day to Edinburgh, after an absence of sixty years: 'I could see none of my old friends,' she said, 'until I went into the Raeburn Gallery, and found them all there.'

It would be difficult to say whether the collection was more interesting on the score of unity or diversity. Where the portraits were all of the same period, almost all of the same race, and all from the same brush, there could not fail to be many points of similarity. And yet the similarity of the handling seems to throw into more vigorous relief those personal distinctions which Raeburn was so quick to seize. He was a born painter of portraits.

He looked people shrewdly between the eyes, surprised their manners in their face, and had possessed himself of what was essential in their character before they had been many minutes in his studio. What he was so swift to perceive, he conveyed to the canvas almost in the moment of conception. He had never any difficulty, he said, about either hands or faces. About draperies or light or composition, he might see room for hesitation or afterthought. But a face or a hand was something plain and legible. There were no two ways about it, any more than about the person's name. And so each of his portraits are not only (in Doctor Johnson's phrase, aptly quoted on the catalogue) 'a piece of history,' but a piece of biography into the bargain. It is devoutly to be wished that all biography were equally amusing, and carried its own credentials equally upon its face. These portraits are racier than many anecdotes, and more complete than many a volume of sententious memoirs. You can see whether you get a stronger and clearer idea of Robertson the historian from Raeburn's palette or Dugald Stewart's woolly and evasive periods. And then the portraits are both signed and countersigned. For you have, first, the authority of the artist, whom you recognise as no mean critic of the looks and manners of men; and next you have the tacit acquiescence of the subject, who sits looking out upon you with inimitable innocence, and apparently under the impression that he is in a room by himself. For Raeburn could plunge at once through all the constraint and embarrassment of the sitter, and present the face, clear, open, and intelligent as at the most disengaged moments. This is best seen in portraits where the sitter is represented in some appropriate action: Neil Gow with his fiddle, Doctor Spens shooting an arrow, or Lord Bannatyne hearing a cause. Above all, from this point of view, the portrait of Lieutenant-Colonel Lyon is notable. A strange enough young man, pink, fat about the lower part of the face, with a lean forehead, a narrow nose and a fine nostril, sits with a drawing-board upon his knees. He has just paused to render himself account of some difficulty, to disentangle some complication of line or compare neighbouring values. And there, without any perceptible wrinkling, you have rendered for you exactly the fixed look in the eyes, and the unconscious compression of the mouth, that befit and signify an effort of the kind. The whole pose, the whole expression, is absolutely direct and simple. You are ready to take your oath to it that Colonel Lyon had no idea he was sitting for his picture, and thought of nothing in the world besides his own occupation of the moment.

Although the collection did not embrace, I understand, nearly the whole of Raeburn's works, it was too large not to contain some that were indifferent, whether as works of art or as portraits. Certainly the standard was remarkably high, and was wonderfully maintained, but there were one or two pictures that might have been almost as well away – one or two that seemed wanting in salt, and some that you can only hope were not successful likenesses. Neither of the portraits of Sir Walter Scott, for instance, were very agreeable to look upon. You do not care to think that Scott looked quite so rustic and puffy. And where is that peaked forehead which, according to all written accounts and many portraits, was the distinguishing characteristic of his face? Again, in spite of his own satisfaction and in spite of Dr John Brown, I cannot consider that Raeburn was very happy in hands. Without doubt, he could paint one if he had taken the trouble to study it; but it was by no means always that he gave himself the trouble. Looking round one of these rooms hung about with his portraits, you were struck with the array of expressive faces, as compared with what you may have seen in looking round a room full of living people. But it was not so with the hands. The portraits differed from each other in face perhaps ten times as much as they differed by the hand; whereas with living people the two go pretty much together; and where one is remarkable, the other will almost certainly not be commonplace.

One interesting portrait was that of Duncan of Camperdown. He stands in uniform beside a table, his feet slightly straddled with the balance of an old sailor, his hand poised upon a chart by the finger tips. The mouth is pursed, the nostril spread and drawn up, the eyebrows very highly arched. The cheeks lie along the jaw in folds of iron, and have the redness that comes from much exposure to salt sea winds. From the whole figure, attitude and countenance, there breathes something precise and decisive, something alert, wiry, and strong. You can understand, from the look of him, that sense, not so much of humour, as of what is grimmest and driest in pleasantry which inspired his address before the fight at Camperdown. He had just overtaken the Dutch fleet under Admiral de Winter. 'Gentlemen,' says he, 'you see a severe winter approaching; I have only to advise you to keep up a good fire.' Somewhat of this same spirit of adamantine drollery must have supported him in the days of the mutiny at the Nore, when he lay off the Texel with his own flagship, the *Venerable*, and only one other vessel, and kept up active signals, as though he had a powerful fleet in the offing, to intimidate the Dutch.

Another portrait which irresistibly attracted the eye, was the half-length of Robert M'Queen, of Braxfield, Lord Justice-Clerk. If I know gusto in painting when I see it, this canvas was painted with rare enjoyment. The tart, rosy, humorous look of the man, his nose like a cudgel, his face resting squarely on the jowl, has been caught and perpetuated with something that looks like brotherly love. A peculiarly subtle expression haunts the lower part, sensual and incredulous, like that of a man tasting good Bordeaux with half a fancy it has been somewhat too long uncorked. From under the pendulous eyelids of old age the eyes look out with a half-youthful, half frosty twinkle. Hands, with no pretence to distinction, are folded on the judge's stomach. So sympathetically is the character conceived by the portrait painter, that it is hardly possible to avoid some movement of sympathy on the part of the spectator. And sympathy is a thing to be encouraged, apart from humane considerations, because it supplies us with the materials for wisdom. It is probably more instructive to entertain a sneaking kindness for any unpopular person, and, among the rest, for Lord Braxfield, than to give way to perfect raptures of moral indignation against his abstract vices. He was the last judge on the Scotch bench to employ the pure Scotch idiom. His opinions, thus given in Doric, and conceived in a lively, rugged, conversational style, were full of point and authority. Out of the bar, or off the bench, he was a convivial man, a lover of wine, and one who 'shone peculiarly' at tavern meetings. He has left behind him an unrivalled reputation for rough and cruel speech; and to this day his name smacks of the gallows. It was he who presided at the trials of Muir and Skirving in 1793 and 1794; and his appearance on these occasions was scarcely cut to the pattern of to-day. His summing up on Muir began thus – the reader must supply for himself 'the growling, blacksmith's voice' and the broad Scotch accent: 'Now this is the question for consideration – Is the panel guilty of sedition, or is he not? Now, before this can be answered, two things must be attended to that require no proof: *First,* that the British constitution is the best that ever was since the creation of the world, and it is not possible to make it better.' It's a pretty fair start, is it not, for a political trial? A little later, he has occasion to refer to the relations of Muir with 'those wretches,' the French. 'I never liked the French all my days,' said his lordship, 'but now I hate them.' And yet a little further on: 'A government in any country should be like a corporation; and in this country it is made up of the landed interest, which alone has a right to be represented. As for the rabble who have nothing but personal property, what hold has the nation of them? They may pack up their property on their backs, and leave the country in the twinkling of an eye.' After having made profession of sentiments so cynically anti-popular as these, when the trials were at an end, which was generally about midnight, Braxfield would walk home to his house in George Square with no better escort than an easy conscience. I think I see him getting his cloak about his shoulders, and, with perhaps a lantern in one hand, steering his way along the streets in the mirk January night. It might have been that very day that Skirving had defied him in these words: 'It is altogether unavailing for your lordship to menace me; for I have long learned to fear not the face of man;' and I can fancy, as Braxfield reflected on the number of what he called *Grumbletonians* in Edinburgh, and of how many of them must bear special malice against so upright and inflexible a judge, nay, and might at that very moment be lurking in the mouth of a dark close with hostile intent – I can fancy that he indulged in a sour smile, as he reflected that he also was not especially afraid of men's faces or men's fists, and had hitherto found no occasion to embody this insensibility in heroic words. For if he was an inhumane old gentleman (and I am afraid it is a fact that he was inhumane), he was also perfectly intrepid. You may look into the queer face of that portrait for as long as you will, but you will not see any hole or corner for timidity to enter in.

Indeed, there would be no end to this paper if I were even to name half of the portraits that were remarkable for this execution, or interesting by association. There was one picture of Mr Wardrop, of Torbane Hill, which you might palm off upon most laymen as a Rembrandt; and close by, you saw the white head of John Clerk, of Eldin, that country gentleman who, playing with pieces of cork on his own dining-table, invented modern naval warfare. There was that portrait of Neil Gow, to sit for which the old fiddler walked daily through the streets of Edinburgh arm in arm with the Duke of Athole. There was good Harry Erskine, with his satirical nose and upper lip, and his mouth just open for a witticism to pop out; Hutton the geologist, in quakerish raiment, and looking altogether trim and narrow, and as if he cared more about fossils than young ladies; full-blown John Robieson, in hyperbolical red dressing-gown, and, every inch of him, a fine old man of the world; Constable the publisher, upright beside a table, and bearing a corporation with commercial dignity; Lord Bannatyne hearing a cause, if ever anybody heard a cause since the world began; Lord Newton just awakened from clandestine slumber on the bench; and the second President Dundas, with every feature so fat that he reminds you, in his wig, of some droll old court officer in an illustrated nursery story-book, and yet all these fat features instinct with meaning, the flat lips curved and compressed, the nose combining somehow the dignity of a beak with the good nature of a bottle, and the very double chin with an air of intelligence and insight. And all these portraits are so pat and telling, and look at you so spiritedly from the walls, that, compared with the sort of living people one sees about the streets, they are as bright new sovereigns to fishy and obliterated sixpences. Some disparaging thoughts upon our own generation could hardly fail to present themselves; but it is perhaps only the *sacer vates* who is wanting; and we also, painted by such a man as Carolus Duran, may look in holiday immortality upon our children and grandchildren.

Raeburn's young women, to be frank, are by no means of the same order of merit. No one, of course, could be insensible to the presence of Miss Janet Suttie or Mrs Campbell of Possil. When things are as pretty as that, criticism is out of season. But, on the whole, it is only with women of a certain age that he can be said to have succeeded, in at all the same sense as we say he succeeded with men. The younger women do not seem to be made of good flesh and blood. They are not painted in rich and unctuous touches. They are dry and diaphanous. And although young ladies in Great Britain are all that can be desired of them, I would fain hope they are not quite so much of that as Raeburn would have us believe. In all these pretty faces, you miss character, you miss fire, you miss that spice of the devil which is worth all the prettiness in the world; and what is worst of all, you miss sex. His young ladies are not womanly to nearly the same degree as his men are masculine; they are so in a negative sense; in short, they are the typical young ladies of the male novelist.

To say truth, either Raeburn was timid with young and pretty sitters; or he had stupefied himself with sentimentalities; or else (and here is about the truth of it) Raeburn and the rest of us labour under an obstinate blindness in one direction, and know very little more about women after all these centuries than Adam when he first saw Eve. This is all the more likely, because we are by no means so unintelligent in the matter of old women. There are some capital old women, it seems to me, in books written by men. And Raeburn has some, such as Mrs Colin Campbell, of Park, or the anonymous 'Old lady with a large cap,' which are done in the same frank, perspicacious spirit as the very best of his men. He could look into their eyes without trouble; and he was not withheld, by any bashful sentimentalism, from recognising what he saw there and unsparingly putting it down upon the canvas. But where people cannot meet without some confusion and a good deal of involuntary humbug, and are occupied, for as long as they are together, with a very different vein of thought, there cannot be much room for intelligent study nor much result in the shape of genuine comprehension. Even women, who understand men so well for practical purposes, do not know them well enough for the purposes of art. Take even the very best of their male creations, take Tito Melema, for instance, and you will find he has an equivocal air, and every now and again remembers he has a comb at the back of his head. Of course, no woman will believe this, and many men will be so very polite as to humour their incredulity.

THE PHILOSOPHY OF UMBRELLAS[1]

It is wonderful to think what a turn has been given to our whole
Society by the fact that we live under the sign of Aquarius, – that
our climate is essentially wet. A mere arbitrary distinction, like the
walking-swords of yore, might have remained the symbol of
foresight and respectability, had not the raw mists and dropping
showers of our island pointed the inclination of Society to another
exponent of those virtues. A ribbon of the Legion of Honour or a
string of medals may prove a person's courage; a title may prove
his birth; a professorial chair his study and acquirement; but it
is the habitual carriage of the umbrella that is the stamp of
Respectability. The umbrella has become the acknowledged
index of social position.

Robinson Crusoe presents us with a touching instance of the
hankering after them inherent in the civilised and educated mind.
To the superficial, the hot suns of Juan Fernandez may sufficiently
account for his quaint choice of a luxury; but surely one who had
borne the hard labour of a seaman under the tropics for all these
years could have supported an excursion after goats or a peaceful
constitutional arm in arm with the nude Friday. No, it was not
this: the memory of a vanished respectability called for some
outward manifestation, and the result was – an umbrella. A pious
castaway might have rigged up a belfry and solaced his Sunday
mornings with the mimicry of church-bells; but Crusoe was
rather a moralist than a pietist, and his leaf-umbrella is as fine an
example of the civilised mind striving to express itself under
adverse circumstances as we have ever met with.

It is not for nothing, either, that the umbrella has become the
very foremost badge of modern civilisation – the Urim and

---

[1]'This paper was written in collaboration with James Walter Ferrier, and if reprinted this is
to be stated, though his principal collaboration was to lie back in an easy-chair and laugh.' –
R.L.S., Oct. 25, 1894.

Thummim of respectability. Its pregnant symbolism has taken its rise in the most natural manner. Consider, for a moment, when umbrellas were first introduced into this country, what manner of men would use them, and what class would adhere to the useless but ornamental cane. The first, without doubt, would be the hypochondriacal, out of solicitude for their health, or the frugal, out of care for their raiment; the second, it is equally plain, would include the fop, the fool, and the Bobadil. Anyone acquainted with the growth of Society, and knowing out of what small seeds of cause are produced great revolutions, and wholly new conditions of intercourse, sees from this simple thought how the carriage of an umbrella came to indicate frugality, judicious regard for bodily welfare, and scorn for mere outward adornment, and, in one word, all those homely and solid virtues implied in the term RESPECTABILITY. Not that the umbrella's costliness has nothing to do with its great influence. Its possession, besides symbolising (as we have already indicated) the change from wild Esau to plain Jacob dwelling in tents, implies a certain comfortable provision of fortune. It is not every one that can expose twenty-six shillings' worth of property to so many chances of loss and theft. So strongly do we feel on this point, indeed, that we are almost inclined to consider all who possess really well-conditioned umbrellas as worthy of the Franchise. They have a qualification standing in their lobbies; they carry a sufficient stake in the common-weal below their arm. One who bears with him an umbrella – such a complicated structure of whalebone, of silk, and of cane, that it becomes a very microcosm of modern industry – is necessarily a man of peace. A half-crown cane may be applied to an offender's head on a very moderate provocation; but a six-and-twenty shilling silk is a possession too precious to be adventured in the shock of war.

These are but a few glances at how umbrellas (in the general) came to their present high estate. But the true Umbrella-philosopher meets with far stranger applications as he goes about the streets.

Umbrellas, like faces, acquire a certain sympathy with the individual who carries them: indeed, they are far more capable of betraying his trust; for whereas a face is given to us so far ready made, and all our power over it is in frowning, and laughing, and grimacing, during the first three or four decades of life, each umbrella is selected from a whole shopful, as being most consonant to the purchaser's disposition. An undoubted power of diagnosis rests with the practised Umbrella-philosopher. O you who lisp, and amble, and change the fashion of your countenances – you who conceal all these, how little do you think that you left a proof of your weakness in our umbrella-stand – that even now, as you shake out the folds to meet the thickening snow, we read in its ivory handle the outward and visible sign of your snobbery, or from the exposed gingham of its cover detect, through coat and waistcoat, the hidden hypocrisy of the 'dickey'! But alas! even the umbrella is no certain criterion. The falsity and the folly of the human race have degraded that graceful symbol to the ends of dishonesty; and while some umbrellas, from carelessness in selection, are not strikingly characteristic (for it is only in what a man loves that he displays his real nature), others, from certain prudential motives, are chosen directly opposite to the person's disposition. A mendacious umbrella is a sign of great moral degradation. Hypocrisy naturally shelters itself below a silk; while the fast youth goes to visit his religious friends armed with the decent and reputable gingham. May it not be said of the bearers of these inappropriate umbrellas that they go about the streets 'with a lie in their right hand'?

The kings of Siam, as we read, besides having a graduated social scale of umbrellas (which was a good thing), prevented the great bulk of their subjects from having any at all, which was certainly a bad thing. We should be sorry to believe that this Eastern legislator was a fool – the idea of an aristocracy of umbrellas is too philosophic to have originated in a nobody – and we have accordingly taken exceeding pains to find out the reason of this harsh restriction. We think we have succeeded; but while admiring the principle at which he aimed, and while cordially recognising in the Siamese potentate the only man before ourselves who had taken a real grasp of the umbrella, we must be allowed to point out how unphilosophically the great man acted in this particular. His object, plainly, was to prevent any unworthy persons from bearing the sacred symbol of domestic virtues. We cannot excuse his limiting these virtues to the circle of his court. We must only remember that such was the feeling of the age in which he lived. Liberalism had not yet raised the war-cry of the working classes. But here was his mistake: it was a needless regulation. Except in a very few cases of hypocrisy joined to a powerful intellect, men, not by nature *umbrellarians*, have tried again and again to become so by art, and yet have failed – have expended their patrimony in the purchase of umbrella after umbrella, and yet have systematically lost them, and have finally, with contrite spirits and shrunken purses, given up their vain struggle, and relied on theft and borrowing for the remainder of their lives. This is the most remarkable fact that we have had occasion to notice; and yet we challenge the candid reader to call it in question. Now, as there cannot be any *moral selection* in a mere dead piece of furniture – as the umbrella cannot be supposed to have an affinity for individual men equal and reciprocal to that which men certainly feel toward individual umbrellas, – we took the trouble of consulting a scientific friend as to whether there was any possible physical explanation of the phenomenon. He was unable to supply a plausible theory, or even hypothesis; but we extract from his letter the following interesting passage relative to the physical peculiarities of umbrellas: 'Not the least important, and by far the most curious property of the umbrella, is the energy which it displays in affecting the atmospheric strata. There is no fact in meteorology better established – indeed, it is almost the only one on which meteorologists are agreed – than that the carriage of an umbrella produces desiccation of the air; while if it be left at home, aqueous vapour is largely produced, and is soon deposited in the form of rain. No theory,' my friend continues, 'competent to explain this hygrometric law has yet been given (as far as I am aware) by Herschel, Dove, Glaisher, Tait, Buchan, or any other writer; nor do I pretend to supply the defect. I venture, however, to throw out the conjecture that it will be ultimately found to belong to the same class of natural laws as that agreeable to which a slice of toast always descends with the buttered surface downwards.'

But it is time to draw to a close. We could expatiate much longer upon this topic, but want of space constrains us to leave unfinished these few desultory remarks – slender contributions towards a subject which has fallen sadly backward, and which, we grieve to say, was better understood by the king of Siam in 1686 than by all the philosophers of today. If, however, we have awakened in any rational mind an interest in the symbolism of umbrellas – in any generous heart a more complete sympathy with the dumb companion of his daily walk, – or in any grasping spirit a pure notion of respectability strong enough to make him expend his six-and-twenty shillings – we shall have deserved well of the world, to say nothing of the many industrious persons employed in the manufacture of the article.

THE CHARACTER OF DOGS

The civilisation, the manners, and the morals of dog-kind are to a great extent subordinated to those of his ancestral master, man. This animal, in many ways so superior, has accepted a position of inferiority, shares the domestic life, and humours the caprices of the tyrant. But the potentate, like the British in India, pays small regard to the character of his willing client, judges him with listless glances, and condemns him in a byword. Listless have been the looks of his admirers, who have exhausted idle terms of praise, and buried the poor soul below exaggerations. And yet more idle and, if possible, more unintelligent has been the attitude of his express detractors; those who are very fond of dogs 'but in their proper place'; who say 'poo' fellow, poo' fellow,' and are themselves far poorer; who whet the knife of the vivisectionist or heat his oven; who are not ashamed to admire 'the creature's instinct'; and flying far beyond folly, have dared to resuscitate the theory of animal machines. The 'dog's instinct' and the 'automaton-dog,' in this age of psychology and science, sound like strange anachronisms. An automaton he certainly is; a machine working independently of his control, the heart like the mill-wheel, keeping all in motion, and the consciousness, like a person shut in the mill garret, enjoying the view out of the window and shaken by the thunder of the stones; an automaton in one corner of which a living spirit is confined: an automaton like man. Instinct again he certainly possesses. Inherited aptitudes are his, inherited frailties. Some things he at once views and understands, as though he were awakened from a sleep, as though he came 'trailing clouds of glory.' But with him, as with man, the field of instinct is limited; its utterances are obscure and occasional; and about the far larger part of life both the dog and his master must conduct their steps by deduction and observation.

The leading distinction between dog and man, after and

perhaps before the different duration of their lives, is that the one can speak and that the other cannot. The absence of the power of speech confines the dog in the development of his intellect. It hinders him from many speculations, for words are the beginning of metaphysic. At the same blow it saves him from many superstitions, and his silence has won for him a higher name for virtue than his conduct justifies. The faults of the dog are many. He is vainer than man, singularly greedy of notice, singularly intolerant of ridicule, suspicious like the deaf, jealous to the degree of frenzy, and radically devoid of truth. The day of an intelligent small dog is passed in the manufacture and the laborious communication of falsehood; he lies with his tail, he lies with his eye, he lies with his protesting paw; and when he rattles his dish or scratches at the door his purpose is other than appears. But he has some apology to offer for the vice. Many of the signs which form his dialect have come to bear an arbitrary meaning, clearly understood both by his master and himself; yet when a new want arises he must either invent a new vehicle of meaning or wrest an old one to a different purpose; and this necessity frequently recurring must tend to lessen his idea of the sanctity of symbols. Meanwhile the dog is clear in his own conscience, and draws, with a human nicety, the distinction between formal and essential truth. Of his punning perversions, his legitimate dexterity with symbols, he is even vain; but when he has told and been detected in a lie, there is not a hair upon his body but confesses guilt. To a dog of gentlemanly feeling theft and falsehood are disgraceful vices. The canine, like the human, gentleman demands in his misdemeanours Montaigne's *'je ne sais quoi de généreux.'* He is never more than half ashamed of having barked or bitten; and for those faults into which he has been led by the desire to shine before a lady of his race, he retains, even under physical correction, a share of pride. But to be caught lying, if he understands it, instantly uncurls his fleece.

Just as among dull observers he preserves a name for truth, the dog has been credited with modesty. It is amazing how the use of language blunts the faculties of man – that because vainglory finds no vent in words, creatures supplied with eyes have been unable to detect a fault so gross and obvious. If a small spoiled dog were suddenly to be endowed with speech, he would prate interminably, and still about himself; when we had friends, we should be forced to lock him in a garret; and what with his whining jealousies and his foible for falsehood, in a year's time he would have gone far to weary out our love. I was about to compare him to Sir Willoughby Patterne, but the Patternes have a manlier sense of their own merits; and the parallel, besides, is ready. Hans Christian Andersen, as we behold him in his startling memoirs, thrilling from top to toe with an excruciating vanity, and scouting even along the street for shadows of offence – here was the talking dog.

It is just this rage for consideration that has betrayed the dog into his satellite position as the friend of man. The cat, an animal of franker appetites, preserves his independence. But the dog, with one eye ever on the audience, has been wheedled into slavery, and praised and patted into the renunciation of his nature. Once he ceased hunting and became man's plate-licker, the Rubicon was crossed. Thenceforth he was a gentleman of leisure; and except the few whom we keep working, the whole race grew more and more self-conscious, mannered and affected. The number of things that a small dog does naturally is strangely small. Enjoying better spirits and not crushed under material cares, he is far more theatrical than average man. His whole life, if he be a dog of any pretension to gallantry, is spent in a vain show, and in the hot pursuit of admiration. Take out your puppy for a walk, and you will find the little ball of fur clumsy, stupid, bewildered, but natural. Let but a few months pass, and when you repeat the process you will find nature buried in convention. He will do nothing plainly; but the simplest processes of our material life will all be bent into the forms of an elaborate and mysterious etiquette. Instinct, says the fool, has awakened. But it is not so. Some dogs – some, at the very least – if they be kept separate from others, remain quite natural; and these, when at length they meet with a companion of experience, and have the game explained to them, distinguish themselves by the severity of their devotion to its rules. I wish I were allowed to tell a story which would radiantly illuminate the point; but men, like dogs, have an elaborate and mysterious etiquette. It is their bond of sympathy that both are the children of convention.

The person, man or dog, who has a conscience is eternally condemned to some degree of humbug; the sense of the law in their members fatally precipitates either towards a frozen and affected bearing. And the converse is true; and in the elaborate and conscious manners of the dog, moral opinions and the love of the ideal stand confessed. To follow for ten minutes in the street some swaggering, canine cavalier, is to receive a lesson in dramatic art and the cultured conduct of the body; in every act and gesture you see him true to a refined conception; and the dullest cur, beholding him, pricks up his ear and proceeds to imitate and parody that charming ease. For to be a high-mannered and high-minded gentleman, careless, affable, and gay, is the inborn pretension of the dog. The large dog, so much lazier, so much more weighed upon with matter, so majestic in repose, so beautiful in effort, is born with the dramatic means to wholly represent the part. And it is more pathetic and perhaps more instructive to consider the small dog in his conscientious and imperfect efforts to outdo Sir Philip Sidney. For the ideal of the dog is feudal and religious; the ever-present polytheism, the whip-bearing Olympus of mankind, rules them on the one hand; on the other, their singular difference of size and strength among themselves effectually prevents the appearance of the democratic notion. Or we might more exactly compare their society to the curious spectacle presented by a school – ushers, monitors, and big and little boys – qualified by one circumstance, the introduction of the other sex. In each, we should observe a somewhat similar tension of manner, and somewhat similar points of honour. In each the larger animal keeps a contemptuous good humour; in each the smaller annoys him with wasp-like impudence, certain of practical immunity; in each we shall find a double life producing double characters, and an excursive and noisy heroism combined with a fair amount of practical timidity. I have known dogs, and I have known school heroes that, set aside the fur, could hardly have been told apart; and if we desire to understand the chivalry of old, we must turn to the school playfields or the dungheap where the dogs are trooping.

Woman, with the dog, has been long enfranchised. Incessant massacre of female innocents has changed the proportions of the sexes and perverted their relations. Thus, when we regard the manners of the dog, we see a romantic and monogamous animal, once perhaps as delicate as the cat, at war with impossible conditions. Man has much to answer for; and the part he plays is yet more damnable and parlous than Corin's in the eyes of Touchstone. But his intervention has at least created an imperial situation for the rare surviving ladies. In that society they reign without a rival: conscious queens; and in the only instance of a canine wife-beater that has ever fallen under my notice, the criminal was somewhat excused by the circumstances of his story. He is a little, very alert, well-bred, intelligent Skye, as black as a hat, with a wet bramble for a nose and two cairngorms for eyes. To the human observer, he is decidedly well-looking; but to the ladies of his race he seems abhorrent. A thorough elaborate gentleman, of the plume and sword-knot order, he was born with a nice sense of gallantry to women. He took at their hands the most outrageous treatment; I have heard him bleating like a sheep, I have seen him streaming blood, and his ear tattered like a regimental banner; and yet he would scorn to make reprisals. Nay more, when a human lady upraised the contumelious whip against the very dame who had been so cruelly misusing him, my little great-heart gave but one hoarse cry and fell upon the tyrant tooth and nail. This is the tale of a soul's tragedy. After three years of unavailing chivalry, he suddenly, in one hour, threw off the yoke of obligation; had he been Shakespeare he would then have written *Troilus and Cressida* to brand the offending sex; but being only a little dog, he began to bite them. The surprise of the ladies whom he attacked indicated the monstrosity of his offence; but he had fairly beaten off his better angel, fairly committed moral suicide; for almost in the same hour, throwing aside the last rags of decency, he proceeded to attack the aged also. The fact is worth remark, showing, as it does, that ethical laws are common both to dogs and men; and that with both a single deliberate violation of the conscience loosens all. 'But while the lamp holds on to burn,' says the paraphrase, 'the greatest sinner may return.' I have been cheered to see symptoms of effectual penitence in my sweet ruffian; and by the handling that he accepted uncomplainingly the other day from an indignant fair one, I begin to hope the period of *Sturm und Drang* is closed.

All these little gentlemen are subtle casuists. The duty to the female dog is plain; but where competing duties rise, down they will sit and study them out, like Jesuit confessors. I knew another little Skye, somewhat plain in manner and appearance, but a creature compact of amiability and solid wisdom. His family going abroad for a winter, he was received for that period by an uncle in the same city. The winter over, his own family home again, and his own house (of which he was very proud) reopened, he found himself in a dilemma between two conflicting duties of loyalty and gratitude. His old friends were not to be neglected, but it seemed hardly decent to desert the new. This was how he solved the problem. Every morning, as soon as the door was opened, off posted Coolin to his uncle's, visited the children in the nursery, saluted the whole family, and was back at home in time for breakfast and his bit of fish. Nor was this done without a sacrifice on his part, sharply felt; for he had to forego the particular honour and jewel of his day – his morning's walk with my father. And, perhaps from this cause, he gradually wearied of and relaxed the practice, and at length returned entirely to his ancient habits. But the same decision served him in another and more distressing case of divided duty, which happened not long after. He was not at all a kitchen dog, but the cook had nursed him with unusual kindness during the distemper; and though he did not adore her as he adored my father – although (born snob) he was critically conscious of her position as 'only a servant' – he still cherished for her a special gratitude. Well, the cook left, and retired some streets away to lodgings of her own; and there was Coolin in precisely the same situation with any young gentleman who has had the inestimable benefit of a faithful nurse. The canine conscience did not solve the problem with a pound of tea at Christmas. No longer content to pay a flying visit, it was the whole forenoon that he dedicated to his solitary friend. And so, day by day, he continued to comfort her solitude until (for some reason which I could never understand and cannot approve) he was kept locked up to break him of the graceful habit. Here, it is not the similarity, it is the difference, that is worthy of remark; the clearly marked degrees of gratitude and the proportional duration of his visits. Anything further removed from instinct it were hard to fancy; and one is even stirred to a certain impatience with a character so destitute of spontaneity, so passionless in justice, and so priggishly obedient to the voice of reason.

There are not many dogs like this good Coolin, and not many people. But the type is one well marked, both in the human and the canine family. Gallantry was not his aim, but a solid and somewhat oppressive respectability. He was a sworn foe to the unusual and the conspicuous, a praiser of the golden mean, a kind of city uncle modified by Cheeryble. And as he was precise and conscientious in all the steps of his own blameless course, he looked for the same precision and an even greater gravity in the bearing of his deity, my father. It was no sinecure to be Coolin's idol: he was exacting like a rigid parent; and at every sign of levity in the man whom he respected, he announced loudly the death of virtue and the proximate fall of the pillars of the earth.

I have called him a snob; but all dogs are so, though in varying degrees. It is hard to follow their snobbery among themselves; for though I think we can perceive distinctions of rank, we cannot grasp what is the criterion. Thus in Edinburgh, in a good part of the town, there were several distinct societies or clubs that met in the morning to – the phrase is technical – to 'rake the backets' in a troop. A friend of mine, the master of three dogs, was one day surprised to observe that they had left one club and joined another; but whether it was a rise or a fall, and the result of an invitation or an expulsion, was more than he could guess. And this illustrates pointedly our ignorance of the real life of dogs, their social ambitions and their social hierarchies. At least, in their dealings with men they are not only conscious of sex, but of the difference of station. And that in the most snobbish manner; for the poor man's dog is not offended by the notice of the rich, and keeps all his ugly feeling for those poorer or more ragged than his master. And again, for every station they have an ideal of behaviour, to which the master, under pain of derogation, will do wisely to conform. How often has not a cold glance of an eye informed me that my dog was disappointed; and how much more gladly would he not have taken a beating than to be thus wounded in the seat of piety!

I knew one disrespectable dog. He was far liker a cat; cared little or nothing for men, with whom he merely co-existed as we do with cattle, and was entirely devoted to the art of poaching. A house would not hold him, and to live in a town was what he refused. He led, I believe, a life of troubled but genuine pleasure, and perished beyond all question in a trap. But this was an exception, a marked reversion to the ancestral type; like the hairy human infant. The true dog of the nineteenth century, to judge by the remainder of my fairly large acquaintance, is in love with respectability. A street-dog was once adopted by a lady. While still an Arab, he had done as Arabs do, gambolling in the mud, charging into butchers' stalls, a cat-hunter, a sturdy beggar, a common rogue and vagabond; but with his rise into society he laid aside these inconsistent pleasures. He stole no more, he hunted no more cats; and conscious of his collar, he ignored his old companions. Yet the canine upper class was never brought to recognise the upstart, and from that hour, except for human countenance, he was alone. Friendless, shorn of his sports and the habits of a lifetime, he still lived in a glory of happiness, content with his acquired respectability, and with no care but to support it solemnly. Are we to condemn or praise this self-made dog? We praise his human brother. And thus to conquer vicious habits is as rare with dogs as with men. With the more part, for all their scruple-mongering and moral thought, the vices that are born with them remain invincible throughout; and they live all their years, glorying in their virtues, but still the slaves of their defects. Thus the sage Coolin was a thief to the last; among a thousand peccadilloes, a whole goose and a whole cold leg of mutton lay upon his conscience; but Woggs,[1] whose soul's shipwreck in the matter of gallantry I have recounted above, has only twice been known to steal, and has often nobly conquered the temptation. The eighth is his favourite commandment. There is something painfully human in these unequal virtues and mortal frailties of the best. Still more painful is the bearing of those 'stammering professors' in the house of sickness and under the terror of death. It is beyond a doubt to me that, somehow or other, the dog connects together, or confounds, the uneasiness of sickness and the consciousness of guilt. To the pains of the body he often adds the tortures of the conscience; and at these times his haggard protestations form, in regard to the human deathbed, a dreadful parody or parallel.

I once supposed that I had found an inverse relation between the double etiquette which dogs obey; and that those who were most addicted to the showy street life among other dogs were less careful in the practice of home virtues for the tyrant man. But the female dog, that mass of carneying affections, shines equally in either sphere; rules her rough posse of attendant swains with unwearying tact and gusto; and with her master and mistress pushes the arts of insinuation to their crowning point. The attention of man and the regard of other dogs flatter (it would thus appear) the same sensibility; but perhaps, if we could read the canine heart, they would be found to flatter it in very different degrees. Dogs live with man as courtiers round a monarch, steeped in the flattery of his notice and enriched with sinecures. To push their favour in this world of pickings and caresses is, perhaps, the business of their lives; and their joys may lie outside. I am in despair at our persistent ignorance. I read in the lives of our companions the same processes of reason, the same antique and fatal conflicts of the right against the wrong, and of unbitted nature with too rigid custom; I see them with our weaknesses, vain, false, inconstant against appetite, and with our one stalk of virtue, devoted to the dream of an

---

[1] Walter, Watty, Woggy, Woggs, Wogg, and lastly Bogue; under which last name he fell in battle some twelve months ago. Glory was his aim and he attained it; for his icon, by the hand of Caldecott, now lies among the treasures of the nation.

ideal; and yet, as they hurry by me on the street with tail in air, or come singly to solicit my regard, I must own the secret purport of their lives is still inscrutable to man. Is man the friend, or is he the patron only? Have they indeed forgotten nature's voice? or are those moments snatched from courtier-ship when they touch noses with the tinker's mongrel, the brief reward and pleasure of their artificial lives? Doubtless, when man shares with his dog the toils of a profession and the pleasures of an art, as with the shepherd or the poacher, the affection warms and strengthens till it fills the soul. But doubtless, also, the masters are, in many cases, the object of a merely interested cultus, sitting aloft like Louis Quatorze, giving and receiving flattery and favour; and the dogs, like the majority of men, have but foregone their true existence and become the dupes of their ambition.

CHILD'S PLAY

The regret we have for our childhood is not wholly justifiable: so much a man may lay down without fear of public ribaldry; for although we shake our heads over the change, we are not unconscious of the manifold advantages of our new state. What we lose in generous impulse, we more than gain in the habit of generously watching others; and the capacity to enjoy Shakespeare may balance a lost aptitude for playing at soldiers. Terror is gone out of our lives, moreover; we no longer see the devil in the bed-curtains nor lie awake to listen to the wind. We go to school no more; and if we have only exchanged one drudgery for another (which is by no means sure), we are set free for ever from the daily fear of chastisement. And yet a great change has overtaken us; and although we do not enjoy ourselves less, at least we take our pleasure differently. We need pickles nowadays to make Wednesday's cold mutton please our Friday's appetite; and I can remember the time when to call it red venison, and tell myself a hunter's story, would have made it more palatable than the best of sauces. To the grown person, cold mutton is cold mutton all the world over; not all the mythology ever invented by man will make it better or worse to him; the broad fact, the clamant reality, of the mutton carries away before it such seductive figments. But for the child it is still possible to weave an enchantment over eatables; and if he has but read of a dish in a story-book, it will be heavenly manna to him for a week.

If a grown man does not like eating and drinking and exercise, if he is not something positive in his tastes, it means he has a feeble body and should have some medicine; but children may be pure spirits, if they will, and take their enjoyment in a world of moonshine. Sensation does not count for so much in our first years as afterwards; something of the swaddling numbness of infancy clings about us; we see and touch and hear through a sort of golden mist. Children, for instance, are able enough to see, but they have no great faculty for looking; they do not use their eyes for the pleasure of using them, but for by-ends of their own; and the things I call to mind seeing most vividly, were not beautiful in themselves, but merely interesting or enviable to me as I thought they might be turned to practical account in play. Nor is the sense of touch so clean and poignant in children as it is in a man. If you will turn over your old memories, I think the sensations of this sort you remember will be somewhat vague, and come to not much more than a blunt, general sense of heat on summer days, or a blunt, general sense of wellbeing in bed. And here, of course, you will understand pleasurable sensations; for overmastering pain – the most deadly and tragical element in life, and the true commander of man's soul and body – alas! pain has its own way with all of us; it breaks in, a rude visitant, upon the fairy garden where the child wanders in a dream, no less surely than it rules upon the field of battle, or sends the immortal war-god whimpering to his father; and innocence, no more than philosophy, can protect us from this sting. As for taste, when we bear in mind the excesses of unmitigated sugar which delight a youthful palate, 'it is surely no very cynical asperity' to think taste a character of the maturer growth. Smell and hearing are perhaps more developed; I remember many scents, many voices, and a great deal of spring singing in the woods. But hearing is capable of vast improvement as a means of pleasure; and there is all the world between gaping wonderment at the jargon of birds, and the emotion with which a man listens to articulate music.

At the same time, and step by step with this increase in the definition and intensity of what we feel which accompanies our growing age, another change takes place in the sphere of intellect, by which all things are transformed and seen through theories and associations as through coloured windows. We make to ourselves day by day, out of history, and gossip, and economical speculations, and God knows what, a medium in which we walk and through which we look abroad. We study shop windows with other eyes than in our childhood, never to wonder, not always to admire, but to make and modify our little incongruous theories about life. It is no longer the uniform of a soldier that arrests our attention; but perhaps the flowing carriage of a woman, or perhaps a countenance that has been vividly stamped with passion and carries an adventurous story written in its lines. The pleasure of surprise is passed away; sugar-loaves and water-carts seem mighty tame to encounter; and we walk the streets to make romances and to sociologise. Nor must we deny that a good many of us walk them solely for the purposes of transit or in the interest of a livelier digestion. These, indeed, may look back with mingled thoughts upon their childhood, but the rest are in a better case; they know more than when they were children, they understand better, their desires and sympathies answer more nimbly to the provocation of the senses, and their minds are brimming with interest as they go about the world.

According to my contention, this is a flight to which children cannot rise. They are wheeled in perambulators or dragged about by nurses in a pleasing stupor. A vague, faint, abiding wonderment possesses them. Here and there some specially remarkable circumstance, such as a water-cart or a guardsman, fairly penetrates into the seat of thought and calls them, for half a moment, out of themselves; and you may see them, still towed forward sideways by the inexorable nurse as by a sort of destiny, but still staring at the bright object in their wake. It may be some minutes before another such moving spectacle reawakens them to the world in which they dwell. For other children, they almost invariably show some intelligent sympathy. 'There is a fine fellow making mud pies,' they seem to say; 'that I can understand, there is some sense in mud pies.' But the doings of their elders, unless where they are speakingly picturesque or recommend themselves by the quality of being easily imitable, they let them go over their heads (as we say) without the least regard. If it were not for this perpetual imitation, we should be tempted to fancy they despised us outright, or only considered us in the light of creatures brutally strong and brutally silly; among whom they condescended to dwell in obedience like a philosopher at a barbarous court. At times, indeed, they display an arrogance of disregard that is truly staggering. Once, when I was groaning aloud with physical pain, a young gentleman came into the room and nonchalantly inquired if I had seen his bow and arrow. He made no account of my groans, which he accepted, as he had to accept so much else, as a piece of the inexplicable conduct of his elders; and like a wise young gentleman, he would waste no wonder on the subject. Those elders, who care so little for rational enjoyment, and are even the enemies of rational enjoyment for others, he had accepted without understanding and without complaint, as the rest of us accept the scheme of the universe.

We grown people can tell ourselves a story, give and take strokes until the bucklers ring, ride far and fast, marry, fall, and die; all the while sitting quietly by the fire or lying prone in bed. This is exactly what a child cannot do, or does not do, at least, when he can find anything else. He works all with lay figures and stage properties. When his story comes to the fighting, he must rise, get something by way of a sword and have a set-to with a piece of furniture, until he is out of breath. When he comes to ride with the king's pardon, he must bestride a chair, which he will so hurry and belabour and on which he will so furiously demean himself, that the messenger will arrive, if not bloody with spurring, at least fiery red with haste. If his romance involves an accident upon a cliff, he must clamber in person about the chest of drawers and fall bodily upon the carpet, before his imagination is satisfied. Lead soldiers, dolls, all toys, in short, are in the same category and answer the same end. Nothing can stagger a child's faith; he accepts the clumsiest substitutes and can swallow the most staring incongruities. The chair he has just been besieging as a castle, or valiantly cutting to the ground as a dragon, is taken away for the accommodation of a morning visitor, and he is nothing abashed; he can skirmish by the hour with a stationary coal-scuttle; in the midst of the enchanted pleasance, he can see, without sensible shock, the gardener soberly digging potatoes for the day's dinner. He can make abstraction of whatever does not fit into his fable; and he puts his eyes into his pocket, just as we hold our noses in an unsavoury lane. And so it is, that although the ways of children cross with those of their elders in a hundred places daily, they never go in the same direction nor so much as lie in the same element. So may the telegraph wires intersect the line of the high-road, or so might a landscape painter and a bagman visit the same country, and yet move in different worlds.

People struck with these spectacles, cry aloud about the power of imagination in the young. Indeed there may be two words to that. It is, in some ways, but a pedestrian fancy that the child exhibits. It is the grown people who make the nursery stories; all the children do, is jealously to preserve the text. One out of a dozen reasons why *Robinson Crusoe* should be so popular with youth, is that it hits their level in this matter to a nicety; Crusoe was always at makeshifts and had, in so many words, to *play* at a great variety of professions; and then the book is all about tools, and there is nothing that delights a child so much. Hammers and saws belong to a province of life that positively calls for imitation.

The juvenile lyrical drama, surely of the most ancient Thespian model, wherein the trades of mankind are successively simulated to the running burthen 'On a cold and frosty morning,' gives a good instance of the artistic taste in children. And this need for overt action and lay figures testifies to a defect in the child's imagination which prevents him from carrying out his novels in the privacy of his own heart. He does not yet know enough of the world and men. His experience is incomplete. That stage-wardrobe and scene-room that we call the memory is so ill provided, that he can overtake few combinations and body out few stories, to his own content, without some external aid. He is at the experimental stage; he is not sure how one would feel in certain circumstances; to make sure, he must come as near trying it as his means permit. And so here is young heroism with a wooden sword, and mothers practise their kind vocation over a bit of jointed stick. It may be laughable enough just now; but it is these same people and these same thoughts, that not long hence, when they are on the theatre of life, will make you weep and tremble. For children think very much the same thoughts and dream the same dreams, as bearded men and marriageable women. No one is more romantic. Fame and honour, the love of young men and the love of mothers, the business man's pleasure in method, all these and others they anticipate and rehearse in their play hours. Upon us, who are further advanced and fairly dealing with the threads of destiny, they only glance from time to time to glean a hint for their own mimetic reproduction. Two children playing at soldiers are far more interesting to each other than one of the scarlet beings whom both are busy imitating. This is perhaps the greatest oddity of all. 'Art for art' is their motto; and the doings of grown folk are only interesting as the raw material for play. Not Théophile Gautier, not Flaubert, can look more callously upon life, or rate the reproduction more highly over the reality; and they will parody an execution, a deathbed, or the funeral of the young man of Nain, with all the cheerfulness in the world.

The true parallel for play is not to be found, of course, in conscious art, which, though it be derived from play, is itself an abstract, impersonal thing, and depends largely upon philosophical interest beyond the scope of childhood. It is when we make castles in the air and personate the leading character in our own romances, that we return to the spirit of our first years. Only, there are several reasons why the spirit is no longer so agreeable to indulge. Nowadays, when we admit this personal element into our divagations we are apt to stir up uncomfortable and sorrowful memories, and remind ourselves sharply of old wounds. Our day-dreams can no longer lie all in the air like a story in the *Arabian Nights;* they read to us rather like the history of a period in which we ourselves had taken part, where we come across many unfortunate passages and find our own conduct smartly reprimanded. And then the child, mind you, acts his parts. He does not merely repeat them to himself; he leaps, he runs, and sets the blood agog over all his body. And so his play breathes him; and he no sooner assumes a passion than he gives it vent. Alas! when we betake ourselves to our intellectual form of play, sitting quietly by the fire or lying prone in bed, we rouse many hot feelings for which we can find no outlet. Substitutes are not acceptable to the mature mind, which desires the thing itself; and even to rehearse a triumphant dialogue with one's enemy, although it is perhaps the most satisfactory piece of play still left within our reach, is not entirely satisfying, and is even apt to lead to a visit and an interview which may be the reverse of triumphant after all.

In the child's world of dim sensation, play is all in all. 'Making believe' is the gist of his whole life, and he cannot so much as take a walk except in character. I could not learn my alphabet without some suitable *mise-en-scène*, and had to act a business man in an office before I could sit down to my book. Will you kindly question your memory, and find out how much you did, work or pleasure, in good faith and soberness, and for how much you had to cheat yourself with some invention? I remember, as though it were yesterday, the expansion of spirit, the dignity and self-reliance, that came with a pair of mustachios in burnt cork, even when there was none to see. Children are even content to forego what we call the realities, and prefer the shadow to the substance. When they might be speaking intelligibly together, they chatter senseless gibberish by the hour, and are quite happy because they are making believe to speak French. I have said already how even the imperious appetite of hunger suffers itself to be gulled and led by the nose with the fag end of an old song. And it goes deeper than this: when children are together even a meal is felt as an interruption in the business of life; and they must find some imaginative sanction, and tell themselves some sort of story, to account for, to colour, to render entertaining, the simple processes of eating and drinking. What wonderful fancies I have heard evolved out of the pattern upon tea-cups! – from which there followed a code of rules and a whole world of excitement, until tea-drinking began to take rank as a game. When my cousin and I took our porridge of a morning, we had a device to enliven the course of the meal. He ate his with sugar, and explained it to be a country continually buried under snow. I took mine with milk, and explained it to be a country suffering gradual inundation. You can imagine us exchanging bulletins; how here was an island still unsubmerged, here a valley not yet covered with snow; what inventions were made; how his population lived in cabins on perches and travelled on stilts, and how mine was always in boats; how the interest grew furious as the last corner of safe ground was cut off on all sides and grew smaller every moment; and how in fine, the food was of altogether secondary importance, and might even have been nauseous, so long as we seasoned it with these dreams. But perhaps the most exciting moments I ever had over a meal, were in the case of calves' feet jelly. It was hardly possible not to believe – and you may be sure, so far from trying, I did all I could to favour the illusion – that some part of it was hollow, and that sooner or later my spoon would lay open the secret tabernacle of the golden rock. There, might some miniature *Red Beard* await his hour; there, might one find the treasures of the *Forty Thieves,* and bewildered Cassim beating about the walls. And so I quarried on slowly, with bated breath, savouring the interest. Believe me, I have little palate left for the jelly; and though I preferred the taste when I took cream with it, I used often to go without, because the cream dimmed the transparent fractures.

Even with games, this spirit is authoritative with right-minded children. It is thus that hide-and-seek has so pre-eminent a sovereignty, for it is the wellspring of romance, and the actions and the excitement to which it gives rise lend themselves to almost any sort of fable. And thus cricket, which is a mere matter of dexterity, palpably about nothing and for no end, often fails to satisfy infantile craving. It is a game, if you like, but not a game of play. You cannot tell yourself a story about cricket; and the activity it calls forth can be justified on no rational theory. Even football, although it admirably simulates the tug and the ebb and flow of battle, has presented difficulties to the mind of young sticklers after verisimilitude; and I knew at least one little boy who was mightily exercised about the presence of the ball, and had to spirit himself up, whenever he came to play, with an elaborate story of enchantment, and take the missile as a sort of talisman bandied about in conflict between two Arabian nations.

To think of such a frame of mind, is to become disquieted about the bringing up of children. Surely they dwell in a mythological epoch, and are not the contemporaries of their parents. What can they think of them? what can they make of these bearded or petticoated giants who look down upon their games? who move upon a cloudy Olympus, following unknown designs apart from rational enjoyment? who profess the tenderest solicitude for children, and yet every now and again reach down out of their altitude and terribly vindicate the prerogatives of age? Off goes the child, corporally smarting, but morally rebellious. Were there ever such unthinkable deities as parents? I would give a great deal to know what, in nine cases out of ten, is the child's unvarnished feeling. A sense of past cajolery; a sense of personal attraction, at best very feeble; above all, I should imagine, a sense of terror for the untried residue of mankind: go to make up the attraction that he feels. No wonder, poor little heart, with such a weltering world in front of him, if he clings to the hand he knows! The dread irrationality of the whole affair, as it seems to children, is a thing we are all too ready to forget. 'O, why,' I remember passionately wondering, 'why can we not all be happy and devote ourselves to play?' And when children do philosophise, I believe it is usually to very much the same purpose.

One thing, at least, comes very clearly out of these considerations; that whatever we are to expect at the hands of children, it should not be any peddling exactitude about matters of fact. They walk in a vain show, and among mists and rainbows; they are passionate after dreams and unconcerned about realities; speech is a difficult art not wholly learned; and there is nothing in their own tastes or purposes to teach them what we mean by abstract truthfulness. When a bad writer is inexact, even if he can look back on half a century of years, we charge him with incompetence and not with dishonesty. And why not extend the same allowance to imperfect speakers? Let a stockbroker be dead stupid about poetry, or a poet inexact in the details of business, and we excuse them heartily from blame. But show us a miserable, unbreeched, human entity, whose whole profession it is to take a tub for a fortified town and a shaving-brush for the deadly stiletto, and who passes three-fourths of his time in a dream and the rest in open self-deception, and we expect him to be as nice upon a matter of fact as a scientific expert bearing evidence. Upon my heart, I think it less than decent. You do not consider how little the child sees, or how swift he is to weave what he has seen into bewildering fiction; and that he cares no more for what you call truth, than you for a gingerbread dragoon.

I am reminded, as I write, that the child is very inquiring as to the precise truth of stories. But indeed this is a very different matter, and one bound up with the subject of play, and the precise amount of playfulness, or playability, to be looked for in the world. Many such burning questions must arise in the course of nursery education. Among the fauna of this planet, which already embraces the pretty soldier and the terrifying Irish beggarman, is, or is not, the child to expect a Bluebeard or a Cormoran? Is he, or is he not, to look out for magicians, kindly and potent? May he, or may he not, reasonably hope to be cast away upon a desert island, or turned to such diminutive proportions that he can live on equal terms with his lead soldiery, and go a cruise in his own toy schooner? Surely all these are practical questions to a neophyte entering upon life with a view to play. Precision upon such a point, the child can understand. But if you merely ask him of his past behaviour, as to who threw such a stone, for instance, or struck such and such a match; or whether he had looked into a parcel or gone by a forbidden path, – why, he can see no moment in the inquiry, and it is ten to one, he has already half forgotten and half bemused himself with subsequent imaginings.

It would be easy to leave them in their native cloudland, where they figure so prettily – pretty like flowers and innocent like dogs. They will come out of their gardens soon enough, and have to go into offices and the witness-box. Spare them yet a while, O conscientious parent! Let them doze among their playthings yet a little! for who knows what a rough, warfaring existence lies before them in the future?

'A PENNY PLAIN AND TWOPENCE COLOURED'

These words will be familiar to all students of Skelt's Juvenile Drama. That national monument, after having changed its name to Park's, to Webb's, to Redington's, and last of all to Pollock's, has now become, for the most part, a memory. Some of its pillars, like Stonehenge, are still afoot, the rest clean vanished. It may be the Museum numbers a full set; and Mr Ionides perhaps, or else her gracious Majesty, may boast their great collections; but to the plain private person they are become, like Raphaels, unattainable. I have, at different times, possessed *Aladdin, The Red Rover, The Blind Boy, The Old Oak Chest, The Wood Dæmon, Jack Sheppard, The Miller and his Men, Der Freischütz, The Smuggler, The Forest of Bondy, Robin Hood, The Waterman, Richard I., My Poll and my Partner Joe, The Inchcape Bell* (imperfect), and *Three-Fingered Jack, the Terror of Jamaica*; and I have assisted others in the illumination of *The Maid of the Inn* and *The Battle of Waterloo*. In this roll-call of stirring names you read the evidences of a happy childhood; and though not half of them are still to be procured of any living stationer, in the mind of their once happy owner all survive, kaleidoscopes of changing pictures, echoes of the past.

There stands, I fancy, to this day (but now how fallen!) a certain stationer's shop at a corner of the wide thoroughfare that joins the city of my childhood with the sea. When, upon any Saturday, we made a party to behold the ships, we passed that corner; and since in those days I loved a ship as a man loves Burgundy or daybreak, this of itself had been enough to hallow it. But there was more than that. In the Leith Walk window, all the year round, there stood displayed a theatre in working order, with a 'forest set,' a 'combat,' and a few 'robbers carousing' in the slides; and below and about, dearer tenfold to me! the plays themselves, those budgets of romance, lay tumbled one upon another. Long and often have I lingered there with empty pockets. One figure, we shall say, was visible in the first plate of characters, bearded, pistol in hand, or drawing to his ear the clothyard arrow; I would spell the name: was it Macaire, or Long Tom Coffin, or Grindoff, 2d dress? O, how I would long to see the rest! how – if the name by chance were hidden – I would wonder in what play he figured, and what immortal legend justified his attitude and strange apparel! And then to go within, to announce yourself as an intending purchaser, and, closely watched, be suffered to undo those bundles and breathlessly devour those pages of gesticulating villains, epileptic combats, bosky forests, palaces and war-ships, frowning fortresses and prison vaults – it was a giddy joy. That shop, which was dark and smelt of Bibles, was a lodestone rock for all that bore the name of boy. They could not pass it by, nor, having entered, leave it. It was a place besieged; the shopmen, like the Jews rebuilding Salem, had a double task. They kept us at the stick's end, frowned us down, snatched each play out of our hand ere we were trusted with another; and, incredible as it may sound, used to demand of us upon our entrance, like banditti, if we came with money or with empty hand. Old Mr Smith himself, worn out with my eternal vacillation, once swept the treasures from before me, with the cry: 'I do not believe, child, that you are an intending purchaser at all!' These were the dragons of the garden; but for such joys of paradise we could have faced the Terror of Jamaica himself. Every sheet we fingered was another lightning glance into obscure, delicious story; it was like wallowing in the raw stuff of story-books. I know nothing to compare with it save now and then in dreams, when I am privileged to read in certain unwrit stories of adventure, from which I awake to find the world all vanity. The *crux* of Buridan's donkey was as nothing to the uncertainty of the boy as he handled and lingered and doted on these bundles of delight; there was a physical pleasure in the sight and touch of them which he would jealously prolong; and when at length the deed was done, the play selected, and the impatient shopman had brushed the rest into the grey portfolio, and the boy was forth again, a little late for dinner, the lamps springing into light in the blue winter's even, and *The Miller*, or *The Rover*, or some kindred drama clutched against his side – on what gay feet he ran, and how he laughed aloud in exultation! I can hear that laughter still. Out of all the years of my life, I can recall but one home-coming to compare with these, and that was on the night when I brought back with me the *Arabian*

Entertainments in the fat, old, double-columned volume with the prints. I was just well into the story of the Hunchback, I remember, when my clergyman-grandfather (a man we counted pretty stiff) came in behind me. I grew blind with terror. But instead of ordering the book away, he said he envied me. Ah, well he might!

The purchase and the first half-hour at home, that was the summit. Thenceforth the interest declined by little and little. The fable, as set forth in the play-book, proved to be not worthy of the scenes and characters: what fable would not? Such passages as: 'Scene 6. The Hermitage. Night set scene. Place back of scene 1, No. 2, at back of stage and hermitage, Fig. 2, out of set piece, R. H. in a slanting direction' – such passages, I say, though very practical, are hardly to be called good reading. Indeed, as literature, these dramas did not much appeal to me. I forget the very outline of the plots. Of *The Blind Boy*, beyond the fact that he was a most injured prince and once, I think, abducted, I know nothing. And *The Old Oak Chest*, what was it all about? that proscript (1st dress), that prodigious number of banditti, that old woman with the broom, and the magnificent kitchen in the third act (was it in the third?) – they are all fallen in a deliquium, swim faintly in my brain, and mix and vanish.

I cannot deny that joy attended the illumination; nor can I quite forgive that child who, wilfully foregoing pleasure, stoops to 'twopence coloured.' With crimson lake (hark to the sound of it – crimson lake! – the horns of elf-land are not richer on the ear) – with crimson lake and Prussian blue a certain purple is to be compounded which, for cloaks especially, Titian could not equal. The latter colour with gamboge, a hated name although an exquisite pigment, supplied a green of such a savoury greenness that today my heart regrets it. Nor can I recall without a tender weakness the very aspect of the water where I dipped my brush. Yes, there was pleasure in the painting. But when all was painted, it is needless to deny it, all was spoiled. You might, indeed, set up a scene or two to look at; but to cut the figures out was simply sacrilege; nor could any child twice court the tedium, the worry, and the long-drawn disenchantment of an actual performance. Two days after the purchase the honey had been sucked. Parents used to complain; they thought I wearied of my play. It was not so: no more than a person can be said to have wearied of his dinner when he leaves the bones and dishes; I had got the marrow of it and said grace.

Then was the time to turn to the back of the play-book and to study that enticing double file of names, where poetry, for the true child of Skelt, reigned happy and glorious like her Majesty the Queen. Much as I have travelled in these realms of gold, I have yet seen, upon that map or abstract, names of El Dorados that still haunt the ear of memory, and are still but names. *The Floating Beacon* – why was that denied me? or *The Wreck Ashore*? *Sixteen-String Jack*, whom I did not even guess to be a highwayman, troubled me awake and haunted my slumbers; and there is one sequence of three from that enchanted calender that I still at times recall, like a loved verse of poetry: *Lodoiska, Silver Palace, Echo of Westminster Bridge*. Names, bare names, are surely more to children than we poor, grown-up, obliterated fools remember.

The name of Skelt itself has always seemed a part and parcel of the charm of his productions. It may be different with the rose, but the attraction of this paper drama sensibly declined when Webb had crept into the rubric: a poor cuckoo, flaunting in Skelt's nest. And now we have reached Pollock, sounding deeper gulfs. Indeed, this name of Skelt appears so stagey and piratic, that I will adopt it boldly to design these qualities. Skeltery, then, is a quality of much art. It is even to be found, with reverence be it said, among the works of nature. The stagey is its generic name; but it is an old, insular, home-bred staginess; not French, domestically British; not of to-day, but smacking of O. Smith, Fitzball, and the great age of melodrama: a peculiar fragrance haunting it; uttering its unimportant message in a tone of voice that has the charm of fresh antiquity. I will not insist upon the art of Skelt's purveyors. These wonderful characters that once so thrilled our soul with their bold attitude, array of deadly engines and incomparable costume, to-day look somewhat pallidly; the extreme hard favour of the heroine strikes me, I had almost said with pain; the villain's scowl no longer thrills me like a trumpet; and the scenes themselves, those once unparalleled landscapes, seem the efforts of a prentice hand. So much of fault we find; but on the other side the impartial critic rejoices to remark the presence of a great unity of gusto; of those direct clap-trap appeals, which a man is dead and buriable when he fails to answer; of the footlight glamour, the ready-made, bare-faced, transpontine picturesque, a thing not one with cold reality, but how much dearer to the mind!

The scenery of Skeltdom – or, shall we say, the kingdom of Transpontus? – had a prevailing character. Whether it set forth Poland as in *The Blind Boy*, or Bohemia with *The Miller and his*

Men, or Italy with *The Old Oak Chest*, still it was Transpontus. A botanist could tell it by the plants. The hollyhock was all pervasive, running wild in deserts; the dock was common, and the bending reed; and overshadowing these were poplar, palm, potato tree, and *Quercus Skeltica* – brave growths. The caves were all embowelled in the Surreyside formation; the soil was all betrodden by the light pump of T. P. Cooke. Skelt, to be sure, had yet another, an oriental string: he held the gorgeous east in fee; and in the new quarter of Hyères, say, in the garden of the Hotel des Iles d'Or, you may behold these blessed visions realised. But on these I will not dwell; they were an outwork; it was in the occidental scenery that Skelt was all himself. It had a strong flavour of England; it was a sort of indigestion of England and drop-scenes, and I am bound to say was charming. How the roads wander, how the castle sits upon the hill, how the sun eradiates from behind the cloud, and how the congregated clouds themselves uproll, as stiff as bolsters! Here is the cottage interior, the usual first flat, with the cloak upon the nail, the rosaries of onions, the gun and powder-horn and corner-cupboard; here is the inn (this drama must be nautical, I foresee Captain Luff and Bold Bob Bowsprit) with the red curtain, pipes, spittoons, and eight-day clock; and there again is that impressive dungeon with the chains, which was so dull to colour. England, the hedgerow elms, the thin brick houses, windmills, glimpses of the navigable Thames – England, when at last I came to visit it, was only Skelt made evident: to cross the border was, for the Scotsman, to come home to Skelt; there was the inn-sign and there the horse-trough, all foreshadowed in the faithful Skelt. If, at the ripe age of fourteen years, I bought a certain cudgel, got a friend to load it, and thenceforward walked the tame ways of the earth my own ideal, radiating pure romance – still I was but a puppet in the hand of Skelt; the original of that regretted bludgeon, and surely the antitype of all the bludgeon kind, greatly improved from Cruikshank, had adorned the hand of Jonathan Wild, pl. I. 'This is mastering me,' as Whitman cries, upon some lesser provocation. What am I? what are life, art, letters, the world, but what my Skelt has made them? He stamped himself upon my immaturity. The world was plain before I knew him, a poor penny world; but soon it was all coloured with romance. If I go to the theatre to see a good old melodrama, 'tis but Skelt a little faded. If I visit a bold scene in nature, Skelt would have been bolder; there had been certainly a castle on that mountain, and the hollow tree – that set piece – I seem to miss it in the foreground. Indeed, out of this cut-and-dry, dull, swaggering, obtrusive and infantile art, I seem to have learned the very spirit of my life's enjoyment; met there the shadows of the characters I was to read about and love in a late future; got the romance of *Der Freischütz* long ere I was to hear of Weber or the mighty Formes; acquired a gallery of scenes and characters with which, in the silent theatre of the brain, I might enact all novels and romances; and took from these rude cuts an enduring and transforming pleasure. Reader – and yourself?

A word of moral: it appears that B. Pollock, late J. Redington, No. 73 Hoxton Street, not only publishes twenty-three of these old stage favourites, but owns the necessary plates and displays a modest readiness to issue other thirty-three. If you love art, folly, or the bright eyes of children, speed to Pollock's, or to Clarke's of Garrick Street. In Pollock's list of publicanda I perceive a pair of my ancient aspirations: *Wreck Ashore* and *Sixteen-String Jack*; and I cherish the belief that when these shall see once more the light of day, B. Pollock will remember this apologist. But, indeed, I have a dream at times that is not all a dream. I seem to myself to wander in a ghostly street – E. W., I think, the postal district – close below the fool's-cap of St Paul's, and yet within easy hearing of the echo of the Abbey bridge. There in a dim shop, low in the roof and smelling strong of glue and footlights, I find myself in quaking treaty with great Skelt himself, the aboriginal, all dusty from the tomb. I buy, with what a choking heart – I buy them all, all but the pantomimes; I pay my mental money, and go forth; and lo! the packets are dust.

I

With the single exception of Falstaff, all Shakespeare's characters are what we call marrying men: Mercutio, as he was own cousin to Benedick and Biron, would have come to the same end in the long run. Even Iago had a wife, and, what is far stranger, he was jealous. People like Jacques and the Fool in *Lear*, although we can hardly imagine they would ever marry, kept single out of a cynical humour or for a broken heart, and not, as we do nowadays, from a spirit of incredulity and preference for the single state. For that matter, if you turn to George Sand's French version of *As You Like It* (and I think I can promise you will like it but little), you will find Jacques marries Celia just as Orlando marries Rosalind.

At least there seems to have been much less hesitation over marriage in Shakespeare's days; and what hesitation there was was of a laughing sort, and not much more serious, one way or the other, than that of Panurge. In modern comedies the heroes are mostly of Benedick's way of thinking, but twice as much in earnest, and not one quarter so confident. And I take this diffidence as a proof of how sincere their terror is. They know they are only human after all; they know what gins and pitfalls lie about their feet; and how the shadow of matrimony waits, resolute and awful, at the cross-roads. They would wish to keep their liberty; but if that may not be, why, God's will be done! 'What, are you afraid of marriage?' asks Cécile, in *Maître Guerin*. 'Oh, mon Dieu, non!' replies Arthur; 'I should take chloroform.' They look forward to marriage much in the same way as they prepare themselves for death: each seems inevitable; each is a great Perhaps, and a leap into the dark, for which, when a man is in the blue devils, he has specially to harden his heart. That splendid scoundrel, Maxime de Trailles, took the news of marriages much as an old man hears the deaths of his contemporaries. 'C'est désespérant,' he cried, throwing himself down in the arm-chair at Madame Schontz's; 'c'est désespérant, nous nous marions tous!' Every marriage was like another grey hair on his head; and the jolly church bells seemed to taunt him with his fifty years and fair round belly.

The fact is, we are much more afraid of life than our ancestors, and cannot find it in our hearts either to marry or not to marry. Marriage is terrifying, but so is a cold and forlorn old age. The friendships of men are vastly agreeable, but they are insecure. You know all the time that one friend will marry and put you to the door; a second accept a situation in China, and become no more to you than a name, a reminiscence, and an occasional crossed letter, very laborious to read; a third will take up with some religious crotchet and treat you to sour looks thenceforward. So, in one way or another, life forces men apart and breaks up the goodly fellowships for ever. The very flexibility and ease which make men's friendships so agreeable while they endure, make them the easier to destroy and forget. And a man who has a few friends, or one who has a dozen (if there be any one so wealthy on this earth), cannot forget on how precarious a base his happiness reposes; and how by a stroke or two of fate – a death, a few light words, a piece of stamped paper, a woman's bright eyes – he may be left, in a month, destitute of all. Marriage is certainly a perilous remedy. Instead of on two or three, you stake your happiness on one life only. But still, as the bargain is more explicit and complete on your part, it is more so on the other; and you have not to fear so many contingencies; it is not every wind that can blow you from your anchorage; and so long as Death withholds his sickle, you will always have a friend at home. People who share a cell in the Bastille, or are thrown together on an uninhabited isle, if they do not immediately fall to fisticuffs, will find some possible ground of compromise. They will learn each other's ways and humours, so as to know where they must go warily, and where they may lean their whole weight. The discretion of the first years becomes the settled habit of the last; and so, with wisdom and patience, two lives may grow indissolubly into one.

But marriage, if comfortable, is not at all heroic. It certainly narrows and damps the spirits of generous men. In marriage, a man becomes slack and selfish, and undergoes a fatty degeneration of his moral being. It is not only when Lydgate misallies himself with Rosamond Vincy, but when Ladislaw marries above him with Dorothea, that this may be exemplified. The air of the fireside withers out all the fine wildings of the husband's heart. He is so comfortable and happy that he begins to prefer comfort and happiness to everything else on earth, his wife included. Yesterday he would have shared his last shilling; to-day 'his first duty is to his family,' and is fulfilled in large measure by laying down vintages and husbanding the health of an invaluable parent. Twenty years ago this man was equally capable of crime or heroism; now he is fit for neither. His soul is asleep, and you may speak without constraint; you will not wake him. It is not for nothing that Don Quixote was a bachelor and Marcus Aurelius married ill. For women, there is less of this danger. Marriage is of so much use to a woman, opens out to her so much more of life, and puts her in the way of so much more freedom and usefulness, that, whether she marry ill or well, she can hardly miss some benefit. It is true, however, that some of the merriest and most genuine of women are old maids; and that those old maids, and wives who are unhappily married, have often most of the true motherly touch. And this would seem to show, even for women, some narrowing influence in comfortable married life. But the rule is none the less certain: if you wish the pick of men and women, take a good bachelor and a good wife.

I am often filled with wonder that so many marriages are passably successful, and so few come to open failure, the more so as I fail to understand the principle on which people regulate their choice. I see women marrying indiscriminately with staring burgesses and ferret-faced, white-eyed boys, and men dwelling in contentment with noisy scullions, or taking into their lives acidulous vestals. It is a common answer to say the good people marry because they fall in love; and of course you may use and misuse a word as much as you please, if you have the world along with you. But love is at least a somewhat hyperbolical expression for such luke-warm preference. It is not here, anyway, that Love employs his golden shafts; he cannot be said, with any fitness of language, to reign here and revel. Indeed, if this be love at all, it is plain the poets have been fooling with mankind since the foundation of the world. And you have only to look these happy couples in the face, to see they have never been in love, or in hate, or in any other high passion, all their days. When you see a dish of fruit at dessert, you sometimes set your affections upon one particular peach or nectarine, watch it with some anxiety as it comes round the table, and feel quite a sensible disappointment when it is taken by some one else. I have used the phrase 'high passion.' Well, I should say this was about as high a passion as generally leads to marriage. One husband hears after marriage that some poor fellow is dying of his wife's love. 'What a pity!' he exclaims; 'you know I could so easily have got another!' And yet that is a very happy union. Or again: A young man was telling me the sweet story of his loves. 'I like it well enough as long as her sisters are there,' said this amorous swain; 'but I don't know what to do when we're alone.' Once more: A married lady was debating the subject with another lady. 'You know, dear,' said the first, 'after ten years of marriage, if he is nothing else, your husband is always an old friend.' 'I have many old friends,' returned the other, 'but I prefer them to be nothing more.' 'Oh, perhaps I might *prefer* that also!' There is a common note in these three illustrations of the modern idyll; and it must be owned the god goes among us with a limping gait and blear eyes. You wonder whether it was so always; whether desire was always equally dull and spiritless, and possession equally cold. I cannot help fancying most people make, ere they marry, some such table of recommendations as Hannah Godwin wrote to her brother William anent her friend, Miss Gay. It is so charmingly comical, and so pat to the occasion, that I must quote a few phrases. 'The young lady is in every sense formed to make one of your disposition really happy. She has a pleasing voice, with which she accompanies her musical instrument with judgement. She has an easy politeness in her manners, neither free nor reserved. She is a good housekeeper and a good economist, and yet of a generous disposition. As to her internal accomplishments, I have reason to speak still more highly of them: good sense without vanity, a penetrating judgement without a disposition to satire, with about as much religion as my William likes, struck me with a wish that she was my William's wife.' That is about the tune: pleasing voice, moderate good looks, unimpeachable internal accomplishments after the style of the copy-book, with about as much religion as my William likes; and then, with all speed, to church.

To deal plainly, if they only married when they fell in love, most people would die unwed; and among the others, there would be not a few tumultuous households. The Lion is the King of Beasts, but he is scarcely suitable for a domestic pet. In the same way, I suspect love is rather too violent a passion to make, in all cases, a good domestic sentiment. Like other violent excitements, it throws up not only what is best, but what is worst and smallest, in men's characters. Just as some people are malicious in drink, or brawling and virulent under the influence of religious feeling, some are moody, jealous, and exacting when they are in love, who are honest, downright, good-hearted fellows enough in the everyday affairs and humours of the world.

How then, seeing we are driven to the hypothesis that people choose in comparatively cold blood, how is it they choose so well? One is almost tempted to hint that it does not much matter whom you marry; that, in fact, marriage is a subjective affection, and if you have made up your mind to it, and once talked yourself fairly over, you could 'pull it through' with anybody. But even if we take matrimony at its lowest, even if we regard it as no more than a sort of friendship recognised by the police, there must be degrees in the freedom and sympathy realised, and some principle to guide simple folk in their selection. Now what should this principle be? Are there no more definite rules than are to be found in the Prayer-book? Law and religion forbid the bans on the ground of propinquity or consanguinity; society steps in to separate classes; and in all this most critical matter, has common sense, has wisdom, never a word to say? In the absence of more magisterial teaching, let us talk it over between friends: even a few guesses may be of interest to youths and maidens.

In all that concerns eating and drinking, company, climate, and ways of life, community of taste is to be sought for. It would be trying, for instance, to keep bed and board with an early riser or a vegetarian. In matters of art and intellect, I believe it is of no consequence. Certainly it is of none in the companionships of men, who will dine more readily with one who has a good heart, a good cellar, and a humorous tongue, than with another who shares all their favourite hobbies and is melancholy withal. If your wife likes Tupper, that is no reason why you should hang your head. She thinks with the majority, and has the courage of her opinions. I have always suspected public taste to be a mongrel product, out of affectation by dogmatism; and felt sure, if you could only find an honest man of no special literary bent, he would tell you he thought much of Shakespeare bombastic and most absurd, and all of him written in very obscure English and wearisome to read. And not long ago I was able to lay by my lantern in content, for I found the honest man. He was a fellow of parts, quick, humorous, a clever painter, and with an eye for certain poetical effects of sea and ships. I am not much of a judge of that kind of thing, but a sketch of his comes before me sometimes at night. How strong, supple, and living the ship seems upon the billows! With what a dip and rake she shears the flying sea! I cannot fancy the man who saw this effect, and took it on the wing with so much force and spirit, was what you call common-place in the last recesses of the heart. And yet he thought, and was not ashamed to have it known of him, that Ouida was better in every way than William Shakespeare. If there were more people of his honesty, this would be about the staple of lay criticism. It is not taste that is plentiful, but courage that is rare. And what have we in place? How many, who think no otherwise than the young painter, have we not heard disbursing second-hand hyperboles? Have you never turned sick at heart, O best of critics! when some of your own sweet adjectives were returned on you before a gaping audience? Enthusiasm about art is become a function of the average female being, which she performs with precision and a sort of haunting sprightliness, like an ingenious and well-regulated machine. Sometimes, alas! the calmest man is carried away in the torrent, bandies adjectives with the best, and out-Herods Herod for some shameful moments. When you remember that, you will be tempted to put things strongly, and say you will marry no one who is not like George the Second, and cannot state openly a distaste for poetry and painting.

The word 'facts' is, in some ways, crucial. I have spoken with Jesuits and Plymouth Brethren, mathematicians and poets, dog-matic republicans and dear old gentlemen in bird's-eye neckcloths; and each understood the word 'facts' in an occult sense of his own. Try as I might, I could get no nearer the principle of their division. What was essential to them, seemed to me trivial or untrue. We could come to no compromise as to what was, or what was not, important in the life of man. Turn as we pleased, we all stood back to back in a big ring, and saw another quarter of the heavens, with different mountain-tops along the sky-line and different constellations overhead. We had each of us some whimsy in the brain, which we believed more than anything else, and which discoloured all experience to its own shade. How would you have people agree, when one is deaf and the other blind? Now this is where there should be community between man and wife. They should be agreed on their catchword in 'facts of religion,' or 'facts of science,' or 'society, my dear'; for without such an agreement all intercourse is a painful strain upon the mind. 'About as much religion as my William likes,' in short, that is what is necessary to make a happy couple of any William and his spouse. For these are differences which no habit nor affection can reconcile, and the Bohemian must not intermarry with the

Pharisee. Imagine Consuelo as Mrs Samuel Budget, the wife of the successful merchant! The best of men and the best of women may sometimes live together all their lives, and, for want of some consent on fundamental questions, hold each other lost spirits to the end.

A certain sort of talent is almost indispensable for people who would spend years together and not bore themselves to death. But the talent, like the agreement, must be for and about life. To dwell happily together, they should be versed in the niceties of the heart, and born with a faculty for willing compromise. The woman must be talented as a woman, and it will not much matter although she is talented in nothing else. She must know her *métier de femme*, and have a fine touch for the affections. And it is more important that a person should be a good gossip, and talk pleasantly and smartly of common friends and the thousand and one nothings of the day and hour, than that she should speak with the tongues of men and angels; for a while together by the fire, happens more frequently in marriage than the presence of a distinguished foreigner to dinner. That people should laugh over the same sort of jests, and have many a story of 'grouse in the gun-room,' many an old joke between them which time cannot wither nor custom stale, is a better preparation for life, by your leave, than many other things higher and better sounding in the world's ears. You could read Kant by yourself, if you wanted; but you must share a joke with some one else. You can forgive people who do not follow you through a philosophical disquisition; but to find your wife laughing when you had tears in your eyes, or staring when you were in a fit of laughter, would go some way towards a dissolution of the marriage.

I know a woman who, from some distaste or disability, could never so much as understand the meaning of the word *politics*, and has given up trying to distinguish Whigs from Tories; but take her on her own politics, ask her about other men or women and the chicanery of everyday existence – the rubs, the tricks, the vanities on which life turns – and you will not find many more shrewd, trenchant, and humorous. Nay, to make plainer what I have in mind, this same woman has a share of the higher and more poetical understanding, frank interest in things for their own sake, and enduring astonishment at the most common. She is not to be deceived by custom, or made to think a mystery solved when it is repeated. I have heard her say she could wonder herself crazy over the human eyebrow. Now in a world where most of us walk very contentedly in the little lit circle of their own reason, and have to be reminded of what lies without by specious and clamant exceptions – earthquakes, eruptions of Vesuvius, banjos floating in mid-air at a *séance,* and the like – a mind so fresh and unsophisticated is no despicable gift. I will own I think it a better sort of mind than goes necessarily with the clearest views on public business. It will wash. It will find something to say at an odd moment. It has in it the spring of pleasant and quaint fancies. Whereas I can imagine myself yawning all night long until my jaws ached and the tears came into my eyes, although my companion on the other side of the hearth held the most enlightened opinions on the franchise or the ballot.

The question of professions, in as far as they regard marriage, was only interesting to women until of late days, but it touches all of us now. Certainly, if I could help it, I would never marry a wife who wrote. The practice of letters is miserably harassing to the mind; and after an hour or two's work, all the more human portion of the author is extinct; he will bully, backbite, and speak daggers. Music, I hear, is not much better. But painting, on the contrary, is often highly sedative; because so much of the labour, after your picture is once begun, is almost entirely manual, and of that skilled sort of manual labour which offers a continual series of successes, and so tickles a man, through his vanity, into good humour. Alas! in letters there is nothing of this sort. You may write as beautiful a hand as you will, you have always something else to think of, and cannot pause to notice your loops and flourishes; they are beside the mark, and the first law stationer could put you to the blush. Rousseau, indeed, made some account of penmanship, even made it a source of livelihood, when he copied out the *Héloïse* for *dilettante* ladies; and therein showed that strange eccentric prudence which guided him among so many thousand follies and insanities. It would be well for all of the *genus irritabile* thus to add something of skilled labour to intangible brain-work. To find the right word is so doubtful a success and lies so near to failure, that there is no satisfaction in a year of it; but we all know when we have formed a letter perfectly; and a stupid artist, right or wrong, is almost equally certain he has found a right tone or a right colour, or made a dexterous stroke with his brush. And, again, painters may work out of doors; and the fresh air, the deliberate seasons, and the 'tranquillising influence' of the green earth, counterbalance the fever of thought, and keep them cool, placable, and prosaic.

A ship captain is a good man to marry if it is a marriage of love, for absences are a good influence in love and keep it bright and delicate; but he is just the worst man if the feeling is more pedestrian, as habit is too frequently torn open and the solder has never time to set. Men who fish, botanise, work with the turning-lathe, or gather sea-weeds, will make admirable husbands; and a little amateur painting in water-colour shows the innocent and quiet mind. Those who have a few intimates are to be avoided; while those who swim loose, who have their hat in their hand all along the street, who can number an infinity of acquaintances and are not chargeable with any one friend, promise an easy disposition and no rival to the wife's influence. I will not say they are the best of men, but they are the stuff out of which adroit and capable women manufacture the best of husbands. It is to be noticed that those who have loved once or twice already are so much the better educated to a woman's hand; the bright boy of fiction is an odd and most uncomfortable mixture of shyness and coarseness, and needs a deal of civilising. Lastly (and this is, perhaps, the golden rule), no woman should marry a teetotaller, or a man who does not smoke. It is not for nothing that this 'ignoble tabagie,' as Michelet calls it, spreads over all the world. Michelet rails against it because it renders you happy apart from thought or work; to provident women this will seem no evil influence in married life. Whatever keeps a man in the front garden, whatever checks wandering fancy and all inordinate ambition, whatever makes for lounging and contentment, makes just so surely for domestic happiness.

These notes, if they amuse the reader at all, will probably amuse him more when he differs than when he agrees with them; at least they will do no harm, for nobody will follow my advice. But the last word is of more concern. Marriage is a step so grave and decisive that it attracts light-headed, variable men by its very awfulness. They have been so tried among the inconstant squalls and currents, so often sailed for islands in the air or lain becalmed with burning heart, that they will risk all for solid ground below their feet. Desperate pilots, they run their sea-sick, weary bark upon the dashing rocks. It seems as if marriage were the royal road through life, and realised, on the instant, what we have all dreamed on summer Sundays when the bells ring, or at night when we cannot sleep for the desire of living. They think it will sober and change them. Like those who join a brotherhood, they fancy it needs but an act to be out of the coil and clamour for ever.

But this is a wile of the devil's. To the end, spring winds will sow disquietude, passing faces leave a regret behind them, and the whole world keep calling and calling in their ears. For marriage is like life in this – that it is a field of battle, and not a bed of roses.

ON FALLING IN LOVE

'Lord, what fools these mortals be!'

There is only one event in life which really astonishes a man and startles him out of his prepared opinions. Everything else befalls him very much as he expected. Event succeeds to event, with an agreeable variety indeed, but with little that is either startling or intense; they form together no more than a sort of background, or running accompaniment to the man's own reflections; and he falls naturally into a cool, curious, and smiling habit of mind, and builds himself up in a conception of life which expects tomorrow to be after the pattern of today and yesterday. He may be accustomed to the vagaries of his friends and acquaintances under the influence of love. He may sometimes look forward to it for himself with an incomprehensible expectation. But it is a subject in which neither intuition nor the behaviour of others will help the philosopher to the truth. There is probably nothing rightly thought or rightly written on this matter of love that is not a piece of the person's experience. I remember an anecdote of a well-known French theorist, who was debating a point eagerly in his *cénacle*. It was objected against him that he had never experienced love. Whereupon he arose, left the society, and made it a point not to return to it until he considered that he had supplied the defect. 'Now,' he remarked, on entering, 'now I am in a position to continue the discussion.' Perhaps he had not penetrated very deeply into the subject after all; but the story indicates right thinking, and may serve as an apologue to readers of this essay.

When at last the scales fall from his eyes, it is not without something of the nature of dismay that the man finds himself in such changed conditions. He has to deal with commanding emotions instead of the easy dislikes and preferences in which he has hitherto passed his days; and he recognises capabilities for pain and pleasure of which he had not yet suspected the existence. Falling in love is the one illogical adventure, the one thing of which we are tempted to think as supernatural, in our trite and reasonable world. The effect is out of all proportion with the cause. Two persons, neither of them, it may be, very amiable or very beautiful, meet, speak a little, and look a little into each other's eyes. That has been done a dozen or so of times in the experience of either with no great result. But on this occasion all is different. They fall at once into that state in which another person becomes to us the very gist and centrepoint of God's creation, and demolishes our laborious theories with a smile; in which our ideas are so bound up with the one master-thought that even the trivial cares of our own person become so many acts of devotion, and the love of life itself is translated into a wish to remain in the same world with so precious and desirable a fellow-creature. And all the while their acquaintances look on in stupor, and ask each other, with almost passionate emphasis, what so-and-so can see in that woman, or such-an-one in that man? I am sure, gentlemen, I cannot tell you. For my part, I cannot think what the women mean. It might be very well, if the Apollo Belvedere should suddenly glow all over into life, and step forward from the pedestal with that godlike air of his. But of the misbegotten changelings who call themselves men, and prate intolerably over dinner-tables, I never saw one who seemed worthy to inspire love – no, nor read of any, except Leonardo de Vinci, and perhaps Goethe in his youth. About women I entertain a somewhat different opinion; but there, I have the misfortune to be a man.

There are many matters in which you may waylay Destiny, and bid him stand and deliver. Hard work, high thinking, adventurous excitement, and a great deal more that forms a part of this or the other person's spiritual bill of fare, are within the reach of almost anyone who can dare a little and be patient. But it is by no means in the way of everyone to fall in love. You know the difficulty Shakespeare was put into when Queen Elizabeth asked him to show Falstaff in love. I do not believe that Henry Fielding was ever in love. Scott, if it were not for a passage or two in *Rob Roy*, would give me very much the same effect. These are great names and (what is more to the purpose) strong, healthy, high-strung, and generous natures, of whom the reverse might have been expected. As for the innumerable army of anaemic and tailorish persons who occupy the face of this planet with so much propriety, it is palpably absurd to imagine them in any such situation as a love-affair. A wet rag goes safely by the fire; and if a man is blind, he cannot expect to be much impressed by romantic scenery. Apart from all this, many lovable people miss each other in the world, or meet under some unfavourable star. There is the nice and critical moment of declaration to be got over. From timidity or lack of opportunity a good half of possible love cases never get so far, and at least another quarter do there cease and determine. A very adroit person, to be sure, manages to prepare the way and out with his declaration in the nick of time. And then there is a fine solid sort of man, who goes on from snub to snub; and if he has to declare forty times, will continue imperturbably declaring, amid the astonished consideration of men and angels, until he has a favourable answer. I daresay, if one were a woman, one would like to marry a man who was capable of doing this, but not quite one who had done so. It is just a little bit abject, and somehow just a little bit gross; and marriages in which one of the parties has been thus battered into consent scarcely form agreeable subjects for meditation. Love should run out to meet love with open arms. Indeed, the ideal story is that of two people who go into love step for step, with a fluttered consciousness, like a pair of children venturing together into a dark room. From the first moment when they see each other, with a pang of curiosity, through stage after stage of growing pleasure and embarrassment, they can read the expression of their own trouble in each other's eyes. There is here no declaration properly so called; the feeling is so plainly shared, that as soon as the man knows what it is in his own heart, he is sure of what it is in the woman's.

This simple accident of falling in love is as beneficial as it is astonishing. It arrests the petrifying influence of years, disproves cold-blooded and cynical conclusions, and awakens dormant sensibilities. Hitherto the man had found it a good policy to disbelieve the existence of any enjoyment which was out of his reach; and thus he turned his back upon the strong sunny parts of nature, and accustomed himself to look exclusively on what was common and dull. He accepted a prose ideal, let himself go blind of many sympathies by disuse; and if he were young and witty, or beautiful, wilfully forewent these advantages. He joined himself to the following of what, in the old mythology of love, was prettily called *nonchaloir*; and in an odd mixture of feelings, a fling of self-respect, a preference for selfish liberty, and a great dash of that fear with which honest people regard serious interests, kept himself back from the straightforward course of life among certain selected activities. And now, all of a sudden, he is unhorsed, like St Paul, from his infidel affectation. His heart, which has been ticking accurate seconds for the last year, gives a bound and begins to beat high and irregularly in his breast. It seems as if he had never heard or felt or seen until that moment; and by the report of his memory, he must have lived his past life between sleep and waking, or with the preoccupied attention of a brown study. He is practically incommoded by the generosity of his feelings, smiles much when he is alone, and develops a habit of looking rather blankly upon the moon and stars. But it is not at all within the province of a prose essayist to give a picture of this hyperbolical frame of mind; and the thing has been done already, and that to admiration. In *Adelaide,* in Tennyson's *Maud,* and in some of Heine's songs, you get the absolute expression of this midsummer spirit. Romeo and Juliet were very much in love; although they tell me some German critics are of a different opinion, probably the same who would have us think Mercutio a dull fellow. Poor Antony was in love, and no mistake. That lay figure Marius, in *Les Misérables,* is also a genuine case in his own way, and worth observation. A good many of George Sand's people are thoroughly in love; and so are a good many of George Meredith's. Altogether, there is plenty to read on the subject. If the root of the matter be in him, and if he has the requisite chords to set in vibration, a young man may occasionally enter, with the key of art, into that land of Beulah which is upon the borders of Heaven and within sight of the City of Love. There let him sit awhile to hatch delightful hopes and perilous illusions.

One thing that accompanies the passion in its first blush is certainly difficult to explain. It comes (I do not quite see how) that from having a very supreme sense of pleasure in all parts of life – in lying down to sleep, in waking, in motion, in breathing, in continuing to be – the lover begins to regard his happiness as beneficial for the rest of the world and highly meritorious in himself. Our race has never been able contentedly to suppose that the noise of its wars, conducted by a few young gentlemen in a corner of an inconsiderable star, does not re-echo among the courts of Heaven with quite a formidable effect. In much the same taste, when people find a great to-do in their own breasts, they imagine it must have some influence in their neighbourhood. The presence of the two lovers is so enchanting to each other that it seems as if it must be the best thing possible for everybody else. They are half inclined to fancy it is because of them and their love that the sky is blue and the sun shines. And certainly the weather is usually fine while people are courting . . . In point of fact, although the happy man feels very kindly towards others of his own sex, there is apt to be something too much of the magnifico in his demeanour. If people grow presuming and self-important over such matters as a dukedom or the Holy See, they will scarcely support the dizziest elevation in life without some suspicion of a strut; and the dizziest elevation is to love and be loved in return. Consequently, accepted lovers are a trifle condescending in their address to other men. An overweening sense of the passion and importance of life hardly conduces to simplicity of manner. To women, they feel very nobly, very purely, and very generously, as if they were so many Joan of Arcs; but this does not come out in their behaviour; and they treat them to Grandisonian airs marked with a suspicion of fatuity. I am not quite certain that women do not like this sort of thing; but really, after having bemused myself over *Daniel Deronda*, I have given up trying to understand what they like.

If it did nothing else, this sublime and ridiculous superstition, that the pleasure of the pair is somehow blessed to others, and everybody is made happier in their happiness, would serve at least to keep love generous and great-hearted. Nor is it quite a baseless superstition after all. Other lovers are hugely interested. They strike the nicest balance between pity and approval, when they see people aping the greatness of their own sentiments. It is an understood thing in the play, that while the young gentlefolk are courting on the terrace, a rough flirtation is being carried on, and a light, trivial sort of love is growing up, between the footman and the singing chambermaid. As people are generally cast for the leading parts in their own imaginations, the reader can apply the parallel to real life without much chance of going wrong. In short, they are quite sure this other love-affair is not so deep-seated as their own, but they like dearly to see it going forward. And love, considered as a spectacle, must have attractions for many who are not of the confraternity. The sentimental old maid is a commonplace of the novelists; and he must be rather a poor sort of human being, to be sure, who can look on at this pretty madness without indulgence and sympathy. For nature commends itself to people with a most insinuating art; the busiest is now and again arrested by a great sunset; and you may be as pacific or as cold-blooded as you will, but you cannot help some emotion when you read of well-disputed battles, or meet a pair of lovers in the lane.

Certainly, whatever it may be with regard to the world at

large, this idea of beneficent pleasure is true as between the sweethearts. To do good and communicate is the lover's grand intention. It is the happiness of the other that makes his own most intense gratification. It is not possible to disentangle the different emotions, the pride, humility, pity and passion, which are excited by a look of happy love or an unexpected caress. To make one's self beautiful, to dress the hair, to excel in talk, to do anything and all things that puff out the character and attributes and make them imposing in the eyes of others, is not only to magnify one's self, but to offer the most delicate homage at the same time. And it is in this latter intention that they are done by lovers; for the essence of love is kindness; and indeed it may be best defined as passionate kindness: kindness, so to speak, run mad and become importunate and violent. Vanity in a merely personal sense exists no longer. The lover takes a perilous pleasure in privately displaying his weak points and having them, one after another, accepted and condoned. He wishes to be assured that he is not loved for this or that good quality, but for himself, or something as like himself as he can contrive to set forward. For, although it may have been a very difficult thing to paint the marriage of Cana, or write the fourth act of *Antony and Cleopatra*, there is a more difficult piece of art before everyone in this world who cares to set about explaining his own character to others. Words and acts are easily wrenched from their true significance; and they are all the language we have to come and go upon. A pitiful job we make of it, as a rule. For better or worse, people mistake our meaning and take our emotions at a wrong valuation. And generally we rest pretty content with our failures; we are content to be misapprehended by cackling flirts; but when once a man is moonstruck with this affection of love, he makes it a point of honour to clear such dubieties away. He cannot have the Best of her Sex misled upon a point of this importance; and his pride revolts at being loved in a mistake.

He discovers a great reluctance to return on former periods of his life. To all that has not been shared with her, rights and duties, bygone fortunes and dispositions, he can look back only by a difficult and repugnant effort of the will. That he should have wasted some years in ignorance of what alone was really important, that he may have entertained the thought of other women with any show of complacency, is a burthen almost too heavy for his self-respect. But it is the thought of another past that rankles in his spirit like a poisoned wound. That he himself made a fashion of being alive in the bald, beggarly days before a certain meeting, is deplorable enough in all good conscience. But that She should have permitted herself the same liberty seems inconsistent with a Divine providence.

A great many people run down jealousy, on the score that it is an artificial feeling, as well as practically inconvenient. This is scarcely fair; for the feeling on which it merely attends, like an ill-humoured courtier, is itself artificial in exactly the same sense and to the same degree. I suppose what is meant by that objection is that jealousy has not always been a character of man; formed no part of that very modest kit of sentiments with which he is supposed to have begun the world; but waited to make its appearance in better days and among richer natures. And this is equally true of love, and friendship, and love of country, and delight in what they call the beauties of nature, and most other things worth having. Love, in particular, will not endure any historical scrutiny: to all who have fallen across it, it is one of the most incontestable facts in the world; but if you begin to ask what it was in other periods and countries, in Greece for instance, the strangest doubts begin to spring up, and everything seems so vague and changing that a dream is logical in comparison. Jealousy, at any rate, is one of the consequences of love; you may like it or not, at pleasure; but there it is.

It is not exactly jealousy, however, that we feel when we reflect on the past of those we love. A bundle of letters found after years of happy union creates no sense of insecurity in the present; and yet it will pain a man sharply. The two people entertain no vulgar doubt of each other: but this pre-existence of both occurs to the mind as something indelicate. To be altogether right, they should have had twin birth together, at the same moment with the feeling that unites them. Then indeed it would be simple and perfect and without reserve or afterthought. Then they would understand each other with a fullness impossible otherwise. There would be no barrier between them of associations that cannot be imparted. They would be led into none of those comparisons that send the blood back to the heart. And they would know that there had been no time lost, and they had been together as much as was possible. For besides terror for the separation that must follow some time or other in the future, men feel anger, and something like remorse, when they think of that other separation which endured until they met. Someone has written that love makes people believe in immortality, because there seems not to be room enough in life for so great a tenderness, and it is inconceivable that the most masterful of our emotions should have no more than the spare moments of a few years. Indeed, it seems strange; but if we call to mind analogies, we can hardly regard it as impossible.

'The blind bow-boy,' who smiles upon us from the end of terraces in old Dutch gardens, laughingly hails his bird-bolts among a fleeting generation. But for as fast as ever he shoots, the game dissolves and disappears into eternity from under his falling arrows; this one is gone ere he is struck; the other has but time to make one gesture and give one passionate cry; and they are all the things of a moment. When the generation is gone, when the play is over, when the thirty years' panorama has been withdrawn in tatters from the stage of the world, we may ask what has become of these great, weighty, and undying loves, and the sweethearts who despised mortal conditions in a fine credulity; and they can only show us a few songs in a bygone taste, a few actions worth remembering, and a few children who have retained some happy stamp from the disposition of their parents.

SOME ASPECTS OF ROBERT BURNS

To write with authority about another man, we must have fellow-feeling and some common ground of experience with our subject. We may praise or blame according as we find him related to us by the best or worst in ourselves; but it is only in virtue of some relationship that we can be his judges, even to condemn. Feelings which we share and understand enter for us into the tissue of the man's character; those to which we are strangers in our own experience we are inclined to regard as blots, exceptions, inconsistencies, and excursions of the diabolic; we conceive them with repugnance, explain them with difficulty, and raise our hands to heaven in wonder when we find them in conjunction with talents that we respect or virtues that we admire. David, king of Israel, would pass a sounder judgement on a man than either Nathaniel or David Hume. Now, Principal Shairp's recent volume, although I believe no one will read it without respect and interest, has this one capital defect — that there is imperfect sympathy between the author and the subject, between the critic and the personality under criticism. Hence an inorganic, if not an incoherent, presentation of both the poems and the man. Of *Holy Willie's Prayer*, Principal Shairp remarks that 'those who have loved most what was best in Burns's poetry must have regretted that it was ever written.' To the *Jolly Beggars*, so far as my memory serves me, he refers but once; and then only to remark on the 'strange, not to say painful,' circumstance that the same hand which wrote the *Cotter's Saturday Night* should have stooped to write the *Jolly Beggars*. The *Saturday Night* may or may not be an admirable poem; but its significance is trebled, and the power and range of the poet first appears, when it is set beside the *Jolly Beggars*. To take a man's work piecemeal, except with the design of elegant extracts, is the way to avoid, and not to perform, the critic's duty. The same defect is displayed in the treatment of

Burns as a man, which is broken, apologetical, and confused. The man here presented to us is not that Burns, *teres atque rotundus* — a burly figure in literature, as, from our present vantage of time, we have begun to see him. This, on the other hand, is Burns as he may have appeared to an indulgent but orderly and orthodox person, anxious to be pleased, but too often hurt and disappointed by the behaviour of his red-hot *protégé,* and solacing himself with the explanation that the poet was 'the most inconsistent of men.' If you are so sensibly pained by the misconduct of your subject, and so paternally delighted with his virtues, you will always be an excellent gentleman, but a somewhat questionable biographer. Indeed, we can only be sorry and surprised that Principal Shairp should have chosen a theme so uncongenial. When we find a man writing on Burns, who likes neither *Holy Willie,* nor the *Beggars,* nor the *Ordination,* nothing is adequate to the situation but the old cry of Géronte: '*Que diable allait-il faire dans cette galère?*' And every merit we find in the book, which is sober and candid in a degree unusual with biographies of Burns, only leads us to regret more heartily that good work should be so greatly thrown away.

It is far from my intention to tell over again a story that has been so often told; but there are certainly some points in the character of Burns that will bear to be brought out, and some chapters in his life that demand a brief rehearsal. The unity of the man's nature, for all its richness, has fallen somewhat out of sight in the pressure of new information and the apologetical ceremony of biographers. Mr Carlyle made an inimitable bust of the poet's head of gold; may I not be forgiven if my business should have more to do with the feet, which were of clay?

YOUTH

Any view of Burns would be misleading which passed over in silence the influences of his home and his father. That father, William Burnes, after having been for many years a gardener, took a farm, married, and, like an emigrant in a new country, built himself a house with his own hands. Poverty of the most distressing sort, with sometimes the near prospect of a gaol, embittered the remainder of his life. Chill, backward, and austere with strangers, grave and imperious in his family, he was yet a man of very unusual parts and of an affectionate nature. On his way through life he had remarked much upon other men, with more result in theory than practice; and he had reflected upon many subjects as he delved the garden. His great delight was in solid conversation; he would leave his work to talk with the schoolmaster Murdoch; and Robert, when he came home late at night, not only turned aside rebuke but kept his father two hours beside the fire by the charm of his merry and vigorous talk. Nothing is more characteristic of the class in general, and William Burnes in particular, than the pains he took to get proper schooling for his boys, and, when that was no longer possible, the sense and resolution with which he set himself to supply the deficiency by his own influence. For many years he was their chief companion; he spoke with them seriously on all subjects as if they had been grown men; at night, when work was over, he taught them arithmetic; he borrowed books for them on history, science, and theology; and he felt it his duty to supplement this last – the trait is laughably Scottish – by a dialogue of his own composition, where his own private shade of orthodoxy was exactly represented. He would go to his daughter as she stayed afield herding cattle, to teach her the names of grasses and wild flowers, or to sit by her side when it thundered. Distance to strangers, deep family tenderness, love of knowledge, a narrow, precise, and formal reading of theology – everything we learn of him hangs well together, and builds up a popular Scotch type. If I mention the name of Andrew Fairservice, it is only as I might couple for an instant Dugald Dalgetty with old Marshal London, to help out the reader's comprehension by a popular but unworthy instance of a class. Such was the influence of this good and wise man that his household became a school to itself, and neighbours who came into the farm at meal-time would find the whole family, father, brothers, and sisters, helping themselves with one hand, and holding a book in the other. We are surprised at the prose style of Robert; that of Gilbert need surprise us no less; even William writes a remarkable letter for a young man of such slender opportunities. One adecdote marks the taste of the family. Murdoch brought *Titus Andronicus,* and, with such dominie elocution as we may suppose, began to read it aloud before this rustic audience; but when he had reached the passage where Tamora insults Lavinia, with one voice and 'in an agony of distress' they refused to hear it to an end. In such a father and with such a home, Robert had already the making of an excellent education; and what Murdoch added, although it may not have been much in amount, was in character the very essence of a literary training. Schools and colleges, for one great man whom they complete, perhaps unmake a dozen; the strong spirit can do well upon more scanty fare.

Robert steps before us, almost from the first, in his complete character – a proud, headstrong, impetuous lad, greedy of pleasure, greedy of notice; in his own phrase 'panting after distinction,' and in his brother's 'cherishing a particular jealousy of people who were richer or of more consequence than himself:' with all this, he was emphatically of the artist nature. Already he made a conspicuous figure in Tarbolton church, with the only tied hair in the parish, 'and his plaid, which was of a particular colour, wrapped in a particular manner round his shoulders.' Ten years later, when a married man, the father of a family, a farmer, and an officer of Excise, we shall find him out fishing in masquerade, with fox-skin cap, belted great-coat, and great Highland broadsword. He liked dressing up, in fact, for its own sake. This is the spirit which leads to the extravagant array of Latin Quarter students, and the proverbial velveteen of the English landscape-painter; and, though the pleasure derived is in itself merely personal, it shows a man who is, to say the least of it, not pained by general attention and remark. His father wrote the family name *Burnes;* Robert early adopted the orthography *Burness* from his cousin in the Mearns; and in his twenty-eighth year changed it once more to *Burns*. It is plain that the last transformation was not made without some qualm; for in addressing his cousin he adheres, in at least one more letter, to spelling number two. And this, again, shows a man preoccupied about the manner of his appearance even down to the name, and little willing to follow custom. Again, he was proud, and justly proud, of his powers in conversation. To no other man's have we the same conclusive testimony from different sources and from every rank of life. It is almost a commonplace that the best of his works was what he said in talk. Robertson the historian 'scarcely ever met any man whose conversation displayed greater vigour;' the Duchess of Gordon declared that he 'carried her off her feet;' and, when he came late to an inn, the servants would get out of bed to hear him talk. But, in these early days at least, he was determined to shine by any means. He made himself feared in the village for his tongue. He would crush weaker men to their faces, or even perhaps – for the statement of Sillar is not absolute – say cutting things of his acquaintances behind their back. At the church door, between sermons, he would parade his religious views amid hisses. These details stamp the man. He had no genteel timidities in the conduct of his life. He loved to force his personality upon the world. He would please himself, and shine. Had he lived in the Paris of 1830, and joined his lot with the Romantics, we can conceive him writing *Jehan* for *Jean,* swaggering in Gautier's red waistcoat, and horrifying Bourgeois in a public café with paradox and gasconnade.

A leading trait throughout his whole career was his desire to be in love. *Ne fait pas ce tour qui veut.* His affections were often enough touched, but perhaps never engaged. He was all his life on a voyage of discovery, but it does not appear conclusively that he ever touched the happy isle. A man brings to love a deal of ready-made sentiment, and even from childhood obscurely prognosticates the symptoms of this vital malady. Burns was formed for love; he had passion, tenderness, and a singular bent in the direction; he could foresee, with the intuition of an artist, what love ought to be; and he could not conceive a worthy life without it. But he had ill-fortune, and was besides so greedy after every shadow of the true divinity, and so much the slave of a strong temperament, that perhaps his nerve was relaxed and his heart had lost the power of self-devotion before an opportunity occurred. The circumstances of his youth doubtless counted for something in the result. For the lads of Ayrshire, as soon as the day's work was over and the beasts were stabled, would take the road, it might be in a winter tempest, and travel perhaps miles by moss and moorland to spend an hour or two in courtship. Rule 10 of the Bachelors' Club at Tarbolton provides that 'every man proper for a member of this Society must be a professed lover of *one or more* of the female sex.' The rich, as Burns himself points out, may have a choice of pleasurable occupations, but these lads had nothing but their 'cannie hour at e'en.' It was upon love and flirtation that this rustic society was built; gallantry was the essence of life among the Ayrshire hills as well as in the Court of Versailles; and the days were distinguished from each other by love-letters, meetings, tiffs, reconciliations, and expansions to the chosen confidant, as in a comedy of Marivaux. Here was a field for a man of Burns's indiscriminate personal ambition, where he might pursue his voyage of discovery in quest of true love, and enjoy temporary triumphs by the way. He was 'constantly the victim of some fair enslaver' – at least, when it was not the other way about; and there were often underplots and secondary fair enslavers in the background. Many – or may we not say most? – of these affairs were entirely artificial. One, he tells us, he began out of 'a vanity of showing his parts in courtship,' for he piqued himself on his ability at a love-letter. But, however they began, these flames of his were fanned into a passion ere the end; and he stands unsurpassed in his power of self-deception, and positively without a competitor in the art, to use his own words, of 'battering himself into a warm affection,' – a debilitating and futile exercise. Once he had worked himself into the vein, 'the agitations of his mind and body' were an astonishment to all who knew him. Such a course as this, however pleasant to a thirsty vanity, was lowering to his nature. He sank more and more towards the professional Don Juan. With a leer of what the French call fatuity, he bids the belles of Mauchline beware of his seductions; and the same cheap self-satisfaction finds a yet uglier vent when he plumes himself on the scandal at the birth of his first bastard. We can well believe what we hear of his facility in striking up an acquaintance with women: he would have conquering manners; he would bear down upon his rustic game with the grace that comes of absolute assurance – the Richelieu of Lochlea or Mossgiel. In yet another manner did these quaint ways of courtship help him into fame. If he were great as principal, he was unrivalled as confidant. He could enter into a passion; he could counsel wary moves, being, in his own phrase, so old a hawk; nay, he could turn a letter for some unlucky swain, or even string a few lines of verse that should clinch the business and fetch the hesitating fair one to the ground. Nor, perhaps, was it only his 'curiosity, zeal, and intrepid dexterity' that recommended him for a second in such affairs; it must have been a distinction to have the assistance and advice of *Rab the Ranter*; and one who was in no way formidable by himself might grow dangerous and attractive through the fame of his associate.

I think we can conceive him, in these early years, in that rough moorland country, poor among the poor with his seven pounds a year, looked upon with doubt by respectable elders, but for all that the best talker, the best letter-writer, the most famous lover and confidant, the laureate poet, and the only man who wore his hair tied in the parish. He says he had then as high a notion of himself as ever after; and I can well believe it. Among the youth he walked *facile princeps*, an apparent god; and even if, from time to time, the Reverend Mr Auld should swoop upon him with the thunders of the Church, and, in company with seven others, Rab the Ranter must figure some fine Sunday on the stool of repentance, would there not be a sort of glory, an infernal apotheosis, in so conspicuous a shame? Was not Richelieu in disgrace more idolised than ever by the dames of Paris? and when was the highwayman most acclaimed but on his way to Tyburn? Or, to take a simile from nearer home, and still more exactly to the point, what could even corporal punishment avail, administered by a cold, abstract, unearthly schoolmaster, against the influence and fame of the school's hero?

And now we come to the culminating point of Burns's early period. He began to be received into the unknown upper world. His fame soon spread from among his fellow-rebels on the benches, and began to reach the ushers and monitors of this great Ayrshire academy. This arose in part from his lax views about religion; for at this time that old war of the creeds and confessors, which is always grumbling from end to end of our poor Scotland, brisked up in these parts into a hot and virulent skirmish; and Burns found himself identified with the opposition party – a clique of roaring lawyers and half-heretical divines, with wit enough to appreciate the value of the poet's help, and not sufficient taste to moderate his grossness and personality. We may judge of their surprise when *Holy Willie* was put into their hand; like the amorous lads of Tarbolton, they recognised in him the best of seconds. His satires began to go the round in manuscript; Mr Aiken, one of the lawyers, 'read him into fame;' he himself was soon welcome in many houses of a better sort, where his admirable talk, and his manners, which he had direct from his Maker, except for a brush he gave them at a country dancing school, completed what his poems had begun. We have a sight of him at his first visit to Adamhill, in his ploughman's shoes, coasting around the carpet as though that were sacred ground. But he soon grew used to carpets and their owners; and he was still the superior of all whom he encountered, and ruled the roost in conversation. Such was the impression made, that a young clergyman, himself a man of ability, trembled and became confused when he saw Robert enter the church in which he was to preach. It is not surprising that the poet determined to publish: he had now stood the test of some publicity, and under this hopeful impulse he composed in six winter months the bulk of his more important poems. Here was a young man who, from a very humble place, was mounting rapidly; from the cynosure of a parish, he had become the talk of a county; once the bard of rural courtships, he was now about to appear as a bound and printed poet in the world's bookshops.

A few more intimate strokes are necessary to complete the sketch. This strong young ploughman, who feared no competitor with the flail, suffered like a fine lady from sleeplessness and vapours; he would fall into the blackest melancholies, and be filled with remorse for the past and terror for the future. He was still not perhaps devoted to religion, but haunted by it; and at a touch of sickness prostrated himself before God in what I can only call unmanly penitence. As he had aspirations beyond his place in the world, so he had tastes, thoughts, and weaknesses to match. He loved to walk under a wood to the sound of a winter tempest; he had a singular tenderness for animals; he carried a book with him in his pocket when he went abroad, and wore out in this service two copies of the *Man of Feeling*. With young people in the field at work he was very long-suffering; and when his brother Gilbert spoke sharply to them – 'O man, ye are no for young folk,' he would say, and give the defaulter a helping hand and a smile. In the hearts of the men whom he met, he read as in a book; and, what is yet more rare, his knowledge of himself equalled his knowledge of others. There are no truer things said of Burns than what is to be found in his own letters. Country Don Juan as he was, he had none of that blind vanity which values itself on what it is not; he knew his own strength and weakness to a hair: he took himself boldly for what he was, and, except in moments of hypochondria, declared himself content.

THE LOVE STORIES

On the night of Mauchline races, 1785, the young men and women of the place joined in a penny ball, according to their custom. In the same set danced Jean Armour, the master-mason's daughter, and our dark-eyed Don Juan. His dog (not the immortal Luath, but a successor unknown to fame, *caret quia vate sacro*), apparently sensible of some neglect, followed his master to and fro, to the confusion of the dancers. Some mirthful comments followed; and Jean heard the poet say to his partner – or, as I should imagine, laughingly launch the remark to the company at large – that 'he wished he could get any of the lasses to like him as well as his dog.' Some time after, as the girl was bleaching clothes on Mauchline green, Robert chanced to go by, still accompanied by his dog; and the dog, 'scouring in long excursion,' scampered with four black paws across the linen. This brought the two into conversation; when Jean, with a somewhat hoydenish advance, inquired if 'he had yet got any of the lasses to like him as well as his dog?' It is one of the misfortunes of the professional Don Juan that his honour forbids him to refuse battle; he is in life like the Roman soldier upon duty, or like the sworn physician who must attend on all diseases. Burns accepted the provocation; hungry hope reawakened in his heart; here was a girl – pretty, simple at least, if not honestly stupid, and plainly not averse to his attentions; it seemed to him once more as if love might here be waiting him. Had he but known the truth! for this facile and empty-headed girl had nothing more in view than a flirtation; and her heart, from the first and on to the end of her story, was engaged by another man. Burns once more commenced the celebrated process of 'battering himself into a warm affection;' and the proofs of his success are to be found in many verses of the period. Nor did he succeed with himself only; Jean, with her heart still elsewhere, succumbed to his fascination, and early in the next year the natural consequence became manifest. It was a heavy stroke for this unfortunate couple. They had trifled with life, and were now rudely reminded of life's serious issues. Jean awoke to the ruin of her hopes; the best she had now to expect was marriage with a man who was a stranger to her dearest thoughts; she might now be glad if she could get what she would never have chosen. As for Burns, at the stroke of the calamity he recognised that his voyage of discovery had led him into a wrong hemisphere – that he was not, and never had been, really in love with Jean. Hear him in the pressure of the hour. 'Against two things,' he writes, 'I am as fixed as fate – staying at home, and owning her conjugally. The first, by heaven, I will not do! – the last, by hell, I will never do!' And then he adds, perhaps already in a more relenting temper: 'If you see Jean, tell her I will meet her, so God help me in my hour of need.' They met accordingly; and Burns, touched with her misery, came down from these heights of independence, and gave her a written acknowledgement of marriage. It is the punishment of Don Juanism to create continually false positions – relations in life which are wrong in themselves, and which it is equally wrong to break or to perpetuate. This was such a case. Worldly Wiseman would have laughed and gone his way; let us be glad that Burns was better counselled by his heart. When we discover that we can be no longer true, the next best is to be kind. I daresay he came away from that interview not very content, but with a glorious conscience; and as he went homeward, he would sing his favourite, 'How are Thy servants blest, O Lord!' Jean, on the other hand, armed with her 'lines,' confided her position to the master-mason, her father, and his wife. Burns and his brother were then in a fair way to ruin themselves in their farm; the poet was an execrable match for any well-to-do country lass; and perhaps old Armour had an inkling of a previous attachment on his daughter's part. At least, he was not so much incensed by her slip from virtue as by the marriage which had been designed to cover it. Of this he would not hear a word. Jean, who had besought the acknowledgement only to appease her parents, and not at all from any violent inclination to the poet, readily gave up the paper for destruction; and all parties imagined, although wrongly, that the marriage was thus dissolved. To a proud man like Burns here was a crushing blow. The concession which had been wrung from his pity was now publicly thrown back in his teeth. The Armour family preferred disgrace to his connection. Since the promise, besides, he had doubtless been busy 'battering himself' back again into his affection for the girl; and the blow would not only take him in his vanity, but wound him at the heart.

He relieved himself in verse; but for such a smarting affront manuscript poetry was insufficient to console him. He must find a more powerful remedy in good flesh and blood, and after this discomfiture, set forth again at once upon his voyage of discovery in quest of love. It is perhaps one of the most touching things in human nature, as it is a commonplace of psychology, that when a man has just lost hope or confidence in one love, he is then most eager to find and lean upon another. The universe could not be yet exhausted; there must be hope and love waiting for him somewhere; and so, with his head down, this poor, insulted poet ran once more upon his fate. There was an innocent and gentle Highland nursery-maid at service in a neighbouring family; and he had soon battered himself and her into a warm affection and a secret engagement. Jean's marriage lines had not been destroyed till March 13, 1786; yet all was settled between Burns and Mary Campbell by Sunday, May 14, when they met for the last time, and said farewell with rustic solemnities upon the banks of Ayr. They each wet their hands in a stream, and, standing one on either bank, held a Bible between them as they vowed eternal faith. Then they exchanged Bibles, on one of which Burns, for greater security, had inscribed texts as to the binding nature of an oath; and surely, if ceremony can do aught to fix the wandering affections, here were two people united for life. Mary came of a superstitious family, so that she perhaps insisted on these rites; but they must have been eminently to the taste of Burns at this period; for nothing would seem superfluous, and no oath great enough, to stay his tottering constancy.

Events of consequence now happened thickly in the poet's life. His book was announced; the Armours sought to summon him at law for the aliment of the child; he lay here and there in hiding to correct the sheets; he was under an engagement for Jamaica, where Mary was to join him as his wife; now, he had 'orders within three weeks at latest to repair aboard the *Nancy*, Captain Smith;' now his chest was already on the road to Greenock; and now, in the wild autumn weather on the moorland, he measures verses of farewell:—

> The bursting tears my heart declare;
> Farewell the bonny banks of Ayr!

But the great master dramatist had secretly another intention for the piece; by the most violent and complicated solution, in which death and birth and sudden fame all play a part as interposing deities, the act-drop fell upon a scene of transformation. Jean was brought to bed of twins, and, by an amicable arrangement, the Burnses took the boy to bring up by hand, while the girl remained with her mother. The success of the book was immediate and emphatic; it put £20 at once into the author's purse; and he was encouraged upon all hands to go to Edinburgh and push his success in a second and larger edition. Third and last in these series of interpositions, a letter came one day to Mossgiel Farm for Robert. He went to the window to read it; a sudden change came over his face, and he left the room without a word. Years afterwards, when the story began to leak out, his family understood that he had then learned the death of Highland Mary. Except in a few poems and a few dry indications purposely misleading as to date, Burns himself made no reference to this passage of his life; it was an adventure of which, for I think sufficient reasons, he desired to bury the details. Of one thing we may be glad; in after years he visited the poor girl's mother, and left her with the impression that he was 'a real warm-hearted chield.'

Perhaps a month after he received this intelligence, he set out for Edinburgh on a pony he had borrowed from a friend. The town that winter was 'agog with the ploughman poet.' Robertson, Dugald Stewart, Blair, 'Duchess Gordon and all the gay world,' were of his acquaintance. Such a revolution is not to be found in literary history. He was now, it must be remembered, twenty-seven years of age; he had fought since his early boyhood an obstinate battle against poor soil, bad seed, and inclement seasons, wading deep in Ayrshire mosses, guiding the plough in the furrow, wielding 'the thresher's weary flingin'-tree;' and his education, his diet, and his pleasures, had been those of a Scotch countryman. Now he stepped forth suddenly among the polite and learned. We can see him as he then was, in his boots and buckskins, his blue coat and waistcoat striped with buff and blue, like a farmer in his Sunday best; the heavy ploughman's figure firmly planted on its burly legs; his face full of sense and shrewdness, and with a somewhat melancholy air of thought, and his large dark eye 'literally glowing' as he spoke. 'I never saw such another eye in a human head,' says Walter Scott, 'though I have seen the most distinguished men of my time.' With men, whether they were lords or omnipotent critics, his manner was plain, dignified, and free from bashfulness or affectation. If he made a slip, he had the social courage to pass on and refrain from explanation. He was not embarrassed in this society, because he read and judged the men; he could spy snobbery in a titled lord; and, as for the critics, he dismissed their system in an epigram. 'These gentlemen,' said he, 'remind me of some spinsters in my country who spin their thread so fine that it is neither fit for weft nor woof.' Ladies, on the other hand, surprised him; he was scarce commander of himself in their society; he was disqualified by his acquired nature as a Don Juan; and he, who had been so much at his ease with country lasses, treated the town dames to an extreme of deference. One lady, who met him at a ball, gave Chambers a speaking sketch of his demeanour. 'His manner was not prepossessing – scarcely, she thinks, manly or natural. It seemed as if he affected a rusticity or *landertness,* so that when he said the music was "bonnie, bonnie," it was like the expression of a child.' These would be company manners; and doubtless on a slight degree of intimacy the affectation would grow less. And his talk to women had always 'a turn either to the pathetic or humorous, which engaged the attention particularly.'

The Edinburgh magnates (to conclude this episode at once) behaved well to Burns from first to last. Were heaven-born genius to revisit us in similar guise, I am not venturing too far when I say that he need expect neither so warm a welcome nor such solid help. Although Burns was only a peasant, and one of no very elegant reputation as to morals, he was made welcome to their homes. They gave him a great deal of good advice, helped him to some five hundred pounds of ready money, and got him, as soon as he asked it, a place in the Excise. Burns, on his part, bore the elevation with perfect dignity; and with perfect dignity returned, when the time had come, into a country privacy of life. His powerful sense never deserted him, and from the first he recognised that his Edinburgh popularity was but an ovation and the affair of a day. He wrote a few letters in a high-flown, bombastic vein of gratitude; but in practice he suffered no man to intrude upon his self-respect. On the other hand, he never turned his back, even for a moment, on his old associates; and he was always ready to sacrifice an acquaintance to a friend, although the acquaintance were a duke. He would be a bold man who should promise similar conduct in equally exacting circumstances. It was, in short, an admirable appearance on the stage of life – socially successful, intimately self-respecting, and like a gentleman from first to last.

In the present study, this must only be taken by the way, while we return to Burns's love affairs. Even on the road to Edinburgh he had seized upon the opportunity of a flirtation, and had carried the 'battering' so far that when next he moved from town, it was to steal two days with this anonymous fair one. The exact importance to Burns of this affair may be gathered from the song in which he commemorated its occurrence. 'I love the dear lassie,' he sings, 'because she loves me;' or, in the tongue of prose: 'Finding an opportunity, I did not hesitate to profit by it; and even now, if it returned, I should not hesitate to profit by it again.' A love thus founded has no interest for mortal man. Meantime, early in the winter, and only once, we find him regretting Jean in his correspondence. 'Because' – such is his reason – 'because he does not think he will ever meet so delicious an armful again;' and then, after a brief excursion into verse, he goes straight on to describe a new episode in the voyage of discovery with the daughter of a Lothian farmer for a heroine. I must ask the reader to follow all these references to his future wife; they are essential to the comprehension of Burns's character and fate. In June, we find him back at Mauchline, a famous man. There, the Armour family greeted him with a 'mean, servile compliance,' which increased his former disgust. Jean was not less compliant; a second time the poor girl submitted to the fascination of the man whom she did not love, and whom she had so cruelly insulted little more than a year ago; and, though Burns took advantage of her weakness, it was in the ugliest and most cynical spirit, and with a heart absolutely indifferent. Judge of this by a letter written some twenty days after his return – a letter to my mind among the most degrading in the whole collection – a letter which seems to have been inspired by a boastful, libertine bagman. 'I am afraid,' it goes, 'I have almost ruined one source, the principal one, indeed, of my former happiness – the eternal propensity I always had to fall in love. My heart no more glows with feverish rapture; I have no paradisiacal evening interviews.' Even the process of 'battering' has failed him, you perceive. Still he had someone in his eye – a lady, if you please, with a fine figure and elegant manners, and who had 'seen the politest quarters in Europe.' 'I frequently visited her,' he writes, 'and after passing regularly the intermediate degrees between the distant formal bow and the familiar grasp round the waist, I ventured, in my careless way, to talk of friendship in rather ambiguous terms; and after her return to — , I wrote her in the same terms. Miss, construing my remarks further than even I intended, flew off in a tangent of female dignity and reserve, like a mounting lark in an April morning; and wrote me an answer which measured out very completely what an immense way I had to travel before I could reach the climate of her favours. But I am an old hawk at the sport, and wrote her such a cool, deliberate, prudent reply, as brought my bird from her aerial towerings, pop, down to my foot, like Corporal Trim's hat.' I avow a carnal longing, after this transcription, to buffet the Old Hawk about the ears. There is little question that to this lady he must have repeated his addresses, and that he was by her (Miss Chalmers) eventually, though not at all unkindly, rejected. One more detail to characterise the period. Six months after the date of this letter, Burns, back in Edinburgh, is served with a writ *in meditatione fugæ*, on behalf of some Edinburgh fair one, probably of humble rank, who declared an intention of adding to his family.

About the beginning of December (1787), a new period opens in the story of the poet's random affections. He met at a tea party one Mrs Agnes M'Lehose, a married woman of about his own age, who, with her two children, had been deserted by an unworthy husband. She had wit, could use her pen, and had read *Werther* with attention. Sociable, and even somewhat frisky, there was a good, sound, human kernel in the woman; a warmth of love, strong dogmatic religious feeling, and a considerable, but not authoritative, sense of the proprieties. Of what biographers refer to daintily as 'her somewhat voluptuous style of beauty,' judging from the silhouette in Mr Scott Douglas's invaluable edition, the reader will be fastidious if he does not approve. Take her for all in all, I believe she was the best woman Burns encountered. The pair took a fancy for each other on the spot; Mrs M'Lehose, in her turn, invited him to tea; but the poet, in his character of the Old Hawk, preferred a *tête-à-tête,* excused himself at the last moment, and offered a visit instead. An accident confined him to his room for nearly a month, and this led to the famous Clarinda and Sylvander correspondence. It was begun in simple sport; they are already at their fifth or sixth exchange, when Clarinda writes: 'It is really curious so much *fun* passing between two persons who saw each other only *once*;' but it is hardly safe for a man and woman in the flower of their years to write almost daily, and sometimes in terms too ambiguous, sometimes in terms too plain, and generally in terms too warm, for mere acquaintance. The exercise partakes a little of the nature of battering, and danger may be apprehended when next they meet. It is difficult to give any account of this remarkable correspondence; it is too far away from us, and perhaps, not yet far enough, in point of time and manner; the imagination is baffled by these stilted literary utterances, warming, in bravura passages, into downright truculent nonsense. Clarinda has one famous sentence in which she bids Sylvander connect the thought of his mistress with the changing phases of the year; it was enthusiastically admired by the swain, but on the modern mind produces mild amazement and alarm. 'Oh, Clarinda,' writes Burns, 'shall we not meet in a state – some yet unknown state – of being, where the lavish hand of Plenty shall minister to the highest wish of Benevolence, and where the chill north wind of Prudence shall never blow over the flowery field of Enjoyment?' The design may be that of an Old Hawk, but the style is more suggestive of a Bird of Paradise. It is sometimes hard to fancy they are not gravely making fun of each other as they write. Religion, poetry, love, and charming sensibility, are the current topics. 'I am delighted, charming Clarinda, with your honest enthusiasm for religion,' writes Burns; and the pair entertained a fiction that this was their 'favourite subject.' 'This is Sunday,' writes the lady, 'and not a word on our favourite subject. O fy! "divine Clarinda!"' I suspect, although quite unconsciously on the part of the lady, who was bent on his redemption, they but used the favourite subject as a stalking-horse. In the meantime, the sportive acquaintance was ripening steadily into a genuine passion. Visits took place, and then became frequent. Clarinda's friends were hurt and suspicious; her clergyman interfered; she herself had smart attacks of conscience; but her heart had gone from her control; it was altogether his, and she 'counted all things but loss – heaven excepted – that she might win and keep him.' Burns himself was transported while in her neighbourhood, but his transports somewhat rapidly declined during an absence. I am tempted to imagine that, womanlike, he took on the colour of his mistress's feeling; that he could not but heat himself at the fire of her unaffected passion; but that, like one who should leave the hearth upon a winter's night, his temperature soon fell when he was out of sight, and in a word, though he could share the symptoms, that he had never shared the disease. At the same time, amid the fustian of the letters there are forcible and true expressions, and the love verses that he wrote upon Clarinda are among the most moving in the language.

We are approaching the solution. In mid-winter, Jean, once more in the family way, was turned out of doors by her family; and Burns had her received and cared for in the house of a friend. For he remained to the last imperfect in his character of Don Juan, and lacked the sinister courage to desert his victim. About the middle of February (1788), he had to tear himself from his Clarinda and make a journey into the south-west on business. Clarinda gave him two shirts for his little son. They were daily to meet in prayer at an appointed hour. Burns, too late for the post at Glasgow, sent her a letter by parcel that she might not have to wait. Clarinda on her part writes, this time with a beautiful simplicity: 'I think the streets look deserted-like since Monday; and there's a certain insipidity in good kind folks I once enjoyed not a little. Miss Wardrobe supped here on Monday. She once named you, which kept me from falling asleep. I drank your health in a glass of ale – as the lasses do at Hallowe'en – "in to mysel".' Arrived at Mauchline, Burns installed Jean Armour in a lodging, and prevailed on Mrs Armour to promise her help and countenance in the approaching confinement. This was kind at least; but hear his expressions: 'I have taken her a room; I have taken her to my arms; I have given her a mahogany bed; I have given her a guinea . . . I swore her privately and solemnly never to attempt any claim on me as a husband, even though anybody should persuade her she had such a claim – which she has not, neither during my life nor after my death. She did all this like a good girl.' And then he took advantage of the situation. To Clarinda he wrote: 'I this morning called for a certain woman. I am disgusted with her; I cannot endure her;' and he accused her of 'tasteless insipidity, vulgarity of soul, and mercenary fawning.'

This was already in March; by the thirteenth of that month he was back in Edinburgh. On the 17th, he wrote to Clarinda: 'Your hopes, your fears, your cares, my love, are mine; so don't mind them. I will take you in my hand through the dreary wilds of this world, and scare away the ravening bird or beast that would annoy you.' Again, on the 21st: 'Will you open, with satisfaction and delight, a letter from a man who loves you, who has loved you, and who will love you, to death, through death, and for ever . . . How rich am I to have such a treasure as you! . . . "The Lord God knoweth," and, perhaps, "Israel he shall know," my love and your merit. Adieu, Clarinda! I am going to remember you in my prayers.' By the 7th of April, seventeen days later, he had already decided to make Jean Armour publicly his wife.

A more astonishing stage-trick is not to be found. And yet his conduct is seen, upon a nearer examination, to be grounded both in reason and in kindness. He was now about to embark on a solid worldly career; he had taken a farm; the affair with Clarinda, however gratifying to his heart, was too contingent to offer any great consolation to a man like Burns, to whom marriage must have seemed the very dawn of hope and self-respect. This is to regard the question from its lowest aspect; but there is no doubt that he entered on this new period of his life with a sincere determination to do right. He had just helped his brother with a loan of a hundred and eighty pounds; should he do nothing for the poor girl whom he had ruined? It was true he could not do as he did without brutally wounding Clarinda; that was the punishment of his bygone fault; he was, as he truly says, 'damned with a choice only of different species of error and misconduct.' To be professional Don Juan, to accept the provocation of any lively lass upon the village green, may thus lead a man through a series of detestable words and actions, and land him at last in an undesired and most unsuitable union for life. If he had been strong enough to refrain or bad enough to persevere in evil; if he had only not been Don Juan at all, or been Don Juan altogether, there had been some possible road for him throughout this troublesome world; but a man, alas! who is equally at the call of his worse and better instincts, stands among changing events without foundation or resource.[1]

DOWNWARD COURSE

It may be questionable whether any marriage could have tamed Burns; but it is at least certain that there was no hope for him in

[1] For the love affairs see, in particular, Mr Scott Douglas's edition under the different dates.

the marriage he contracted. He did right, but then he had done wrong before; it was, as I said, one of those relations in life which it seems equally wrong to break or to perpetuate. He neither loved nor respected his wife. 'God knows,' he writes, 'my choice was as random as blind man's buff.' He consoles himself by the thought that he has acted kindly to her; that she 'has the most sacred enthusiasm of attachment to him;' that she has a good figure; that she has a 'wood-note wild,' 'her voice rising with ease to B natural,' no less. The effect on the reader is one of unmingled pity for both parties concerned. This was not the wife who (in his own words) could 'enter into his favourite studies or relish his favourite authors;' this was not even a wife, after the affair of the marriage lines, in whom a husband could joy to place his trust. Let her manage a farm with sense, let her voice rise to B natural all day long, she would still be a peasant to her lettered lord, and an object of pity rather than of equal affection. She could now be faithful, she could now be forgiving, she could now be generous even to a pathetic and touching degree; but coming from one who was unloved, and who had scarce shown herself worthy of the sentiment, these were all virtues thrown away, which could neither change her husband's heart nor affect the inherent destiny of their relation. From the outset, it was a marriage that had no root in nature; and we find him, ere long, lyrically regretting Highland Mary, renewing correspondence with Clarinda in the warmest language, on doubtful terms with Mrs Riddel, and on terms unfortunately beyond any question with Anne Park.

Alas! this was not the only ill circumstance in his future. He had been idle for some eighteen months, superintending his new edition, hanging on to settle with the publisher, travelling in the Highlands with Willie Nichol, or philandering with Mrs M'Lehose; and in this period the radical part of the man had suffered irremediable hurt. He had lost his habits of industry, and formed the habit of pleasure. Apologetical biographers assure us of the contrary; but from the first, he saw and recognised the danger for himself; his mind, he writes, is 'enervated to an alarming degree' by idleness and dissipation; and again, 'my mind has been vitiated with idleness.' It never fairly recovered. To business he could bring the required diligence and attention without difficulty; but he was thenceforward incapable, except in rare instances, of that superior effort of concentration which is required for serious literary work. He may be said, indeed, to have worked no more, and only amused himself with letters. The man who had written a volume of masterpieces in six months, during the remainder of his life rarely found courage for any more sustained effort than a song. And the nature of the songs is itself characteristic of these idle later years; for they are often as polished and elaborate as his earlier works were frank, and headlong, and colloquial; and this sort of verbal elaboration in short flights is, for a man of literary turn, simply the most agreeable of pastimes. The change in manner coincides exactly with the Edinburgh visit. In 1786 he had written the *Address to a Louse,* which may be taken as an extreme instance of the first manner; and already, in 1787, we come upon the rosebud pieces to Miss Cruikshank, which are extreme examples of the second. The change was, therefore, the direct and very natural consequence of his great change in life; but it is not the less typical of his loss of moral courage that he should have given up all larger ventures, nor the less melancholy that a man who first attacked literature with a hand that seemed capable of moving mountains, should have spent his later years in whittling cherry-stones.

Meanwhile, the farm did not prosper; he had to join to it the salary of an exciseman; at last he had to give it up, and rely altogether on the latter resource. He was an active officer; and, though he sometimes tempered severity with mercy, we have local testimony oddly representing the public feeling of the period, that, while 'in everything else he was a perfect gentleman, when he met with anything seizable he was no better than any other gauger.'

There is but one manifestation of the man in these last years which need delay us: and that was the sudden interest in politics which arose from his sympathy with the great French Revolution. His only political feeling had been hitherto a sentimental Jacobitism, not more or less respectable than that of Scott, Aytoun, and the rest of what George Borrow has nicknamed the 'Charlie over the water' Scotchmen. It was a sentiment almost entirely literary and picturesque in its origin, built on ballads and the adventures of the Young Chevalier; and in Burns it is the more excusable, because he lay out of the way of active politics in his youth. With the great French Revolution, something living, practical, and feasible appeared to him for the first time in this realm of human action. The young ploughman who had desired so earnestly to rise, now reached out his sympathies to a whole nation animated with the same desire. Already in 1788 we find the old Jacobitism hand in hand with the new popular doctrine, when, in a letter of indignation against the zeal of a Whig clergyman, he writes: 'I daresay the American Congress in 1776 will be allowed to be as able and as enlightened as the English Convention was in 1688; and that their posterity will celebrate the centenary of their deliverance from us, as duly and sincerely as we do ours from the oppressive measures of the wrong-headed house of Stuart.' As time wore on, his sentiments grew more pronounced and even violent; but there was a basis of sense and generous feeling to his hottest excess. What he asked was a fair chance for the individual in life; an open road to success and distinction for all classes of men. It was in the same spirit that he had helped to found a public library in the parish where his farm was situated, and that he sang his fervent snatches against tyranny and tyrants. Witness, were it alone, this verse:—

> Here's freedom to him that wad read,
> Here's freedom to him that wad write;
> There's nane ever feared that the truth should be heard
> But them wham the truth wad indite.

Yet his enthusiasm for the cause was scarce guided by wisdom. Many stories are preserved of the bitter and unwise words he used in country coteries; how he proposed Washington's health as an amendment to Pitt's, gave as a toast 'the last verse of the last chapter of Kings,' and celebrated Dumouriez in a doggerel impromptu full of ridicule and hate. Now his sympathies would inspire him with *Scots, wha hae*; now involve him in a drunken broil with a loyal officer, and consequent apologies and explanations, hard to offer for a man of Burns's stomach. Nor was this the front of his offending. On February 27, 1792, he took part in the capture of an armed smuggler, bought at the subsequent sale four carronades, and despatched them with a letter to the French Assembly. Letter and guns were stopped at Dover by the English officials; there was trouble for Burns with his superiors; he was reminded firmly, however delicately, that, as a paid official, it was his duty to obey and to be silent; and all the blood of this poor, proud, and falling man must have rushed to his head at the humiliation. His letter to Mr Erskine, subsequently Earl of Mar, testifies, in its turgid, turbulent phrases, to a perfect passion of alarmed self-respect and vanity. He had been muzzled, and muzzled, when all was said, by his paltry salary as a exciseman; alas! had he not a family to keep? Already, he wrote, he looked forward to some such judgement from a hackney scribbler as this:

'Burns, notwithstanding the *fanfaronnade* of independence to be found in his works, and after having been held forth to view and to public estimation as a man of some genius, yet, quite destitute of resources within himself to support his borrowed dignity, he dwindled into a paltry exciseman, and shrunk out the rest of his insignificant existence in the meanest of pursuits, and among the vilest of mankind.' And then on he goes, in a style of rodomontade, but filled with living indignation, to declare his right to a political opinion, and his willingness to shed his blood for the political birthright of his sons. Poor, perturbed spirit! he was indeed exercised in vain; those who share and those who differ from his sentiments about the Revolution, alike understand and sympathise with him in this painful strait; for poetry and human manhood are lasting like the race, and politics, which are but a wrongful striving after right, pass and change from year to year and age to age. The *Twa Dogs* has already outlasted the constitution of Siéyès and the policy of the Whigs; and Burns is better known among English-speaking races than either Pitt or Fox.

Meanwhile, whether as a man, a husband, or a poet, his steps led downward. He knew, knew bitterly, that the best was out of him; he refused to make another volume, for he felt that it would be a disappointment; he grew petulantly alive to criticism, unless he was sure it reached him from a friend. For his songs, he would take nothing; they were all that he could do; the proposed Scotch play, the proposed series of Scotch tales in verse, all had gone to water; and in a fling of pain and disappointment, which is surely noble with the nobility of a viking, he would rather stoop to borrow than to accept money for these last and inadequate efforts of his muse. And this desperate abnegation rises at times near to the height of madness; as when he pretended that he had not written, but only found and published, his immortal *Auld Lang Syne*. In the same spirit he became more scrupulous as an artist; he was doing so little, he would fain do that little well; and about two months before his death, he asked Thomson to send back all his manuscripts for revisal, saying that he would rather write five songs to his taste than twice that number otherwise. The battle of his life was lost; in forlorn efforts to do well, in desperate submissions to evil, the last years flew by. His temper is dark and explosive, launching epigrams, quarrelling with his friends, jealous of young puppy officers. He tries to be a good father; he boasts himself a libertine. Sick, sad, and jaded, he can refuse no occasion of temporary pleasure, no opportunity to shine; and he who had once refused the invitations of lords and ladies is now whistled to the inn by any curious stranger. His death (July 21, 1796), in his thirty-seventh year, was indeed a kindly dispensation. It is the fashion to say he died of drink; many a man has drunk more and yet lived with reputation, and reached a good age. That drink and debauchery helped to destroy his constitution, and were the means of his unconscious suicide, is doubtless true; but he had failed in life, had lost his power of work, and was already married to the poor, unworthy, patient Jean, before he had shown his inclination to convivial nights, or at least before that inclination had become dangerous either to his health or his self-respect. He had trifled with life, and must pay the penalty. He had chosen to be Don Juan, he had grasped at temporary pleasures, and substantial happiness and solid industry had passed him by. He died of being Robert Burns, and there is no levity in such a statement of the case; for shall we not, one and all, deserve a similar epitaph?

WORKS

The somewhat cruel necessity which has lain upon me throughout this paper only to touch upon those points in the life of Burns where correction or amplification seemed desirable, leaves me little opportunity to speak of the works which have made his name so famous. Yet, even here, a few observations seem necessary.

At the time when the poet made his appearance and great first success, his work was remarkable in two ways. For, first, in an age when poetry had become abstract and conventional, instead of continuing to deal with shepherds, thunderstorms, and personifications, he dealt with the actual circumstances of his life, however matter-of-fact and sordid these might be. And, second, in a time when English versification was particularly stiff, lame, and feeble, and words were used with ultra-academical timidity, he wrote verses that were easy, racy, graphic, and forcible, and used language with absolute tact and courage as it seemed most fit to give a clear impression. If you take even those English authors whom we know Burns to have most admired and studied, you will see at once that he owed them nothing but a warning. Take Shenstone, for instance, and watch that elegant author as he tries to grapple with the facts of life. He has a description, I remember, of a gentleman engaged in sliding or walking on thin ice, which is a little miracle of incompetence. You see my memory fails me, and I positively cannot recollect whether his hero was sliding or walking; as though a writer should describe a skirmish, and the reader, at the end, be still uncertain whether it were a charge of cavalry or a slow and stubborn advance of foot. There could be no such ambiguity in Burns; his work is at the opposite pole from such indefinite and stammering performances; and a whole lifetime passed in the study of Shenstone would only lead a man further and further from writing the *Address to a Louse*. Yet Burns, like most great artists, proceeded from a school and continued a tradition; only the school and tradition were Scotch, and not English. While the English language was becoming daily more pedantic and inflexible, and English letters more colourless and slack, there was another dialect in the sister country, and a different school of poetry tracing its descent, through King James I, from Chaucer. The dialect alone accounts for much; for it was then written colloquially, which kept it fresh and supple; and, although not shaped for heroic flights, it was a direct and vivid medium for all that had to do with social life. Hence, whenever Scotch poets left their laborious imitations of bad English verses, and fell back on their own dialect, their style would kindle, and they would write of their convivial and somewhat gross existences with pith and point. In Ramsay, and far more in the poor lad Fergusson, there was mettle, humour, literary courage, and a power of saying what they wished to say definitely and brightly, which in the latter case should have justified great anticipations. Had Burns died at the same age as Fergusson, he would have left us literally nothing worth remark. To Ramsay and to Fergusson, then, he was indebted in a very uncommon degree, not only following their tradition and using their measures, but directly and avowedly imitating their pieces. The same tendency to borrow a hint, to work on someone else's foundation, is notable in Burns from first to last, in the period of song-writing as well as in that of the early poems; and strikes one oddly in a man of such deep originality, who left so strong a print on all he touched, and whose work is so greatly distinguished by that character of 'inevitability' which Wordsworth denied to Goethe.

When we remember Burns's obligations to his predecessors, we must never forget his immense advances on them. They had already 'discovered' nature; but Burns discovered poetry – a higher and more intense way of thinking of the things that go to make up nature, a higher and more ideal key of words in which to speak of them. Ramsay and Fergusson excelled at making a popular – or shall we say vulgar? – sort of society verses, comical and prosaic, written, you would say, in taverns while a supper party waited for its laureate's word; but on the appearance of Burns, this coarse and laughing literature was touched to finer issues, and learned gravity of thought and natural pathos.

What he had gained from his predecessors was a direct, speaking style, and to walk on his own feet instead of on academical stilts. There was never a man of letters with more absolute command of his means; and we may say of him, without excess, that his style was his slave. Hence that energy of epithet, so concise and telling, that a foreigner is tempted to explain it by some special richness or aptitude in the dialect he wrote. Hence that Homeric justice and completeness of description which gives us the very physiognomy of nature, in body and detail, as nature is. Hence, too, the unbroken literary quality of his best pieces, which keeps him from any slip into the weariful trade of word-painting, and presents everything, as everything should be presented by the art of words, in a clear, continuous medium of thought. Principal Shairp, for instance, gives us a paraphrase of one tough verse of the original; and for those who know the Greek poets only by paraphrase, this has the very quality they are accustomed to look for and admire in Greek. The contemporaries of Burns were surprised that he should visit so many celebrated mountains and waterfalls, and not seize the opportunity to make a poem. Indeed, it is not for those who have a true command of the art of words, but for peddling, professional amateurs, that these pointed occasions are most useful and inspiring. As those who speak French imperfectly are glad to dwell on any topic they may have talked upon or heard others talk upon before, because they know appropriate words for it in French, so the dabbler in verse rejoices to behold a waterfall, because he has learned the sentiment and knows appropriate words for it in poetry. But the dialect of Burns was fitted to deal with any subject; and whether it was a stormy night, a shepherd's collie, a sheep struggling in the snow, the conduct of cowardly soldiers in the field, the gait and cogitations of a drunken man, or only a village cockcrow in the morning, he could find language to give it freshness, body, and relief. He was always ready to borrow the hint of a design, as though he had a difficulty in commencing – a difficulty, let us say, in choosing a subject out of a world which seemed all equally living and significant to him; but once he had the subject chosen, he could cope with nature single-handed, and make every stroke a triumph. Again, his absolute mastery in his art enabled him to express each and all of his different humours, and to pass smoothly and congruously from one to another. Many men invent a dialect for only one side of their nature – perhaps their pathos or their humour, or the delicacy of their senses – and, for lack of a medium, leave all the others unexpressed. You meet such an one, and find him in conversation full of thought, feeling, and experience, which he has lacked the art to employ in his writings. But Burns was not thus hampered in the practice of the literary art; he could throw the whole weight of his nature into his work, and impregnate it from end to end. If Doctor Johnson, that stilted and accomplished stylist, had lacked the sacred Boswell, what should we have known of him? and how should we have delighted in his acquaintance as we do? Those who spoke with Burns tell us how much we have lost who did not. But I think they exaggerate their privilege: I think we have the whole Burns in our possession set forth in his comsummate verses.

It was by his style, and not by his matter, that he affected Wordsworth and the world. There is, indeed, only one merit worth considering in a man of letters – that he should write well; and only one damning fault – that he should write ill. We are little the better for the reflections of the sailor's parrot in the story. And so, if Burns helped to change the course of literary history, it was by his frank, direct, and masterly utterance, and not by his homely choice of subjects. That was imposed upon him, not chosen upon a principle. He wrote from his own experience, because it was his nature so to do, and the tradition of the school from which he proceeded was fortunately not opposed to homely subjects. But to these homely subjects he communicated the rich commentary of his nature; they were all steeped in Burns; and they interest us not in themselves, but because they have been passed through the spirit of so genuine and vigorous a man. Such is the stamp of living literature; and there was never any more alive than that of Burns.

What a gust of sympathy there is in him sometimes flowing out in byways hitherto unused, upon mice, and flowers, and the devil himself; sometimes speaking plainly between human hearts; sometimes ringing out in exultation like a peal of bells! When we compare the *Farmer's Salutation to his Auld Mare Maggie,* with the clever and inhumane production of half a century earlier, *The Auld Man's Mare's dead,* we see in a nutshell the spirit of the change introduced by Burns. And as to its manner, who that has read it can forget how the collie, Luath, in the *Twa Dogs,* describes and enters into the merry-making in the cottage?

> The luntin' pipe an' sneeshin' mill,
> Are handed round wi' richt guid will;
> The canty auld folks crackin' crouse,
> The young anes rantin' through the house –
> My heart has been sae fain to see them
> That I for joy hae barkit wi' them.

It was this ardent power of sympathy that was fatal to so many women, and, through Jean Armour, to himself at last. His humour comes from him in a stream so deep and easy that I will venture to call him the best of humorous poets. He turns about in the midst to utter a noble sentiment or a trenchant remark on human life, and the style changes and rises to the occasion. I think it is Principal Shairp who says, happily, that Burns would have been no Scotchman if he had not loved to moralise; neither, may we add, would he have been his father's son; but (what is worthy of note) his moralisings are to a large extent the moral of his own career. He was among the least impersonal of artists. Except in the *Jolly Beggars*, he shows no gleam of dramatic instinct. Mr Carlyle has complained that *Tam o' Shanter* is, from the absence of this quality, only a picturesque and external piece of work; and I may add that in the *Twa Dogs* it is precisely in the infringement of dramatic propriety that a great deal of the humour of the speeches depends for its existence and effect. Indeed, Burns was so full of his identity that it breaks forth on every page; and there is scarce an appropriate remark either in praise or blame of his own conduct, but he has put it himself into verse. Alas! for the tenor of these remarks! They are, indeed, his own pitiful apology for such a marred existence and talents so misused and stunted; and they seem to prove for ever how small a part is played by reason in the conduct of man's affairs. Here was one, at least, who with unfailing judgement predicted his own fate; yet his knowledge could not avail him, and with open eyes he must fulfil his tragic destiny. Ten years before the end he had written his epitaph; and neither subsequent events, nor the critical eyes of posterity, have shown us a word in it to alter. And, lastly, has he not put in for himself the last unanswerable plea? —

> Then gently scan your brother man,
>   Still gentler sister woman;
> Though they may gang a kennin wrang,
>   To step aside is human;
> One point must still be greatly dark –

SAMUEL PEPYS

In two books a fresh light has recently been thrown on the character and position of Samuel Pepys. Mr Mynors Bright has given us a new transcription of the Diary, increasing it in bulk by near a third, correcting many errors, and completing our knowledge of the man in some curious and important points. We can only regret that he has taken liberties with the author and the public. It is no part of the duties of the editor of an established classic to decide what may or may not be 'tedious to the reader.' The book is either an historical document or not, and in condemning Lord Braybrooke Mr Bright condemns himself. As for the time-honoured phrase, 'unfit for publication,' without being cynical, we may regard it as the sign of a precaution more or less commercial; and we may think, without being sordid, that when we purchase six huge and distressingly expensive volumes, we are entitled to be treated rather more like scholars and rather less like children. But Mr Bright may rest assured: while we complain, we are still grateful. Mr Wheatley, to divide our obligation, brings together, clearly and with no lost words, a body of illustrative material. Sometimes we might ask a little more; never, I think, less. And as a matter of fact, a great part of Mr Wheatley's volume might be transferred, by a good editor of Pepys, to the margin of the text, for it is precisely what the reader wants.

In the light of these two books, at least, we have now to read our author. Between them they contain all we can expect to learn for, it may be, many years. Now, if ever, we should be able to form some notion of that unparalleled figure in the annals of mankind – unparalleled for three good reasons: first, because he was a man known to his contemporaries in a halo of almost historical pomp, and to his remote descendants with an indecent familiarity, like a tap-room comrade; second, because he has outstripped all competitors in the art or virtue of a conscious honesty about oneself; and, third, because, being in many ways a very ordinary person, he has yet placed himself before the public eye with such a fullness and such an intimacy of detail as might be envied by a genius like Montaigne. Not then for his own sake only, but as a character in a unique position, endowed with a unique talent, and shedding a unique light upon the lives of the mass of mankind, he is surely worthy of prolonged and patient study.

THE DIARY

That there should be such a book as Pepys's Diary is incomparably strange. Pepys, in a corrupt and idle period, played the man in public employments, toiling hard and keeping his honour bright. Much of the little good that is set down to James the Second comes by right to Pepys; and if it were little for a king, it is much for a subordinate. To his clear, capable head was owing somewhat of the greatness of England on the seas. In the exploits of Hawke, Rodney, or Nelson, this dead Mr Pepys of the Navy Office had some considerable share. He stood well by his business in the appalling plague of 1666. He was loved and respected by some of the best and wisest men in England. He was President of the Royal Society; and when he came to die, people said of his conduct in that solemn hour – thinking it needless to say more – that it was answerable to the greatness of his life. Thus he walked in dignity, guards of soldiers sometimes attending him in his walks, subalterns bowing before his periwig; and when he uttered his thoughts they were suitable to his state and services. On February 8, 1668, we find him writing to Evelyn, his mind bitterly occupied with the late Dutch war, and some thoughts of the different story of the repulse of the Great Armada:

Sir, you will not wonder at the backwardness of my thanks for the present you made me, so many days since, of the Prospect of the Medway, while the Hollander rode master in it, when I have told you that the sight of it hath led me to such reflections on my particular interest, by my employment, in the reproach due to that miscarriage, as have given me little less disquiet than he is fancied to have who found his face in Michael Angelo's hell. The same should serve me also in excuse for my silence in celebrating your mastery shown in the design and draught, did not indignation rather than courtship urge me so far to commend them, as to wish the furniture of our House of Lords changed from the story of '88 to that of '67 (of Evelyn's designing), till the pravity of this were reformed to the temper of that age, wherein

God Almighty found his blessings more operative than, I fear, he doth in ours his judgments.

This is a letter honourable to the writer, where the meaning rather than the words is eloquent. Such was the account he gave of himself to his contemporaries; such thoughts he chose to utter, and in such language: giving himself out for a grave and patriotic public servant. We turn to the same date in the Diary by which he is known, after two centuries, to his descendants. The entry begins in the same key with the letter, blaming the 'madness of the House of Commons' and 'the base proceedings, just the epitome of all our public proceedings in this age, of the House of Lords;' and then, without the least transition, this is how our diarist proceeds:

> To the Strand, to my bookseller's, and there bought an idle, rogueish French book, *L'escholle des Filles,* which I have bought in plain binding, avoiding the buying of it better bound, because I resolve, as soon as I have read it, to burn it, that it may not stand in the list of books, nor among them, to disgrace them, if it should be found.

Even in our day, when responsibility is so much more clearly apprehended, the man who wrote the letter would be notable; but what about the man, I do not say who bought a roguish book, but who was ashamed of doing so, yet did it, and recorded both the doing and the shame in the pages of his daily journal?

We all, whether we write or speak, must somewhat drape ourselves when we address our fellows; at a given moment we apprehend our character and acts by some particular side; we are merry with one, grave with another, as befits the nature and demands of the relation. Pepys's letter to Evelyn would have little in common with that other one to Mrs Knipp which he signed by the pseudonym of *Dapper Dicky*; yet each would be suitable to the character of his correspondent. There is no untruth in this, for man, being a Protean animal, swiftly shares and changes with his company and surroundings; and these changes are the better part of his education in the world. To strike a posture once for all, and to march through life like a drum-major, is to be highly disagreeable to others and a fool for oneself into the bargain. To Evelyn and to Knipp we understand the double facing; but to whom was he posing in the Diary, and what, in the name of astonishment, was the nature of the pose? Had he suppressed all mention of the book, or had he bought it, gloried in the act, and cheerfully recorded his glorification, in either case we should have made him out. But no; he is full of precautions to conceal the 'disgrace' of the purchase, and yet speeds to chronicle the whole affair in pen and ink. It is a sort of anomaly in human action, which we can exactly parallel from another part of the Diary.

Mrs Pepys had written a paper of her too just complaints against her husband, and written it in plain and very pungent English. Pepys, in an agony lest the world should come to see it, brutally seizes and destroys the tell-tale document; and then – you disbelieve your eyes – down goes the whole story with unsparing truth and in the cruellest detail. It seems he has no design but to appear respectable, and here he keeps a private book to prove he was not. You are at first faintly reminded of some of the vagaries of the morbid religious diarist; but at a moment's thought the resemblance disappears. The design of Pepys is not at all to edify; it is not from repentance that he chronicles his peccadilloes, for he tells us when he does repent, and, to be just to him, there often follows some improvement. Again, the sins of the religious diarist are of a very formal pattern, and are told with an elaborate whine. But in Pepys you come upon good, substantive misdemeanours; beams in his eye of which he alone remains unconscious; healthy outbreaks of the animal nature, and laughable subterfuges to himself that always command belief and often engage the sympathies.

Pepys was a young man for his age, came slowly to himself in the world, sowed his wild oats late, took late to industry, and preserved till nearly forty the headlong gusto of a boy. So, to come rightly at the spirit in which the Diary was written, we must recall a class of sentiments which with most of us are over and done before the age of twelve. In our tender years we still preserve a freshness of surprise at our prolonged existence; events make an impression out of all proportion to their consequence; we are unspeakably touched by our own past adventures, and look forward to our future personality with sentimental interest. It was something of this, I think, that clung to Pepys. Although not sentimental in the abstract, he was sweetly sentimental about himself. His own past clung about his heart, an evergreen. He was the slave of an association. He could not pass by Islington, where his father used to carry him to cakes and ale, but he must light at the 'King's Head' and eat and drink 'for remembrance of the old house sake.' He counted it good fortune to lie a night at Epsom to renew his old walks, 'where Mrs Hely and I did use to walk and talk, with whom I had the first sentiments of love and pleasure in a woman's company, discourse and taking her by the hand, she being a pretty woman.' He goes about weighing up the *Assurance,* which lay near Woolwich under water, and cries in a parenthesis, 'Poor ship, that I have been twice merry in, in Captain Holland's time;' and after revisiting the *Naseby,* now changed into the *Charles,* he confesses 'it was a great pleasure to myself to see the ship that I began my good fortune in.' The stone that he was cut for he preserved in a case; and to the Turners he kept alive such gratitude for their assistance that for years, and after he had begun to mount himself into higher zones, he continued to have that family to dinner on the anniversary of the operation. Not Hazlitt nor Rousseau had a more romantic passion for their past, although at times they might express it more romantically; and if Pepys shared with them this childish fondness, did not Rousseau, who left behind him the *Confessions,* or Hazlitt, who wrote the *Liber Amoris,* and loaded his essays with loving personal detail, share with Pepys in his unwearied egotism? For the two things go hand in hand; or, to be more exact, it is the first that makes the second either possible or pleasing.

But, to be quite in sympathy with Pepys, we must return once more to the experience of children. I can remember to have written, in the fly-leaf of more than one book, the date and the place where I then was – if, for instance, I was ill in bed or sitting in a certain garden; these were jottings for my future self; if I should chance on such a note in after years, I thought it would cause me a particular thrill to recognise myself across the intervening distance. Indeed, I might come upon them now, and not be moved one tittle – which shows that I have comparatively failed in life, and grown older than Samuel Pepys. For in the Diary we can find more than one such note of perfect childish egotism; as when he explains that his candle is going out, 'which makes me write thus slobberingly;' or as in this incredible particularity, 'To my study, where I only wrote thus much of this day's passages to this *, and so out again;' or lastly, as here, with more of circumstance: 'I staid up till the bellman came by with his bell under my window, *as I was writing of this very line,* and cried, "Past one of the clock, and a cold, frosty, windy morning."' Such passages are not to be misunderstood. The appeal to Samuel Pepys years hence is unmistakable. He desires that dear, though unknown, gentleman keenly to realise his predecessor; to remember why a passage was uncleanly written; to recall (let us fancy, with a sigh) the tones of the bellman, the chill of the early, windy morning, and the very line his own romantic self was scribing at the moment. The man, you will perceive, was making reminiscences – a sort of pleasure by ricochet, which comforts many in distress, and turns some others into sentimental libertines: and the whole book, if you will but look at it in that way, is seen to be a work of art to Pepys's own address.

Here, then, we have the key to that remarkable attitude preserved by him throughout his Diary, to that unflinching – I had almost said, that unintelligent – sincerity which makes it a miracle among human books. He was not unconscious of his errors – far from it; he was often startled into shame, often reformed, often made and broke his vows of change. But whether he did ill or well, he was still his own unequalled self; still that entrancing *ego* of whom alone he cared to write; and still sure of his own affectionate indulgence, when the parts should be changed, and the writer come to read what he had written. Whatever he did, or said, or thought, or suffered, it was still a trait of Pepys, a character of his career; and as, to himself, he was more interesting than Moses or than Alexander, so all should be faithfully set down. I have called his Diary a work of art. Now when the artist has found something, word or deed, exactly proper to a favourite character in play or novel, he will neither suppress nor diminish it, though the remark be silly or the act mean. The hesitation of Hamlet, the credulity of Othello, the baseness of Emma Bovary, or the irregularities of Mr Swiveller, caused neither disappointment nor disgust to their creators. And so with Pepys and his adored protagonist; adored not blindly, but with trenchant insight and enduring, human toleration. I have gone over and over the greater part of the Diary; and the points where, to the most suspicious scrutiny, he has seemed not perfectly sincere, are so few, so doubtful, and so petty, that I am ashamed to name them. It may be said that we all of us write such a diary in airy characters upon our brain; but I fear there is a distinction to be made; I fear that as we render to our consciousness an account of our daily fortunes and behaviour, we too often weave a tissue of romantic compliments and dull excuses; and even if Pepys were the ass and coward that men call him, we must take rank as sillier and more cowardly than he. The bald truth about oneself, what we are all too timid to admit when we are not too dull to see it, that was what he saw clearly and set down unsparingly.

It is improbable that the Diary can have been carried on in the same single spirit in which it was begun. Pepys was not such an ass, but he must have perceived, as he went on, the extraordinary nature of the work he was producing. He was a great reader, and he knew what other books were like. It must, at least, have crossed his mind that someone might ultimately decipher the manuscript, and he himself, with all his pains and pleasures, be resuscitated in some later day; and the thought, although discouraged, must have warmed his heart. He was not such an ass, besides, but he must have been conscious of the deadly explosives, the gun-cotton and the giant powder, he was hoarding in his drawer. Let some contemporary light upon the Journal, and Pepys was plunged for ever in social and political disgrace. We can trace the growth of his terrors by two facts. In 1660, while the Diary was still in its youth, he tells about it, as a matter of course, to a lieutenant in the navy; but in 1669, when it was already near an end, he could have bitten his tongue out, as the saying is, because he had let slip his secret to one so grave and friendly as Sir William Coventry. And from two other facts I think we may infer that he had entertained, even if he had not acquiesced in, the thought of a far-distant publicity. The first is of capital importance: the Diary was not destroyed. The second – that he took unusual precautions to confound the cipher in 'rogueish' passages – proves, beyond question, that he was thinking of some other reader besides himself. Perhaps while his friends were admiring the 'greatness of his behaviour' at the approach of death, he may have had a twinkling hope of immortality. *Mens cujusque is est quisque,* said his chosen motto; and, as he had stamped his mind with every crook and foible in the pages of the Diary, he might feel that what he left behind him was indeed himself. There is perhaps no other instance so remarkable of the desire of man for publicity and an enduring name. The greatness of his life was open, yet he longed to communicate its smallness also; and, while contemporaries bowed before him, he must buttonhole posterity with the news that his periwig was once alive with nits. But this thought, although I cannot doubt he had it, was neither his first nor his deepest; it did not colour one word that he wrote; and the Diary, for as long as he kept it, remained what it was when he began, a private pleasure for himself. It was his bosom secret; it added a zest to all his pleasures; he lived in and for it, and might well write these solemn words, when he closed that confidant for ever:

> And so I betake myself to that course which is almost as much as to see myself go into the grave; for which, and all the discomforts that will accompany my being blind, the good God prepare me.

A LIBERAL GENIUS

Pepys spent part of a certain winter Sunday, when he had taken physic, composing 'a song in praise of a liberal genius (such as I take my own to be) to all studies and pleasures.' The song was unsuccessful, but the Diary is, in a sense, the very song that he was seeking; and his portrait by Hales, so admirably reproduced in Mynors Bright's edition, is a confirmation of the Diary. Hales, it would appear, had known his business; and though he put his sitter to a deal of trouble, almost breaking his neck 'to have the portrait full of shadows,' and draping him in an Indian gown hired expressly for the purpose, he was preoccupied about no merely picturesque effects, but to portray the essence of the man. Whether we read the picture by the Diary or the Diary by the picture, we shall at least agree that Hales was among the number of those who can 'surprise the manners in the face.' Here we have a mouth pouting, moist with desires; eyes greedy, protuberant, and yet apt for weeping too; a nose great alike in character and dimensions; and altogether a most fleshly, melting countenance. The face is attractive by its promise of reciprocity. I have used the word *greedy*, but the reader must not suppose that he can change it for that closely kindred one of *hungry*, for there is here no aspiration, no waiting for better things, but an animal joy in all that comes. It could never be the face of an artist; it is the face of a *viveur* – kindly, pleased and pleasing, protected from excess and upheld in contentment by the shifting versatility of his desires. For a single desire is more rightly to be called a lust; but there is health in a variety, where one may balance and control another.

The whole world, town or country, was to Pepys a garden of Armida. Wherever he went his steps were winged with the most eager expectation; whatever he did, it was done with the most lively pleasure. An insatiable curiosity in all the shows of the world and all the secrets of knowledge, filled him brimful of the longing to travel, and supported him in the toils of study. Rome was the dream of his life; he was never happier than when he read or talked of the Eternal City. When he was in Holland, he was 'with child' to see any strange thing. Meeting some friends and singing with them in a palace near the Hague, his pen fails him to express his passion of delight, 'the more so because in a heaven of pleasure and in a strange country.' He must go to see all famous executions. He must needs visit the body of a murdered man, defaced 'with a broad wound,' he says, 'that makes my hand now shake to write of it.' He learned to dance, and was 'like to make a dancer.' He learned to sing, and walked about Gray's Inn Fields 'humming to myself (which is now my constant practice) the trillo.' He learned to play the lute, the flute, the flageolet, and the theorbo, and it was not the fault of his intention if he did not learn the harpsichord or the spinet. He learned to compose songs, and burned to give forth 'a scheme and theory of music not yet ever made in the world.' When he heard 'a fellow whistle like a bird exceeding well,' he promised to return another day and give an angel for a lesson in the art. Once, he writes, 'I took the Bezan back with me, and with a brave gale and tide reached up that night to the Hope, taking great pleasure in learning the seamen's manner of singing when they sound the depths.' If he found himself rusty in his Latin grammar, he must fall to it like a schoolboy. He was a member of Harrington's Club till its dissolution, and of the Royal Society before it had received the name. Boyle's *Hydrostatics* was 'of infinite delight' to him, walking in Barnes Elms. We find him comparing Bible concordances, a captious judge of sermons, deep in Descartes and Aristotle. We find him, in a single year, studying timber and the measurement of timber; tar and oil, hemp, and the process of preparing cordage; mathematics and accounting; the hull and the rigging of ships from a model; and 'looking and improving himself of the (naval) stores with' – hark to the fellow! – 'great delight.' His familiar spirit of delight was not the same with Shelley's; but how true it was to him through life! He is only copying something, and behold, he 'takes great pleasure to rule the lines, and have the capital words wrote with red ink;' he has only had his coal-cellar emptied and cleaned, and behold, 'it do please him exceedingly.' A hog's harslett is 'a piece of meat he loves.' He cannot ride home in my Lord Sandwich's coach, but he must exclaim, with breathless gusto, 'his noble, rich coach.' When he is bound for a supper party, he anticipates a 'glut of pleasure.' When he has a new watch, 'to see my childishness,' says he, 'I could not forbear carrying it in my hand and seeing what o'clock it was an hundred times.' To go to Vauxhall, he says, and 'to hear the nightingales and other birds, hear fiddles, and there a harp and here a Jew's trump, and here laughing, and there fine people walking, is mighty divertising.' And the nightingales, I take it, were particularly dear to him; and it was again 'with great pleasure' that he paused to hear them as he walked to Woolwich, while the fog was rising and the April sun broke through.

He must always be doing something agreeable, and, by preference, two agreeable things at once. In his house he had a box of carpenter's tools, two dogs, an eagle, a canary, and a blackbird that whistled tunes, lest, even in that full life, he should chance upon an empty moment. If he had to wait for a dish of poached eggs, he must put in the time by playing on the flageolet; if a sermon were dull, he must read in the book of Tobit or divert his mind with sly advances on the nearest women. When he walked, it must be with a book in his pocket to beguile the way in case the nightingales were silent; and even along the streets of London, with so many pretty faces to be spied for and dignitaries to be saluted, his trail was marked by little debts 'for wine, pictures, etc.,' the true headmark of a life intolerant of any joyless passage. He had a kind of idealism in pleasure; like the princess in the fairy story, he was conscious of a rose-leaf out of place. Dearly as he loved to talk, he could not enjoy nor shine in a conversation when he thought himself unsuitably dressed. Dearly as he loved eating, he 'knew not how to eat alone;' pleasure for him must heighten pleasure; and the eye and ear must be flattered like the palate ere he avow himself content. He had no zest in a good dinner when it fell to be eaten 'in a bad street and in a periwig-maker's house;' and a collation was spoiled for him by indifferent music. His body was indefatigable, doing him yeoman's service in this breathless chase of pleasures. On April 11, 1662, he mentions that he went to bed 'weary, *which I seldom am*;' and already over thirty, he would sit up all night cheerfully to see a comet. But it is never pleasure that exhausts the pleasure-seeker; for in that career, as in all others, it is failure that kills. The man who enjoys so wholly and bears so impatiently the slightest widowhood from joy, is just the man to lose a night's rest over some paltry question of his right to fiddle on the leads, or to be 'vexed to the blood' by a solecism in his wife's attire; and we find in consequence that he was always peevish when he was hungry, and that his head 'aked mightily' after a dispute. But nothing could divert him from his aim in life; his remedy in care was the same as his delight in prosperity; it was with pleasure, and with pleasure only, that he sought to drive out sorrow; and, whether he was jealous of his wife or skulking from a bailiff, he would equally take refuge in the theatre. There, if the house be full and the company noble, if the songs be tunable, the actors perfect, and the play diverting, this odd hero of the secret Diary, this private self-adorer, will speedily be healed of his distresses.

Equally pleased with a watch, a coach, a piece of meat, a tune upon the fiddle, or a fact in hydrostatics, Pepys was pleased yet more by the beauty, the worth, the mirth, or the mere scenic attitude in life of his fellow-creatures. He shows himself throughout a sterling humanist. Indeed, he who loves himself, not in idle vanity, but with a plenitude of knowledge, is the best equipped of all to love his neighbours. And perhaps it is in this sense that charity may be most properly said to begin at home. It does not matter what quality a person has: Pepys can appreciate and love him for it. He 'fills his eyes' with the beauty of Lady Castlemaine; indeed, he may be said to dote upon the thought of her for years; if a woman be good-looking and not painted, he will walk miles to have another sight of her; and even when a lady by a mischance spat upon his clothes, he was immediately consoled when he had observed that she was pretty. But, on the other hand, he is delighted to see Mrs Pett upon her knees, and speaks thus of his Aunt James: 'a poor, religious, well-meaning, good soul, talking of nothing but God Almighty, and that with so much innocence that mightily pleased me.' He is taken with Pen's merriment and loose songs, but not less taken with the sterling worth of Coventry. He is jolly with a drunken sailor, but listens with interest and patience, as he rides the Essex roads, to the story of a Quaker's spiritual trials and convictions. He lends a critical ear to the discourse of kings and royal dukes. He spends an evening at Vauxhall with 'Killigrew and young Newport – loose company,' says he, 'but worth a man's being in for once, to know the nature of it, and their manner of talk and lives.' And when a rag-boy lights him home, he examines him about his business and other ways of livelihood for destitute children. This is almost half-way to the beginning of philanthropy; had it only been the fashion, as it is at present, Pepys had perhaps been a man famous for good deeds. And it is through this quality that he rises, at times, superior to his surprising egotism; his interest in the love affairs of others is, indeed, impersonal; he is filled with concern for my Lady Castlemaine, whom he only knows by sight, shares in her very jealousies, joys with her in her successes; and it is not untrue, however strange it seems in his abrupt presentment, that he loved his maid Jane because she was in love with his man Tom.

Let us hear him, for once, at length:

So the women and W. Hewer and I walked upon the Downes, where a flock of sheep was; and the most pleasant and innocent sight that ever I saw in my life. We found a shepherd and his little boy reading, far from any houses or sight of people, the Bible to him; so I made the boy read to me, which he did with the forced tone that children do usually read, that was mighty pretty; and then I did give him something, and went to the father, and talked with him. He did content himself mightily in my liking his boy's reading, and did bless God for him, the most like one of the old patriarchs that ever I saw in my life, and it brought those thoughts of the old age of the world in my mind for two or three days after. We took notice of his woolen knit stockings of two colours mixed, and of his shoes shod with iron, both at the toe and heels, and with great nails in the soles of his feet, which was mighty pretty; and taking notice of them, 'Why,' says the poor man, 'the downes, you see, are full of stones, and we are faine to shoe ourselves thus; and these,' says he, 'will make the stones fly till they ring before me.' I did give the poor man something, for which he was mighty thankful, and I tried to cast stones with his horne crooke. He values his dog mightily, that would turn a sheep any way which he would have him, when he goes to fold them; told me there was about eighteen score sheep in his flock, and that he hath four shillings a week the year round for keeping of them; and Mrs Turner, in the common fields here, did gather one of the prettiest nosegays that ever I saw in my life.

And so the story rambles on to the end of that day's pleasuring; with cups of milk, and glowworms, and people walking at sundown with their wives and children, and all the way home Pepys still dreaming 'of the old age of the world' and the early innocence of man. This was how he walked through life, his eyes and ears wide open, and his hand, you will observe, not shut; and thus he observed the lives, the speech, and the manners of his fellow-men, with prose fidelity of detail and yet a lingering glamour of romance.

It was 'two or three days after' that he extended this passage in the pages of his Journal, and the style has thus the benefit of some reflection. It is generally supposed that, as a writer, Pepys must rank at the bottom of the scale of merit. But a style which is indefatigably lively, telling, and picturesque through six large volumes of everyday experience, which deals with the whole matter of a life, and yet is rarely wearisome, which condescends to the most fastidious particulars, and yet sweeps all away in the forthright current of the narrative, – such a style may be ungrammatical, it may be inelegant, it may be one tissue of mistakes, but it can never be devoid of merit. The first and the true function of the writer has been thoroughly performed through-out; and though the manner of his utterance may be childishly awkward, the matter has been transformed and assimilated by his unfeigned interest and delight. The gusto of the man speaks out fierily after all these years. For the difference between Pepys and Shelley, to return to that half-whimsical approximation, is one of quality but not one of degree; in his sphere, Pepys felt as keenly, and his is the true prose of poetry – prose because the spirit of the man was narrow and earthly, but poetry because he was delightedly alive. Hence, in such a passage as this about the Epsom shepherd, the result upon the reader's mind is entire conviction and unmingled pleasure. So, you feel, the thing fell out, not otherwise; and you would no more change it than you would change a sublimity of Shakespeare's, a homely touch of Bunyan's, or a favoured reminiscence of your own.

There never was a man nearer being an artist, who yet was not one. The tang was in the family; while he was writing the journal for our enjoyment in his comely house in Navy Gardens, no fewer than two of his cousins were tramping the fens, kit under arm, to make music to the country girls. But he himself, though he could play so many instruments and pass judgement in so many fields of art, remained an amateur. It is not given to anyone so keenly to enjoy, without some greater power to understand. That he did not like Shakespeare as an artist for the stage may be a fault, but it is not without either parallel or excuse. He certainly admired him as a poet; he was the first beyond mere actors on the rolls of that innumerable army who have got 'To be or not to be' by heart. Nor was he content with that; it haunted his mind; he quoted it to himself in the pages of the Diary, and, rushing in where angels fear to tread, he set it to music. Nothing, indeed, is more notable than the heroic quality of the verses that our little sensualist in a periwig chose out to marry with his own mortal strains. Some gust from brave Elizabethan times must have warmed his spirit, as he sat tuning his sublime theorbo. 'To be or not to be. Whether 'tis nobler' – 'Beauty retire, thou dost my pity move' – 'It is decreed, nor shall thy fate, O Rome;' – open and dignified in the sound, various and majestic in the sentiment, it was no inapt, as it was certainly no timid, spirit that selected such a range of themes. Of 'Gaze not on Swans,' I know no more than these four words; yet that also seems to promise well. It was, however, on a probable suspicion, the work of his master, Mr Berkenshaw – as the drawings that figure at the breaking up of a young ladies' seminary are the work of the professor attached to the establishment. Mr Berkenshaw was not altogether happy in his pupil. The amateur cannot usually rise into the artist, some leaven of the world still clogging him; and we find Pepys behaving like a pickthank to the man who taught him composition. In relation to the stage, which he so warmly loved and understood, he was not only more hearty, but more generous to others. Thus he encounters Colonel Reames, 'a man,' says he, 'who understands and loves a play as well as I, and I love him for it.' And again, when he and his wife had seen a most ridiculous insipid piece, 'Glad we were,' he writes, 'that Betterton had no part in it.' It is by such a zeal and loyalty to those who labour for his delight that the amateur grows worthy of the artist. And it should be kept in mind that, not only in art, but in morals, Pepys rejoiced to recognise his betters. There was not one speck of envy in the whole human-hearted egotist.

RESPECTABILITY

When writers inveigh against respectability, in the present degraded meaning of the word, they are usually suspected of a taste for clay pipes and beer cellars; and their performances are thought to hail from the *Owl's Nest* of the comedy. They have something more, however, in their eye than the dullness of a round million dinner parties that sit down yearly in old England. For to do anything because others do it, and not because the thing is good, or kind, or honest in its own right, is to resign all moral control and captaincy upon yourself, and go post-haste to the devil with the greater number. We smile over the ascendency of priests; but I had rather follow a priest than what they call the leaders of society. No life can better than that of Pepys illustrate the dangers of this respectable theory of living. For what can be more untoward than the occurrence, at a critical period and while the habits are still pliable, of such a sweeping transformation as the return of Charles the Second? Round went the whole fleet of England on the other tack; and while a few tall pintas, Milton or Pen, still sailed a lonely course by the stars and their own private compass, the cock-boat, Pepys, must go about with the majority among 'the stupid starers and the loud huzzas.'

The respectable are not led so much by any desire of applause as by a positive need for countenance. The weaker and the tamer the man, the more will he require this support; and any positive quality relieves him, by just so much, of this dependence. In a dozen ways, Pepys was quite strong enough to please himself without regard for others; but his positive qualities were not coextensive with the field of conduct; and in many parts of life he followed, with gleeful precision, in the footprints of the contemporary Mrs Grundy. In morals, particularly, he lived by the countenance of others; felt a slight from another more keenly than a meanness in himself; and then first repented when he was found out. You could talk of religion or morality to such a man; and by the artist side of him, by his lively sympathy and apprehension, he could rise, as it were dramatically, to the significance of what you said. All that matter in religion which has been nicknamed other-worldliness was strictly in his gamut; but a rule of life that should make a man rudely virtuous, following right in good report and ill report, was foolishness and a stumbling-block to Pepys. He was much thrown across the Friends; and nothing can be more instructive than his attitude towards these most interesting people of that age. I have mentioned how he conversed with one as he rode; when he saw some brought from a meeting under arrest, 'I would to God,' said he, 'they would either conform, or be more wise and not be catched;' and to a Quaker in his own office he extended a timid though effectual protection. Meanwhile there was growing up next door to him that beautiful nature, William Pen. It is odd that Pepys condemned him for a fop; odd, though natural enough when you see Pen's portrait, that Pepys was jealous of him with his wife. But the cream of the story is when Pen publishes his *Sandy Foundation Shaken,* and Pepys has it read aloud by his wife. 'I find it,' he says, 'so well writ as, I think, it is too good for him ever to have writ it; and it is a serious sort of book, and *not fit for everybody to read.*' Nothing is more galling to the merely respectable than to be brought in contact with religious ardour. Pepys had his own foundation, sandy enough, but dear to him from practical considerations, and he would read the book with true uneasiness of spirit; for conceive the blow if, by some plaguy accident, this Pen were to convert him! It was a different kind of doctrine that he judged profitable for himself and others.

> A good sermon of Mr Gifford's at our church, upon 'Seek ye first the kingdom of heaven.' A very excellent and persuasive, good and moral sermon. He showed, like a wise man, that righteousness is a surer moral way of being rich than sin and villainy.

It is thus that respectable people desire to have their Greathearts address them, telling, in mild accents, how you may make the best of both worlds, and be a moral hero without courage, kindness, or troublesome reflection; and thus the Gospel, cleared of Eastern metaphor, becomes a manual of worldly prudence, and a handybook for Pepys and the successful merchant.

The respectability of Pepys was deeply grained. He has no idea of truth except for the Diary. He has no care that a thing shall be, if it but appear; gives out that he has inherited a good estate, when he has seemingly got nothing but a lawsuit; and is pleased to be thought liberal when he knows he has been mean. He is conscientiously ostentatious. I say conscientiously, with reason. He could never have been taken for a fop, like Pen, but arrayed himself in a manner nicely suitable to his position. For long he hesitated to assume the famous periwig; for a public man should travel gravely with the fashions, not foppishly before, nor dowdily behind, the central movement of his age. For long he durst not keep a carriage; that, in his circumstances, would have been improper; but a time comes, with the growth of his fortune, when the impropriety has shifted to the other side, and he is 'ashamed to be seen in a hackney.' Pepys talked about being 'a Quaker or some very melancholy thing;' for my part, I can imagine nothing so melancholy, because nothing half so silly, as to be concerned about such problems. But so respectability and the duties of society haunt and burden their poor devotees; and what seems at first the very primrose path of life, proves difficult and thorny like the rest. And the time comes to Pepys, as to all the merely respectable, when he must not only order his pleasures, but even clip his virtuous movements, to the public pattern of the age. There was some juggling among officials to avoid direct taxation; and Pepys, with a noble impulse, growing ashamed of this dishonesty, designed to charge himself with £1000; but finding none to set him an example, 'nobody of our ablest merchants' with this moderate liking for clean hands, he judged it 'not decent;' he feared it would 'be thought vain glory;' and, rather than appear singular, cheerfully remained a thief. One able merchant's countenance, and Pepys had dared to do an honest act! Had he found one brave spirit, properly recognised by society, he might have gone far as a disciple. Mrs Turner, it is true, can fill him full of sordid scandal, and make him believe, against the testimony of his senses, that Pen's venison pasty stank like the devil; but, on the other hand, Sir William Coventry can raise him by a word into another being. Pepys, when he is with Coventry, talks in the vein of an old Roman. What does he care for office or emolument? 'Thank God, I have enough of my own,' says he, 'to

buy me a good book and a good fiddle, and I have a good wife.'
And again, we find this pair projecting an old age when an
ungrateful country shall have dismissed them from the field of
public service; Coventry living retired in a fine house, and Pepys
dropping in, 'it may be, to read a chapter of Seneca.'

Under this influence, the only good one in his life, Pepys
continued zealous and, for the period, pure in his employment. He
would not be 'bribed to be unjust,' he says, though he was 'not so
squeamish as to refuse a present after,' suppose the king to have
received no wrong. His new arrangement for the victualling of
Tangier, he tells us with honest complacency, will save the king a
thousand and gain Pepys three hundred pounds a year, – a
statement which exactly fixes the degree of the age's enlighten-
ment. But for his industry and capacity no praise can be too high.
It was an unending struggle for the man to stick to his business in
such a garden of Armida as he found this life; and the story of his
oaths, so often broken, so courageously renewed, is worthy rather
of admiration than the contempt it has received.

Elsewhere, and beyond the sphere of Coventry's influence, we
find him losing scruples and daily complying further with the age.
When he began the Journal, he was a trifle prim and puritanic;
merry enough, to be sure, over his private cups, and still
remembering Magdalene ale and his acquaintance with Mrs
Ainsworth of Cambridge. But youth is a hot season with all; when
a man smells April and May he is apt at times to stumble; and in
spite of a disordered practice, Pepys's theory, the better things
that he approved and followed after, we may even say were strict.
Where there was 'tag, rag, and bobtail, dancing, singing, and
drinking,' he felt 'ashamed, and went away;' and when he slept in
church, he prayed God forgive him. In but a little while we find
him with some ladies keeping each other awake 'from spite,' as
though not to sleep in church were an obvious hardship; and yet
later he calmly passes the time of service, looking about him, with
a perspective glass, on all the pretty women. His favourite
ejaculation, 'Lord!' occurs but once that I have observed in 1660,
never in '61, twice in '62, and at least five times in '63; after which
the 'Lords' may be said to pullulate like herrings, with here and
there a solitary 'damned,' as it were a whale among the shoal. He
and his wife, once filled with dudgeon by some innocent freedoms
at a marriage, are soon content to go pleasuring with my Lord
Brouncker's mistress, who was not even, by his own account, the
most discreet of mistresses. Tag, rag, and bobtail, dancing,

singing, and drinking, become his natural element; actors and actresses and drunken, roaring courtiers are to be found in his society; until the man grew so involved with Saturnalian manners and companions that he was shot almost unconsciously into the grand domestic crash of 1668.

That was the legitimate issue and punishment of years of staggering walk and conversation. The man who has smoked his pipe for half a century in a powder magazine finds himself at last the author and the victim of a hideous disaster. So with our pleasant-minded Pepys and his peccadilloes. All of a sudden, as he still trips dexterously enough among the dangers of a double-faced career, thinking no great evil, humming to himself the trillo, Fate takes the further conduct of that matter from his hands, and brings him face to face with the consequences of his acts. For a man still, after so many years, the lover, although not the constant lover, of his wife, – for a man, besides, who was so greatly careful of appearances, – the revelation of his infidelities was a crushing blow. The tears that he shed, the indignities that he endured, are not to be measured. A vulgar woman, and now justly incensed, Mrs Pepys spared him no detail of suffering. She was violent, threatening him with the tongs; she was careless of his honour, driving him to insult the mistress whom she had driven him to betray and to discard; worst of all, she was hopelessly inconsequent, in word and thought and deed, now lulling him with reconciliations, and anon flaming forth again with the original anger. Pepys had not used his wife well; he had wearied her with jealousies, even while himself unfaithful; he had grudged her clothes and pleasures, while lavishing both upon himself; he had abused her in words; he had bent his fist at her in anger; he had once blacked her eye; and it is one of the oddest particulars in that odd Diary of his, that, while the injury is referred to once in passing, there is no hint as to the occasion or the manner of the blow. But now, when he is in the wrong, nothing can exceed the long-suffering affection of this impatient husband. While he was still sinning and still undiscovered, he seems not to have known a touch of penitence stronger than what might lead him to take his wife to the theatre, or for an airing, or to give her a new dress, by way of compensation. Once found out, however, and he seems to himself to have lost all claim to decent usage. It is perhaps the strongest instance of his externality. His wife may do what she pleases, and though he may groan, it will never occur to him to blame her; he has no weapon left but tears and the most abject submission. We should perhaps have respected him more had he not given way so utterly – above all, had he refused to write, under his wife's dictation, an insulting letter to his unhappy fellow-culprit, Miss Willet; but somehow I believe we like him better as he was.

The death of his wife, following so shortly after, must have stamped the impression of this episode upon his mind. For the remaining years of his long life we have no Diary to help us, and we have seen already how little stress is to be laid upon the tenor of his correspondence; but what with the recollection of the catastrophe of his married life, what with the natural influence of his advancing years and reputation, it seems not unlikely that the period of gallantry was at an end for Pepys; and it is beyond a doubt that he sat down at last to an honoured and agreeable old age among his books and music, the correspondent of Sir Isaac Newton, and, in one instance at least, the poetical counsellor of Dryden. Through all this period, that Diary which contained the secret memoirs of his life, with all its inconsistencies and escapades, had been religiously preserved; nor, when he came to die, does he appear to have provided for its destruction. So we may conceive him faithful to the end to all his dear and early memories; still mindful of Mrs Hely in the woods at Epsom; still lighting at Islington for a cup of kindness to the dead; still, if he heard again that air that once so much disturbed him, thrilling at the recollection of the love that bound him to his wife.

WALT WHITMAN

Of late years the name of Walt Whitman has been a good deal bandied about in books and magazines. It has become familiar both in good and ill repute. His works have been largely bespattered with praise by his admirers, and cruelly mauled and mangled by irreverent enemies. Now, whether his poetry is good or bad as poetry, is a matter that may admit of a difference of opinion without alienating those who differ. We could not keep the peace with a man who should put forward claims to taste and yet depreciate the choruses in *Samson Agonistes*; but, I think, we may shake hands with one who sees no more in Walt Whitman's volume, from a literary point of view, than a farrago of incompetent essays in a wrong direction. That may not be at all our own opinion. We may think that, when a work contains many unforgettable phrases, it cannot be altogether devoid of literary merit. We may even see passages of a high poetry here and there among its eccentric contents. But when all is said, Walt Whitman is neither a Milton nor a Shakespeare; to appreciate his works is not a condition necessary to salvation; and I would not disinherit a son upon the question, nor even think much the worse of a critic, for I should always have an idea what he meant.

What Whitman has to say is another affair from how he says it. It is not possible to acquit anyone of defective intelligence, or else stiff prejudice, who is not interested by Whitman's matter and the spirit it represents. Not as a poet, but as what we must call (for lack of a more exact expression) a prophet, he occupies a curious and prominent position. Whether he may greatly influence the future or not, he is a notable symptom of the present. As a sign of the times, it would be hard to find his parallel. I should hazard a large wager, for instance, that he was not unacquainted with the works of Herbert Spencer; and yet where, in all the history books, shall we lay our hands on two more incongruous contemporaries?

Mr Spencer so decorous – I had almost said, so dandy – in dissent; and Whitman, like a large shaggy dog, just unchained, scouring the beaches of the world and baying at the moon. And when was an echo more curiously like a satire, than when Mr Spencer found his Synthetic Philosophy reverberated from the other shores of the Atlantic in the 'barbaric yawp' of Whitman?

I

Whitman, it cannot be too soon explained, writes up to a system. He was a theoriser about society before he was a poet. He first perceived something wanting, and then sat down squarely to supply the want. The reader, running over his works, will find that he takes nearly as much pleasure in critically expounding his theory of poetry as in making poems. This is as far as it can be from the case of the spontaneous village minstrel dear to elegy, who has no theory whatever, although sometimes he may have fully as much poetry as Whitman. The whole of Whitman's work is deliberate and preconceived. A man born into a society comparatively new, full of conflicting elements and interests, could not fail, if he had any thoughts at all, to reflect upon the tendencies around him. He saw much good and evil on all sides, not yet settled down into some more or less unjust compromise as in older nations, but still in the act of settlement. And he could not but wonder what it would turn out; whether the compromise would be very just or very much the reverse, and give great or little scope for healthy human energies. From idle wonder to active speculation is but a step; and he seems to have been early struck with the inefficacy of literature and its extreme unsuitability to the conditions. What he calls 'Feudal Literature' could have little living action on the tumult of American democracy; what he calls the 'Literature of Woe,' meaning the whole tribe of Werther and Byron, could have no action for good in any time or place. Both propositions, if art had none but a direct moral influence, would be true enough; and as this seems to be Whitman's view, they were true enough for him. He conceived the idea of a Literature which was to inhere in the life of the present; which was to be, first, human, and next, American; which was to be brave and cheerful as per contract; to give culture in a popular and poetical presentment; and, in so doing, catch and stereotype some democratic ideal of humanity which should be equally natural to all grades of wealth and education, and suited, in one of his favourite phrases, to 'the average man.' To the formation of some such literature as this his poems are to be regarded as so many contributions, one sometimes explaining, sometimes superseding, the other: and the whole together not so much a finished work as a body of suggestive hints. He does not profess to have built the castle, but he pretends he has traced the lines of the foundation. He has not made the poetry, but he flatters himself he has done something towards making the poets.

His notion of the poetic function is ambitious, and coincides roughly with what Schopenhauer has laid down as the province of the metaphysician. The poet is to gather together for men, and set in order, the materials of their existence. He is 'The Answerer;' he is to find some way of speaking about life that shall satisfy, if only for the moment, man's enduring astonishment at his own position. And besides having an answer ready, it is he who shall provoke the question. He must shake people out of their indifference, and force them to make some election in the world, instead of sliding dully forward in a dream. Life is a business we are all apt to mismanage; either living recklessly from day to day, or suffering ourselves to be gulled out of our moments by the inanities of custom. We should despise a man who gave as little activity and forethought to the conduct of any other business. But in this, which is the one thing of all others, since it contains them all, we cannot see the forest for the trees. One brief impression obliterates another. There is something stupefying in the recurrence of unimportant things. And it is only on rare provocations that we can rise to take an outlook beyond daily concerns, and comprehend the narrow limits and great possibilities of our existence. It is the duty of the poet to induce such moments of clear sight. He is the declared enemy of all living by reflex action, of all that is done betwixt sleep and waking, of all the pleasureless pleasurings and imaginary duties in which we coin away our hearts and fritter invaluable years. He has to electrify his readers into an instant unflagging activity, founded on a wide and eager observation of the world, and make them direct their ways by a superior prudence, which has little or nothing in common with the maxims of the copy-book. That many of us lead such lives as they would heartily disown after two hours' serious reflection on the subject is, I am afraid, a true, and, I am sure, a very galling thought. The Enchanted Ground of dead-alive respectability is next, upon the map, to the Beulah of considerate virtue. But there they all slumber and take their rest in the middle of God's beautiful and wonderful universe; the drowsy heads have nodded together in the same position since first their fathers fell asleep; and not even the sound of the last trumpet can wake them to a single active thought. The poet has a hard task before him to stir up such fellows to a sense of their own and other people's principles in life.

And it happens that literature is, in some ways, but an indifferent means to such an end. Language is but a poor bull's-eye lantern wherewith to show off the vast cathedral of the world; and yet a particular thing once said in words is so definite and memorable, that it makes us forget the absence of the many which remain unexpressed; like a bright window in a distant view, which dazzles and confuses our sight of its surroundings. There are not words enough in all Shakespeare to express the merest fraction of a man's experience in an hour. The speed of the eyesight and the hearing, and the continual industry of the mind, produce, in ten minutes, what it would require a laborious volume to shadow forth by comparisons and roundabout approaches. If verbal logic were sufficient, life would be as plain sailing as a piece of Euclid. But, as a matter of fact, we make a travesty of the simplest process of thought when we put it into words; for the words are all coloured and forsworn, apply inaccurately, and bring with them, from former uses, ideas of praise and blame that have nothing to do with the question in hand. So we must always see to it nearly, that we judge by the realities of life and not by the partial terms that represent them in man's speech; and at times of choice, we must leave words upon one side, and act upon those brute convictions, unexpressed and perhaps inexpressible, which cannot be flourished in an argument, but which are truly the sum and fruit of our experience. Words are for communication, not for judgement. This is what every thoughtful man knows for himself, for only fools and silly schoolmasters push definitions over far into the domain of conduct; and the majority of women, not learned in these scholastic refinements, live all-of-a-piece and unconsciously, as a tree grows, without caring to put a name upon their acts or motives. Hence, a new difficulty for Whitman's scrupulous and argumentative poet; he must do more than waken up the sleepers to his words; he must persuade them to look over the book and at life with their own eyes.

This side of truth is very present to Whitman; it is this that he means when he tells us that 'To glance with an eye confounds the learning of all times.' But he is not unready. He is never weary of descanting on the undebatable conviction that is forced upon our minds by the presence of other men, of animals, or of inanimate things. To glance with an eye, were it only at a chair or a park railing, is by far a more persuasive process, and brings us to a far more exact conclusion, than to read the works of all the logicians extant. If both, by a large allowance, may be said to end in certainty, the certainty in the one case transcends the other to an incalculable degree. If people see a lion, they run away; if they only apprehend a deduction, they keep wandering around in an experimental humour. Now, how is the poet to convince like nature, and not like books? Is there no actual piece of nature that he can show the man to his face, as he might show him a tree if they were walking together? Yes, there is one: the man's own thoughts. In fact, if the poet is to speak efficaciously, he must say what is already in his hearer's mind. That, alone, the hearer will believe; that, alone, he will be able to apply intelligently to the facts of life. Any conviction, even if it be a whole system or a whole religion, must pass into the condition of common-place, or postulate, before it becomes fully operative. Strange excursions and high-flying theories may interest, but they cannot rule behaviour. Our faith is not the highest truth that we perceive, but the highest that we have been able to assimilate into the very texture and method of our thinking. It is not, therefore, by flashing before a man's eyes the weapons of dialectic; it is not by induction, deduction, or construction; it is not by forcing him on from one stage of reasoning to another, that the man will be effectually renewed. He cannot be made to believe anything; but he can be made to see that he has always believed it. And this is the practical canon. It is when the reader cries, 'Oh, I know!' and is, perhaps, half irritated to see how nearly the author has forestalled his own thoughts, that he is on the way to what is called in theology a Saving Faith.

Here we have the key to Whitman's attitude. To give a certain unity of ideal to the average population of America – to gather their activities about some conception of humanity that shall be central and normal, if only for the moment – the poet must portray that population as it is. Like human law, human poetry is simply declaratory. If any ideal is possible, it must be already in the thoughts of the people; and, by the same reason, in the thoughts of the poet, who is one of them. And hence Whitman's own formula: 'The poet is individual – he is complete in himself: the others are as good as he; only he sees it, and they do not.' To show them how good they are, the poet must study his fellow-countrymen and himself somewhat like a traveller on the hunt for his book of travels. There is a sense, of course, in which all true books are books of travel; and all genuine poets must run their risk of being charged with the traveller's exaggeration; for to whom are such books more surprising than to those whose own life is faithfully and smartly pictured? But this danger is all upon one side; and you may judiciously flatter the portrait without any likelihood of the sitter's disowning it for a faithful likeness. And so Whitman has reasoned: that by drawing at first hand from himself and his neighbours, accepting without shame the inconsistencies and brutalities that go to make up man, and yet treating the whole in a high, magnanimous spirit, we would make sure of belief, and at the same time encourage people forward by the means of praise.

II

We are accustomed nowadays to a great deal of puling over the circumstances in which we are placed. The great refinement of many poetical gentlemen has rendered them practically unfit for the jostling and ugliness of life, and they record their unfitness at considerable length. The bold and awful poetry of Job's complaint produces too many flimsy imitators; for there is always something consolatory in grandeur, but the symphony transposed for the piano becomes hysterically sad. This literature of woe, as Whitman calls it, this *Maladie de René,* as we like to call it in Europe, is in many ways a most humiliating and sickly phenomenon. Young gentlemen with three or four hundred a year of private means look down from a pinnacle of doleful experience on all the grown and hearty men who have dared to say a good word for life since the beginning of the world. There is no prophet but the melancholy Jacques, and the blue devils dance on all our literary wires.

It would be a poor service to spread culture, if this be its result, among the comparatively innocent and cheerful ranks of men. When our little poets have to be sent to look at the ploughman and learn wisdom, we must be careful how we tamper with our ploughmen. Where a man in not the best of circumstances preserves composure of mind, and relishes ale and tobacco, and his wife and children, in the intervals of dull and unremunerative labour; where a man in this predicament can afford a lesson by the way to what are called his intellectual superiors, there is plainly something to be lost, as well as something to be gained, by teaching him to think differently. It is better to leave him as he is than to teach him whining. It is better that he should go without the cheerful lights of culture, if cheerless doubt and paralysing sentimentalism are to be the consequence. Let us, by all means, fight against that hide-bound stolidity of sensation and sluggishness of mind which blurs and decolorises for poor natures the wonderful pageant of consciousness. Let us teach people, as much as we can, to enjoy, and they will learn for themselves to sympathise; but let us see to it, above all, that we give these lessons in a brave, vivacious note, and build the man up in courage while we demolish its substitute, indifference.

Whitman is alive to all this. He sees that, if the poet is to be of any help, he must testify to the livableness of life. His poems, he tells us, are to be 'hymns of the praise of things.' They are to make for a certain high joy in living, or what he calls himself 'a brave delight fit for freedom's athletes.' And he has had no difficulty in introducing his optimism: it fitted readily enough with his system; for the average man is truly a courageous person and truly fond of living. One of Whitman's remarks upon this head is worth quotation, as he is there perfectly successful, and does precisely what he designs to do throughout: Takes ordinary and even commonplace circumstances; throws them out, by a happy turn of thinking, into significance and something like beauty; and tacks a hopeful moral lesson to the end.

'The passionate tenacity of hunters, woodmen, early risers, cultivators of gardens and orchards and fields,' he says, 'the love of healthy women for the manly form, seafaring persons, drivers of horses, the passion for light and the open air, – all is an old unvaried sign of the unfailing perception of beauty, and of a residence of the poetic in outdoor people.'

There seems to me something truly original in this choice of trite examples. You will remark how adroitly Whitman begins, hunters and woodmen being confessedly romantic. And one thing more. If he had said 'the love of healthy men for the female form,' he would have said almost a silliness; for the thing has never been dissembled out of delicacy, and is so obvious as to be a public nuisance. But by reversing it, he tells us something not unlike news; something that sounds quite freshly in words; and, if the reader be a man, gives him a moment of great self-satisfaction and spiritual aggrandisement. In many different authors you may find passages more remarkable for grammar, but few of a more ingenious turn, and none that could be more to the point in our connection. The tenacity of many ordinary people in ordinary pursuits is a sort of standing challenge to everybody else. If one man can grow absorbed in delving his garden, others may grow absorbed and happy over something else. Not to be upsides in this with any groom or gardener, is to be very meanly organised. A man should be ashamed to take his food if he has not alchemy enough in his stomach to turn some of it into intense and enjoyable occupation.

Whitman tries to reinforce this cheerfulness by keeping up a sort of outdoor atmosphere of sentiment. His book, he tells us, should be read 'among the cooling influences of external nature;' and this recommendation, like that other famous one which Hawthorne prefixed to his collected tales, is in itself a character of the work. Everyone who has been upon a walking or a boating tour, living in the open air, with the body in constant exercise and the mind in fallow, knows true ease and quiet. The irritating action of the brain is set at rest; we think in a plain, unfeverish temper; little things seem big enough, and great things no longer portentous; and the world is smilingly accepted as it is. This is the spirit that Whitman inculcates and parades. He thinks very ill of the atmosphere of parlours or libraries. Wisdom keeps school outdoors. And he has the art to recommend this attitude of mind by simply pluming himself upon it as a virtue; so that the reader, to keep the advantage over his author which most readers enjoy, is tricked into professing the same view. And this spirit, as it is his chief lesson, is the greatest charm of his work. Thence, in spite of an uneven and emphatic key of expression, something trenchant and straightforward, something simple and surprising, distinguishes his poems. He has sayings that come home to one like the Bible. We fall upon Whitman, after the works of so many men who write better, with a sense of relief from strain, with a sense of touching nature, as when one passes out of the flaring, noisy thoroughfares of a great city into what he himself has called, with unexcelled imaginative justice of language, 'the huge and thoughtful night.' And his book in consequence, whatever may be the final judgement of its merit, whatever may be its influence on the future, should be in the hands of all parents and guardians as a specific for the distressing malady of being seventeen years old. Green-sickness yields to his treatment as to a charm of magic; and the youth, after a short course of reading, ceases to carry the universe upon his shoulders.

III

Whitman is not one of those who can be deceived by familiarity. He considers it just as wonderful that there are myriads of stars, as that one man should rise from the dead. He declares 'a hair on the back of his hand just as curious as any special revelation.' His whole life is to him what it was to Sir Thomas Browne, one perpetual miracle. Everything is strange, everything unaccountable, everything beautiful; from a bug to the moon, from the sight of the eyes to the appetite for food. He makes it his business to see things as if he saw them for the first time, and professes astonishment on principle. But he has no leaning towards mythology; avows his contempt for what he calls 'unregenerate poetry;' and does not mean by nature

> The smooth walks, trimmed hedges, butterflies, posies, and nightingales of the English poets, but the whole orb, with its geologic history, the Kosmos, carrying fire and snow, that rolls through the illimitable areas, light as a feather though weighing billions of tons.

Nor is this exhaustive; for in his character of idealist all impressions, all thoughts, trees and people, love and faith, astronomy, history, and religion, enter upon equal terms into his notion of the universe. He is not against religion; not, indeed, against any religion. He wishes to drag with a larger net, to make a more comprehensive synthesis, than any or than all of them put together. In feeling after the central type of man, he must embrace all eccentricities; his cosmology must subsume all cosmologies, and the feelings that gave birth to them; his statement of facts must include all religion and all irreligion, Christ and Boodha, God and the devil. The world as it is, and the whole world as it is, physical, and spiritual, and historical, with its good and bad, with its manifold inconsistencies, is what he wishes to set forth, in strong, picturesque, and popular lineaments, for the understanding of the average man. One of his favourite endeavours is to get the whole matter into a nutshell; to knock the four corners of the universe, one after another, about his reader's ears; to hurry him, in breathless phrases, hither and thither, back and forward, in time and space; to focus all this about his own momentary personality; and then, drawing the ground from under his feet, as

if by some cataclysm of nature, to plunge him into the un-
fathomable abyss sown with enormous suns and systems, and
among the inconceivable numbers and magnitudes and velocities
of the heavenly bodies. So that he concludes by striking into us
some sense of that disproportion of things which Shelley has
illuminated by the ironical flash of these eight words: The desire
of the moth for the star.

The same truth, but to what a different purpose! Whitman's
moth is mightily at his ease about all the planets in heaven, and
cannot think too highly of our sublunary tapers. The universe is
so large that imagination flags in the effort to conceive it; but
here, in the meantime, is the world under our feet, a very warm
and habitable corner. 'The earth, that is sufficient; I do not want
the constellations any nearer,' he remarks. And again: 'Let your
soul stand cool and composed,' says he, 'before a million
universes.' It is the language of a transcendental common sense,
such as Thoreau held and sometimes uttered. But Whitman, who
has a somewhat vulgar inclination for technical talk and the
jargon of philosophy, is not content with a few pregnant hints;
he must put the dots upon his i's; he must corroborate the songs
of Apollo by some of the darkest talk of human metaphysic. He
tells his disciples that they must be ready 'to confront the
growing arrogance of Realism.' Each person is, for himself, the
keystone and the occasion of this universal edifice. 'Nothing, not
God,' he says, 'is greater to one than oneself is;' a statement with
an irreligious smack at the first sight; but like most startling
sayings, a manifest truism on a second. He will give effect to his
own character without apology; he sees 'that the elementary
laws never apologise.' 'I reckon,' he adds, with quaint colloquial
arrogance, 'I reckon I behave no prouder than the level I plant
my house by, after all.' The level follows the law of its being; so,
unrelentingly, will he; everything, every person, is good in his
own place and way; God is the maker of all, and all are in one
design. For he believes in God, and that with a sort of blasphem-
ous security. 'No array of terms,' quoth he, 'no array of terms
can say how much at peace I am about God and about death.'
There certainly never was a prophet who carried things with a
higher hand; he gives us less a body of dogmas than a series of
proclamations by the grace of God; and language, you will
observe, positively fails him to express how far he stands above
the highest human doubts and trepidations.

But next in order of truths to a person's sublime conviction of himself, comes the attraction of one person for another, and all that we mean by the word love:

The dear love of man for his comrade – the attraction of friend for friend,
Of the well-married husband and wife, of children and parents,
Of city for city and land for land.

The solitude of the most sublime idealist is broken in upon by other people's faces; he sees a look in their eyes that corresponds to something in his own heart; there comes a tone in their voices which convicts him of a startling weakness for his fellow-creatures. While he is hymning the *ego* and commercing with God and the universe, a woman goes below his window; and at the turn of her skirt or the colour of her eyes, Icarus is recalled from heaven by the run. Love is so startlingly real that it takes rank upon an equal footing of reality with the consciousness of personal existence. We are as heartily persuaded of the identity of those we love as of our own identity. And so sympathy pairs with self-assertion, the two gerents of human life on earth; and Whitman's ideal man must not only be strong, free, and self-reliant in himself, but his freedom must be bounded and his strength perfected by the most intimate, eager, and long-suffering love for others. To some extent this is taking away with the left hand what has been so generously given with the right. Morality has been ceremoniously extruded from the door only to be brought in again by the window. We are told, on one page, to do as we please; and on the next we are sharply upbraided for not having done as the author pleases. We are first assured that we are the finest fellows in the world in our own right; and then it appears that we are only fine fellows in so far as we practise a most quixotic code of morals. The disciple who saw himself in clear ether a moment before is plunged down again among the fogs and complications of duty. And this is all the more overwhelming because Whitman insists not only on love between sex and sex, and between friends of the same sex, but in the field of the less intense political sympathies; and his ideal man must not only be a generous friend but a conscientious voter into the bargain.

His method somewhat lessens the difficulty. He is not, the reader will remember, to tell us how good we ought to be, but to remind us how good we are. He is to encourage us to be free and kind, by proving that we are free and kind already. He passes our corporate life under review, to show that it is upheld by the very virtues of which he makes himself the advocate. 'There is no object so soft,' he says somewhere in his big, plain way, 'there is no object so soft but it makes a hub for the wheel'd universe.' Rightly understood, it is on the softest of all objects, the sympathetic heart, that the wheel of society turns easily and securely as on a perfect axle. There is no room, of course, for doubt or discussion, about conduct, where everyone is to follow the law of his being with exact compliance. Whitman hates doubt, deprecates discussion, and discourages to his utmost the craving, carping sensibilities of the conscience. We are to imitate, to use one of his absurd and happy phrases, 'the satisfaction and aplomb of animals.' If he preaches a sort of ranting Christianity in morals, a fit consequent to the ranting optimism of his cosmology, it is because he declares it to be the original deliverance of the human heart; or at least, for he would be honestly historical in method, of the human heart as at present Christianised. His is a morality without a prohibition; his policy is one of encouragement all round. A man must be a born hero to come up to Whitman's standard in the practice of any of the positive virtues; but of a negative virtue, such as temperance or chastity, he has so little to say, that the reader need not be surprised if he drops a word or two upon the other side. He would lay down nothing that would be a clog; he would prescribe nothing that cannot be done ruddily, in a heat. The great point is to get people under way. To the faithful Whitmanite this would be justified by the belief that God made all, and that all was good; the prophet, in this doctrine, has only to cry 'Tally-ho,' and mankind will break into a gallop on the road to El Dorado. Perhaps, to another class of minds, it may look like the result of the somewhat cynical reflection that you will not make a kind man out of one who is unkind by any precepts under heaven; tempered by the belief that, in natural circumstances, the large majority is well disposed. Thence it would follow, that if you can only get everyone to feel more warmly and act more courageously, the balance of results will be for good.

So far, you see, the doctrine is pretty coherent as a doctrine; as a picture of man's life it is incomplete and misleading, although eminently cheerful. This he is himself the first to acknowledge; for if he is prophetic in anything, it is in his noble disregard of consistency. 'Do I contradict myself?' he asks somewhere; and then pat comes the answer, the best answer ever given in print, worthy of a sage, or rather of a woman: 'Very well, then, I contradict myself!' with this addition, not so feminine and perhaps not altogether so satisfactory: 'I am large – I contain multitudes.' Life, as a matter of fact, partakes largely of the nature of tragedy. The gospel according to Whitman, even if it be not so logical, has this advantage over the gospel according to Pangloss, that it does not utterly disregard the existence of temporal evil. Whitman accepts the fact of disease and wretchedness like an honest man; and instead of trying to qualify it in the interest of his optimism, sets himself to spur people up to be helpful. He expresses a conviction, indeed, that all will be made up to the victims in the end; that 'what is untried and afterward' will fail no one, not even 'the old man who has lived without purpose and feels it with bitterness worse than gall.' But this is not to palliate our sense of what is hard or melancholy in the present. Pangloss, smarting under one of the worst things that ever was supposed to come from America, consoled himself with the reflection that it was the price we have to pay for cochineal. And with that murderous parody, logical optimism and the praises of the best of possible worlds went irrevocably out of season, and have been no more heard of in the mouths of reasonable men. Whitman spares us all allusions to the cochineal; he treats evil and sorrow in a spirit almost as of welcome; as an old sea-dog might have welcomed the sight of the enemy's topsails off the Spanish Main. There, at least, he seems to say, is something obvious to be done. I do not know many better things in literature than the brief pictures – brief and vivid like things seen by lightning – with which he tries to stir up the world's heart upon the side of mercy. He braces us, on the one hand, with examples of heroic duty and helpfulness; on the other, he touches us with pitiful instances of people needing help. He knows how to make the heart beat at a brave story; to inflame us with just resentment over the hunted slave; to stop our mouths for shame when he tells of the drunken prostitute. For all the afflicted, all the weak, all the wicked, a good word is said in a spirit which I can only call one of ultra-Christianity; and however wild, however contradictory, it may be in parts, this at least may be said for his book, as it may be said of the Christian Gospels, that no one will read it, however respectable, but he gets a knock upon his conscience; no one however fallen, but he finds a kindly and supporting welcome.

IV

Nor has he been content with merely blowing the trumpet for the battle of well-doing; he has given to his precepts the authority of his own brave example. Naturally a grave, believing man, with little or no sense of humour, he has succeeded as well in life as in his printed performances. The spirit that was in him has come forth most eloquently in his actions. Many who have only read his poetry have been tempted to set him down as an ass, or even as a charlatan; but I never met anyone who had known him personally who did not profess a solid affection and respect for the man's character. He practises as he professes; he feels deeply that Christian love for all men, that toleration, that cheerful delight in serving others, which he often celebrates in literature with a doubtful measure of success. And perhaps, out of all his writings, the best and the most human and convincing passages are to be found in 'these soil'd and creas'd little livraisons, each composed of a sheet or two of paper, folded small to carry in the pocket, and fastened with a pin,' which he scribbled during the war by the bedsides of the wounded or in the excitement of great events. They are hardly literature in the formal meaning of the word; he has left his jottings for the most part as he made them; a homely detail, a word from the lips of a dying soldier, a business memorandum, the copy of a letter – short, straightforward, to the point, with none of the trappings of composition; but they breathe a profound sentiment, they give us a vivid look at one of the sides of life, and they make us acquainted with a man whom it is an honour to love.

Whitman's intense Americanism, his unlimited belief in the future of These States (as, with reverential capitals, he loves to call them), made the war a period of great trial to his soul. The new virtue, Unionism, of which he is the sole inventor, seemed to have fallen into premature unpopularity. All that he loved, hoped, or hated, hung in the balance. And the game of war was not only momentous to him in its issues; it sublimated his spirit by its heroic displays, and tortured him intimately by the spectacle of its horrors. It was a theatre, it was a place of education, it was like a season of religious revival. He watched Lincoln going daily to his work; he studied and fraternised with young soldiery passing to the front; above all, he walked the hospitals, reading the Bible, distributing clean clothes, or apples, or tobacco; a patient, helpful, reverend man, full of kind speeches.

His memoranda of this period are almost bewildering to read. From one point of view they seem those of a district visitor; from another, they look like the formless jottings of an artist in the picturesque. More than one woman, on whom I tried the experiment, immediately claimed the writer for a fellow-woman. More than one literary purist might identify him as a shoddy newspaper correspondent without the necessary faculty of style. And yet the story touches home; and if you are of the weeping order of mankind, you will certainly find your eyes fill with tears, of which you have no reason to be ashamed. There is only one way to characterise a work of this order, and that is to quote. Here is a passage from a letter to a mother, unknown to Whitman, whose son died in hospital:

Frank, as far as I saw, had everything requisite in surgical treatment, nursing, etc. He had watches much of the time. He was so good and well-behaved, and affectionate, I myself liked him very much. I was in the habit of coming in afternoons and sitting by him, and he liked to have me – liked to put out his arm and lay his hand on my knee – would keep it so a long while. Toward the last he was more restless and flighty at night – often fancied himself with his regiment – by his talk sometimes seem'd as if his feelings were hurt by being blamed by his officers for something he was entirely innocent of – said 'I never in my life was thought capable of such a thing, and never was.' At other times he would fancy himself talking as it seem'd to children or such like, his relatives, I suppose, and giving them good advice; would talk to them a long while. All the time he was out of his head not one single bad word, or thought, or idea escaped him. It was remark'd that many a man's conversation in his senses was not half so good as Frank's delirium.

He was perfectly willing to die – he had become very weak, and had suffer'd a good deal, and was perfectly resign'd, poor boy. I do not know his past life, but I feel as if it must have been good. At any rate what I saw of him here, under the most trying circumstances, with a painful wound, and among strangers, I can say that he behaved so brave, so composed, and so sweet and affectionate, it could not be surpassed. And now, like many other noble and good men, after serving his country as a soldier, he has yielded up his young life at the very outset in her service. Such things are gloomy – yet there is a text, 'God doeth all things well,' the meaning of which, after due time, appears to the soul.

I thought perhaps a few words, though from a stranger, about your son, from one who was with him at the last, might be worth while, for I loved the young man, though I but saw him immediately to lose him.

It is easy enough to pick holes in the grammar of this letter, but what are we to say of its profound goodness and tenderness? It is written as though he had the mother's face before his eyes, and saw her wincing in the flesh at every word. And what, again, are we to say of its sober truthfulness, not exaggerating, not running to phrases, not seeking to make a hero out of what was only an ordinary but good and brave young man? Literary reticence is not Whitman's stronghold; and this reticence is not literary, but humane; it is not that of a good artist but that of a good man. He knew that what the mother wished to hear about was Frank; and he told her about her Frank as he was.

V

Something should be said of Whitman's style, for style is of the essence of thinking. And where a man is so critically deliberate as our author, and goes solemnly about his poetry for an ulterior end, every indication is worth notice. He has chosen a rough, unrhymed, lyrical verse; sometimes instinct with a fine processional movement; often so rugged and careless that it can only be described by saying that he has not taken the trouble to write prose. I believe myself that it was selected principally because it was easy to write, although not without recollections of the marching measures of some of the prose in our English Old Testament. According to Whitman, on the other hand, 'the time has arrived to essentially break down the barriers of form between Prose and Poetry . . . for the most cogent purposes of those great inland states, and for Texas, and California, and Oregon;' – a statement which is among the happiest achievements of American humour. He calls his verses 'recitatives,' in easily followed allusion to a musical form. 'Easily-written, loose-fingered chords,' he cries, 'I feel the thrum of your climax and close.' Too often, I fear, he is the only one who can perceive the rhythm; and in spite of Mr Swinburne, a great part of his work considered as verses is poor bald stuff. Considered, not as verse, but as speech, a great part of it is full of strange and admirable merits. The right detail is seized; the right word, bold and trenchant, is thrust into its place. Whitman has small regard to literary decencies, and is totally free from literary timidities. He is neither afraid of being slangy nor of being dull; nor, let me add, of being ridiculous. The result is a most surprising compound of plain grandeur, sentimental affectation, and downright nonsense. It would be useless to follow his detractors and give instances of how bad he can be at his worst; and perhaps it would be not much wiser to give extracted specimens of how happily he can write when he is at his best. These come in to most advantage in their own place; owing something, it may be, to the offset of their curious surroundings.

And one thing is certain, that no one can appreciate Whitman's excellences until he has grown accustomed to his faults. Until you are content to pick poetry out of his pages almost as you must pick it out of a Greek play in Bohn's translation, your gravity will be continually upset, your ears perpetually disappointed, and the whole book will be no more to you than a particularly flagrant production by the Poet Close.

A writer of this uncertain quality was, perhaps, unfortunate in taking for thesis the beauty of the world as it now is, not only on the hill-tops but in the factory; not only by the harbour full of stately ships, but in the magazine of the hopelessly prosaic hatter. To show beauty in common things is the work of the rarest tact. It is not to be done by the wishing. It is easy to posit as a theory, but to bring it home to men's minds is the problem of literature, and is only accomplished by rare talent, and in comparatively rare instances. To bid the whole world stand and deliver, with a dogma in one's right hand by way of pistol; to cover reams of paper in a galloping, headstrong vein; to cry louder and louder over everything as it comes up, and make no distinction in one's enthusiasm over the most incomparable matters; to prove one's entire want of sympathy for the jaded, literary palate, by calling, not a spade a spade, but a hatter a hatter, in a lyrical apostrophe;—this, in spite of all the airs of inspiration, is not the way to do it. It may be very wrong, and very wounding to a respectable branch of industry, but the word 'hatter' cannot be used seriously in emotional verse; not to understand this, is to have no literary tact; and I would, for his own sake, that this were the only inadmissible expression with which Whitman had bedecked his pages. The book teems with similar comicalities; and, to a reader who is determined to take it from that side only, presents a perfect carnival of fun.

A good deal of this is the result of theory playing its usual vile trick upon the artist. It is because he is a Democrat that Whitman must have in the hatter. If you may say Admiral, he reasons, why may you not say Hatter? One man is as good as another, and it is the business of the 'great poet' to show poetry in the life of the one as well as the other. A most incontrovertible sentiment surely, and one which nobody would think of controverting, where – and here is the point – where any beauty has been shown. But how, where that is not the case? where the hatter is simply introduced, as God made him and as his fellow-men have miscalled him, at the crisis of a high-flown rhapsody? And what are we to say, where a man of Whitman's notable capacity for putting things in a bright, picturesque, and novel way, simply gives up the attempt, and indulges, with apparent exultation, in an inventory of trades or implements, with no more colour or coherence than so many index-words out of a dictionary? I do not know that we can say anything, but that it is a prodigiously amusing exhibition for a line or so. The worst of it is, that Whitman must have known better. The man is a great critic, and, so far as I can make out, a good one; and how much criticism does it require to know that capitulation is not description, or that fingering on a dumb keyboard, with whatever show of sentiment and execution, is not at all the same thing as discoursing music? I wish I could believe he was quite honest with us; but, indeed, who was ever quite honest who wrote a book for a purpose? It is a flight beyond the reach of human magnanimity.

One other point, where his means failed him, must be touched upon, however shortly. In his desire to accept all facts loyally and simply, it fell within his programme to speak at some length and with some plainness on what is, for I really do not know what reason, the most delicate of subjects. Seeing in that one of the most serious and interesting parts of life, he was aggrieved that it should be looked upon as ridiculous or shameful. No one speaks of maternity with his tongue in his cheek; and Whitman made a bold push to set the sanctity of fatherhood beside the sanctity of motherhood, and introduce this also among the things that can be spoken of without either a blush or a wink. But the Philistines have been too strong; and, to say truth, Whitman has rather played the fool. We may be thoroughly conscious that his end is improving; that it would be a good thing if a window were opened on these close privacies of life; that on this subject, as on all others, he now and then lets fall a pregnant saying. But we are not satisfied. We feel that he was not the man for so difficult an enterprise. He loses our sympathy in the character of a poet by attracting too much of our attention in that of a Bull in a China Shop. And where, by a little more art, we might have been solemnised ourselves, it is too often Whitman alone who is solemn in the face of an audience somewhat indecorously amused.

VI

Lastly, as most important, after all, to human beings in our disputable state, what is that higher prudence which was to be the aim and issue of these deliberate productions?

Whitman is too clever to slip into a succinct formula. If he could have adequately said his say in a single proverb, it is to be presumed he would not have put himself to the trouble of writing several volumes. It was his programme to state as much as he could of the world with all its contradictions, and leave the upshot with God who planned it. What he has made of the world and the world's meanings is to be found at large in his poems. These altogether give his answers to the problems of belief and conduct; in many ways righteous and high-spirited, in some ways loose and contradictory. And yet there are two passages from the preface to the *Leaves of Grass* which do pretty well condense his teaching on all essential points, and yet preserve a measure of his spirit.

'This is what you shall do,' he says in the one, 'love the earth, and sun, and animals, despise riches, give alms to everyone that asks, stand up for the stupid and crazy, devote your income and labour to others, hate tyrants, argue not concerning God, have patience and indulgence towards the people, take off your hat to nothing known or unknown, or to any man or number of men; go freely with powerful uneducated persons, and with the young, and mothers of families, read these leaves (his own works) in the open air every season of every year of your life; re-examine all you have been told at school or church, or in any book, and dismiss whatever insults your own soul.'

'The prudence of the greatest poet,' he adds in the other – and the greatest poet is, of course, himself – 'knows that the young man who composedly perilled his life and lost it, has done exceeding well for himself; while the man who has not perilled his life, and retains it to old age in riches and ease, has perhaps achieved nothing for himself worth mentioning; and that only that person has no great prudence to learn, who has learnt to prefer real long-lived things, and favours body and soul the same, and perceives the indirect surely following the direct, and what evil or good he does leaping onward and waiting to meet him again, and who in his spirit, in any emergency whatever, neither hurries nor avoids death.'

There is much that is Christian in these extracts, startlingly Christian. Any reader who bears in mind Whitman's own advice and 'dismisses whatever insults his own soul' will find plenty that is bracing, brightening, and chastening to reward him for a little patience at first. It seems hardly possible that any being should get evil from so healthy a book as the *Leaves of Grass,* which is simply comical wherever it falls short of nobility; but if there be any such, who cannot both take and leave, who cannot let a single opportunity pass by without some unworthy and unmanly thought, I should have as great difficulty, and neither more nor less, in recommending the works of Whitman as in lending them Shakespeare, or letting them go abroad outside of the grounds of a private asylum.

TALK AND TALKERS (I)

Sir, we had a good talk. JOHNSON

As we must account for every idle word, so we must for
every idle silence. FRANKLIN

There can be no fairer ambition than to excel in talk; to be affable, gay, ready, clear and welcome; to have a fact, a thought, or an illustration, pat to every subject; and not only to cheer the flight of time among our intimates, but bear our part in that great international congress, always sitting, where public wrongs are first declared, public errors first corrected, and the course of public opinion shaped, day by day, a little nearer to the right. No measure comes before Parliament but it has been long ago prepared by the grand jury of the talkers; no book is written that has not been largely composed by their assistance. Literature in many of its branches is no other than the shadow of good talk; but the imitation falls far short of the original in life, freedom and effect. There are always two to a talk, giving and taking, comparing experience and according conclusions. Talk is fluid, tentative, continually 'in further search and progress;' while written words remain fixed, become idols even to the writer, found wooden dogmatisms, and preserve flies of obvious error in the amber of the truth. Last and chief, while literature, gagged with linsey-woolsey, can only deal with a fraction of the life of man, talk goes fancy free and may call a spade a spade. Talk has none of the freezing immunities of the pulpit. It cannot, even if it would, become merely æsthetic or merely classical like literature. A jest intervenes, the solemn humbug is dissolved in laughter, and speech runs forth out of the contemporary groove into the open fields of nature, cheery and cheering, like schoolboys out of school. And it is in talk alone that we can learn our period and ourselves. In short, the first duty of a man is to speak; that is his chief business in this world; and talk, which is the harmonious speech of two or more, is by far the most accessible of pleasures. It costs nothing in money; it is all profit; it completes our education, founds and fosters our friendships, and can be enjoyed at any age and in almost any state of health.

The spice of life is battle; the friendliest relations are still a kind of contest; and if we would not forego all that is valuable in our lot, we must continually face some other person, eye to eye, and wrestle a fall whether in love or enmity. It is still by force of body, or power of character or intellect, that we attain to worthy pleasures. Men and women contend for each other in the lists of love, like rival mesmerists; the active and adroit decide their challenges in the sports of the body; and the sedentary sit down to chess or conversation. All sluggish and pacific pleasures are, to the same degree, solitary and selfish; and every durable bond between human beings is founded in or heightened by some element of competition. Now, the relation that has the least root in matter is undoubtedly that airy one of friendship; and hence, I suppose, it is that good talk most commonly arises among friends. Talk is, indeed, both the scene and instrument of friendship. It is in talk alone that the friends can measure strength, and enjoy that amicable counter-assertion of personality which is the gauge of relations and the sport of life.

A good talk is not to be had for the asking. Humours must first be accorded in a kind of overture or prologue; hour, company and circumstance be suited; and then, at a fit juncture, the subject, the quarry of two heated minds, spring up like a deer out of the wood. Not that the talker has any of the hunter's pride, though he has all and more than all his ardour. The genuine artist follows the stream of conversation as an angler follows the windings of a brook, not dallying where he fails to 'kill.' He trusts implicitly to hazard; and he is rewarded by continual variety, continual pleasure, and those changing prospects of the truth that are the best of education. There is nothing in a subject, so called, that we should regard it as an idol, or follow it beyond the promptings of desire. Indeed, there are few subjects; and so far as they are truly talkable, more than the half of them may be reduced to three: that I am I, that you are you, and that there are other people dimly understood to be not quite the same as either. Wherever talk may range, it still runs half the time on these eternal lines. The theme being set, each plays on himself as on an instrument; asserts and justifies himself; ransacks his brain for instances and opinions, and brings them forth new-minted, to his own surprise and the admiration of his adversary. All natural talk is a festival of ostentation; and by the laws of the game each accepts and fans the vanity of the other. It is from that reason that we venture to lay ourselves so open, that we dare to be so warmly eloquent, and that we swell in each other's eyes to such a vast proportion. For talkers, once launched, begin to overflow the limits of their ordinary selves, tower up to the height of their secret pretensions, and give themselves out for the heroes, brave, pious, musical and wise, that in their most shining moments they aspire to be. So they weave for themselves with words and for a while inhabit a palace of delights, temple at once and theatre, where they fill the round of the world's dignities, and feast with the gods, exulting in Kudos. And when the talk is over, each goes his way, still flushed with vanity and admiration, still trailing clouds of glory; each declines from the height of his ideal orgie, not in a moment, but by slow declension. I remember, in the *entr'acte* of an afternoon performance, coming forth into the sunshine, in a beautiful green, gardened corner of a romantic city; and as I sat and smoked, the music moving in my blood, I seemed to sit there and evaporate *The Flying Dutchman* (for it was that I had been hearing) with a wonderful sense of life, warmth, well-being and pride; and the noises of the city, voices, bells and marching feet, fell together in my ears like a symphonious orchestra. In the same way, the excitement of a good talk lives for a long while after in the blood, the heart still hot within you, the brain still simmering, and the physical earth swimming around you with the colours of the sunset.

Natural talk, like ploughing, should turn up a large surface of life, rather than dig mines into geological strata. Masses of experience, anecdote, incident, cross-lights, quotation, historical instances, the whole flotsam and jetsam of two minds forced in and in upon the matter in hand from every point of the compass, and from every degree of mental elevation and abasement – these are the material with which talk is fortified, the food on which the talkers thrive. Such argument as is proper to the exercise should still be brief and seizing. Talk should proceed by instances; by the apposite, not the expository. It should keep close along the lines of humanity, near the bosoms and businesses of men, at the level where history, fiction and experience intersect and illuminate each other. I am I, and You are You, with all my heart; but conceive how these lean propositions change and brighten when, instead of words, the actual you and I sit cheek by jowl, the spirit housed in the live body, and the very clothes uttering voices to corroborate the story in the face. Not less surprising is the change when we leave off to speak of generalities – the bad, the good, the miser, and all the characters of Theophrastus – and call up other men, by anecdote or instance, in their very trick and feature; or trading on a common knowledge, toss each other famous names, still glowing with the hues of life. Communication is no longer by words, but by the instancing of whole biographies, epics, systems of philosophy, and epochs of history, in bulk. That which is understood excels that which is spoken in quantity and quality alike; ideas thus figured and personified, change hands, as we may say, like coin; and the speakers imply without effort the most obscure and intricate thoughts. Strangers who have a large common ground of reading will, for this reason, come the sooner to the grapple of genuine converse. If they know Othello and Napoleon, Consuelo and Clarissa Harlowe, Vautrin and Steenie Steenson, they can leave generalities and begin at once to speak by figures.

Conduct and art are the two subjects that arise most frequently and that embrace the widest range of facts. A few pleasures bear discussion for their own sake, but only those which are most social or most radically human; and even these can only be discussed among their devotees. A technicality is always welcome to the expert, whether in athletics, art or law; I have heard the best kind of talk on technicalities from such rare and happy persons as both know and love their business. No human being ever spoke of scenery for above two minutes at a time, which makes me suspect we hear too much of it in literature. The weather is regarded as the very nadir and scoff of conversational topics. And yet the weather, the dramatic element in scenery, is far more tractable in language, and far more human both in import and suggestion than the stable features of the landscape. Sailors and shepherds, and the people generally of coast and mountain, talk well of it; and it is often excitingly presented in literature. But the tendency of all living talk draws it back and back into the common focus of humanity. Talk is a creature of the street and marketplace, feeding on gossip; and its last resort is still in a discussion on morals. That is the heroic form of gossip; heroic in virtue of its high pretensions; but still gossip, because it turns on personalities. You can keep no men long, nor Scotchmen at all, off moral or theological discussion. These are to all the world what law is to lawyers; they are everybody's technicalities; the medium through which all consider life, and the dialect in which they express their judgements. I knew three young men who walked together daily for some two months in a solemn and beautiful forest and in cloudless summer weather; daily they talked with unabated zest, and yet scarce wandered that whole time beyond two subjects – theology and love. And perhaps neither a court of love nor an assembly of divines would have granted their premises or welcomed their conclusions.

Conclusions, indeed, are not often reached by talk any more than by private thinking. That is not the profit. The profit is in the exercise, and above all in the experience; for when we reason at large on any subject, we review our state and history in life. From time to time, however, and specially, I think, in talking art, talk becomes effective, conquering like war, widening the boundaries of knowledge like an exploration. A point arises; the question takes a problematical, a baffling, yet a likely air; the talkers begin to feel lively presentiments of some conclusion near at hand; towards this they strive with emulous ardour, each by his own path, and struggling for first utterance; and then one leaps upon the summit of that matter with a shout, and almost at the same moment the other is beside him; and behold they are agreed. Like enough, the progress is illusory, a mere cat's cradle having been wound and unwound out of words. But the sense of joint discovery is none the less giddy and inspiriting. And in the life of the talker such triumphs, though imaginary, are neither few nor far apart; they are attained with speed and pleasure, in the hour of mirth; and by the nature of the process, they are always worthily shared.

There is a certain attitude, combative at once and deferential, eager to fight yet most averse to quarrel, which marks out at once the talkable man. It is not eloquence, not fairness, not obstinacy, but a certain proportion of all of these that I love to encounter in my amicable adversaries. They must not be pontiffs holding doctrine, but huntsmen questing after elements of truth. Neither must they be boys to be instructed, but fellow-teachers with whom I may wrangle and agree on equal terms. We must reach some solution, some shadow of consent; for without that, eager talk becomes a torture. But we do not wish to reach it cheaply, or quickly, or without the tussle and effort wherein pleasure lies.

The very best talker, with me, is one whom I shall call Spring-Heel'd Jack. I say so, because I never knew any one who mingled so largely the possible ingredients of converse. In the Spanish proverb, the fourth man necessary to compound a salad, is a madman to mix it: Jack is that madman. I know not which is more remarkable; the insane lucidity of his conclusions, the humorous eloquence of his language, or his power of method, bringing the whole of life into the focus of the subject treated, mixing the conversational salad like a drunken god. He doubles like the serpent, changes and flashes like the shaken kaleidoscope, transmigrates bodily into the views of others, and so, in the twinkling of an eye and with a heady rapture, turns questions inside out and flings them empty before you on the ground, like a triumphant conjuror. It is my common practice when a piece of conduct puzzles me, to attack it in the presence of Jack with such grossness, such partiality and such wearing iteration, as at length shall spur him up in its defence. In a moment he transmigrates, dons the required character, and with moonstruck philosophy justifies the act in question. I can fancy nothing to compare with the *vim* of these impersonations, the strange scale of language, flying from Shakespeare to Kant, and from Kant to Major Dyngwell —

> As fast as a musician scatters sounds
> Out of an instrument —

the sudden, sweeping generalisations, the absurd irrelevant particularities, the wit, wisdom, folly, humour, eloquence and bathos, each startling in its kind, and yet all luminous in the admired disorder of their combination. A talker of a different calibre, though belonging to the same school, is Burly. Burly is a man of a great presence; he commands a larger atmosphere, gives the impression of a grosser mass of character than most men. It has been said of him that his presence could be felt in a room you entered blindfold; and the same, I think, has been said of other powerful constitutions condemned to much physical inaction. There is something boisterous and piratic in Burly's manner of talk which suits well enough with this impression. He will roar you down, he will bury his face in his hands, he will undergo passions of revolt and agony; and meanwhile his attitude of mind is really both conciliatory and receptive; and after Pistol has been out-Pistol'd, and the welkin rung for hours, you begin to perceive a certain subsidence in these spring torrents, points of agreement issue, and you end arm-in-arm, and in a glow of mutual admiration. The outcry only serves to make your final union the more unexpected and precious. Throughout there has been perfect sincerity, perfect intelligence, a desire to hear although not always to listen, and an unaffected eagerness to meet concessions. You have, with Burly, none of the dangers that attend debate with Spring-Heel'd Jack; who may at any moment turn his powers of transmigration on yourself, create for you a view you never held, and then furiously fall on you for holding it. These, at least, are my two favourites, and both are loud, copious, intolerant talkers. This argues that I myself am in the same category; for if we love talking at all, we love a bright, fierce adversary, who will hold his ground, foot by foot, in much our own manner, sell his attention dearly, and give us our full measure of the dust and exertion of battle. Both these men can be beat from a position, but it takes six hours to do it; a high and hard adventure, worth attempting. With both you can pass days in an enchanted country of the mind, with people, scenery and manners of its own; live a life apart, more arduous, active and glowing than any real existence; and come forth again when the talk is over, as out of a theatre or a dream, to find the east wind still blowing and the chimney-pots of the old battered city still around you. Jack has the far finer mind, Burly the far more honest; Jack gives us the animated poetry, Burly the romantic prose, of similar themes; the one glances high like a meteor and makes a light in darkness; the other, with many changing hues of fire, burns at the sea-level, like a conflagration; but both have the same humour and artistic interests, the same unquenched ardour in pursuit, the same gusts of talk and thunderclaps of contradiction.

Cockshot[1] is a different article, but vastly entertaining, and has been meat and drink to me for many a long evening. His manner is dry, brisk and pertinacious, and the choice of words not much. The point about him is his extraordinary readiness and spirit. You can propound nothing but he has either a theory about it ready-made, or will have one instantly on the stocks, and proceed to lay its timbers and launch it in your presence. 'Let me see,' he will say. 'Give me a moment. I *should* have some theory for that.' A blither spectacle than the vigour with which he sets about the task, it were hard to fancy. He is possessed by a demoniac energy, welding the elements for his life, and bending ideas, as an athlete bends a horseshoe, with a visible and lively effort. He has, in theorising, a compass, an art; what I would call the synthetic gusto; something of a Herbert Spencer, who should see the fun of the thing. You are not bound, and no more is he, to place your faith in these brand-new opinions. But some of them are right enough, durable even for life; and the poorest serve for a cock-shy – as when idle people, after picnics, float a bottle on a pond and

---

[1] Professor Fleeming Jenkin – see note on p. 162.

have an hour's diversion ere it sinks. Whichever they are, serious opinions or humours of the moment, he still defends his ventures with indefatigable wit and spirit, hitting savagely himself, but taking punishment like a man. He knows and never forgets that people talk, first of all, for the sake of talking; conducts himself in the ring, to use the old slang, like a thorough 'glutton,' and honestly enjoys a telling facer from his adversary. Cockshot is bottled effervescency, the sworn foe of sleep. Three-in-the-morning Cockshot, says a victim. His talk is like the driest of all imaginable dry champagnes. Sleight of hand and inimitable quickness are the qualities by which he lives. Athelred, on the other hand, presents you with the spectacle of a sincere and somewhat slow nature thinking aloud. He is the most unready man I ever knew to shine in conversation. You may see him sometimes wrestle with a refractory jest for a minute or two together, and perhaps fail to throw it in the end. And there is something singularly engaging, often instructive, in the simplicity with which he thus exposes the process as well as the result, the works as well as the dial of the clock. Withal he has his hours of inspiration. Apt words come to him as if by accident, and, coming from deeper down, they smack the more personally, they have the more of fine old crusted humanity, rich in sediment and humour. There are sayings of his in which he has stamped himself into the very grain of the language; you would think he must have worn the words next his skin and slept with them. Yet it is not as a sayer of particular good things that Athelred is most to be regarded, rather as the stalwart woodman of thought. I have pulled on a light cord often enough, while he has been wielding the broad-axe; and between us, on this unequal division, many a specious fallacy has fallen. I have known him to battle the same question night after night for years, keeping it in the reign of talk, constantly applying it and re-applying it to life with humorous or grave intention, and all the while, never hurrying, nor flagging, nor taking an unfair advantage of the facts. Jack at a given moment, when arising, as it were, from the tripod, can be more radiantly just to those from whom he differs; but then the tenor of his thoughts is even calumnious; while Athelred, slower to forge excuses, is yet slower to condemn, and sits over the welter of the world, vacillating but still judicial, and still faithfully contending with his doubts.

Both the last talkers deal much in points of conduct and religion studied in the 'dry light' of prose. Indirectly and as if against his will the same elements from time to time appear in the troubled and poetic talk of Opalstein. His various and exotic knowledge, complete although unready sympathies, and fine, full, discriminative flow of language, fit him out to be the best of talkers; so perhaps he is with some, not *quite* with me – *proxime accessit*, I should say. He sings the praises of the earth and the arts, flowers and jewels, wine and music, in a moonlight, serenading manner, as to the light guitar; even wisdom comes from his tongue like singing; no one is, indeed, more tuneful in the upper notes. But even while he sings the song of the Sirens, he still hearkens to the barking of the Sphinx. Jarring Byronic notes interrupt the flow of his Horatian humours. His mirth has something of the tragedy of the world for its perpetual background; and he feasts like Don Giovanni to a double orchestra, one lightly sounding for the dance, one pealing Beethoven in the distance. He is not truly reconciled either with life or with himself; and this instant war in his members sometimes divides the man's attention. He does not always, perhaps not often, frankly surrender himself in conversation. He brings into the talk other thoughts than those which he expresses; you are conscious that he keeps an eye on something else, that he does not shake off the world, nor quite forget himself. Hence arise occasional disappointments; even an occasional unfairness for his companions, who find themselves one day giving too much, and the next, when they are wary out of season, giving perhaps too little. Purcel is in another class from any I have mentioned. He is no debater, but appears in conversation, as occasion rises, in two distinct characters, one of which I admire and fear, and the other love. In the first, he is radiantly civil and rather silent, sits on a high, courtly hilltop, and from that vantage-ground drops you his remarks like favours. He seems not to share in our sublunary contentions; he wears no sign of interest; when on a sudden there falls in a crystal of wit, so polished that the dull do not perceive it, but so right that the sensitive are silenced. True talk should have more body and blood, should be louder, vainer and more declaratory of the man; the true talker should not hold so steady an advantage over whom he speaks with; and that is one reason out of a score why I prefer my Purcel in his second character, when he unbends into a strain of graceful gossip, singing like the fireside kettle. In these moods he has an elegant homeliness that rings of the true Queen Anne. I know another person who attains, in his moments, to the insolence of a Restoration comedy, speaking, I declare, as Congreve wrote; but that is a sport of nature, and scarce falls under the rubric, for there is none, alas! to give him answer.

One last remark occurs: It is the mark of genuine conversation that the sayings can scarce be quoted with their full effect beyond the circle of common friends. To have their proper weight they should appear in a biography, and with the portrait of the speaker. Good talk is dramatic; it is like an impromptu piece of acting where each should represent himself to the greatest advantage; and that is the best kind of talk where each speaker is most fully and candidly himself, and where, if you were to shift the speeches round from one to another, there would be the greatest loss in significance and perspicuity. It is for this reason that talk depends so wholly on our company. We should like to introduce Falstaff and Mercutio, or Falstaff and Sir Toby; but Falstaff in talk with Cordelia seems even painful. Most of us, by the Protean quality of man, can talk to some degree with all; but the true talk, that strikes out all the slumbering best of us, comes only with the peculiar brethren of our spirits, is founded as deep as love in the constitution of our being, and is a thing to relish with all our energy, while yet we have it, and to be grateful for for ever.

Editorial Note

The identities of the 'talkers' in this essay are as follows: 'Spring Heel'd Jack', R. A. M. Stevenson; 'Burly', W. E. Henley; 'Cockshot', Professor Fleeming Jenkin; 'Athelred', Walter Simpson; 'Opalstein', John Addington Symonds; 'Purcel', Edmund Gosse.

TALK AND TALKERS (II)[1]

In the last paper there was perhaps too much about mere debate; and there was nothing said at all about that kind of talk which is merely luminous and restful, a higher power of silence, the quiet of the evening shared by ruminating friends. There is something, aside from personal preference, to be alleged in support of this omission. Those who are no chimney-cornerers, who rejoice in the social thunderstorm, have a ground in reason for their choice. They get little rest indeed; but restfulness is a quality for cattle; the virtues are all active, life is alert, and it is in repose that men prepare themselves for evil. On the other hand, they are bruised into a knowledge of themselves and others; they have in a high degree the fencer's pleasure in dexterity displayed and proved; what they get they get upon life's terms, paying for it as they go; and once the talk is launched, they are assured of honest dealing from an adversary eager like themselves. The aboriginal man within us, the cave-dweller, still lusty as when he fought tooth and nail for roots and berries, scents this kind of equal battle from afar; it is like his old primæval days upon the crags, a return to the sincerity of savage life from the comfortable fictions of the civilised. And if it be delightful to the Old Man, it is none the less profitable to his younger brother, the conscientious gentleman. I feel never quite sure of your urbane and smiling coteries; I fear they indulge a man's vanities in silence, suffer him to encroach, encourage him on to be an ass, and send him forth again, not merely contemned for the moment, but radically more contemptible than when he entered. But if I have a flushed, blustering fellow for my opposite, bent on carrying a point, my vanity is sure to have its ears rubbed, once at least, in the course of the debate. He will not spare me when we differ; he will not fear to demonstrate my folly to my face.

[1]This sequel was called forth by an excellent article in *The Spectator*.

For many natures there is not much charm in the still, chambered society, the circle of bland countenances, the digestive silence, the admired remark, the flutter of affectionate approval. They demand more atmosphere and exercise; 'a gale upon their spirits,' as our pious ancestors would phrase it; to have their wits well breathed in an uproarious Valhalla. And I suspect that the choice, given their character and faults, is one to be defended. The purely wise are silenced by facts; they talk in a clear atmosphere, problems lying around them like a view in nature; if they can be shown to be somewhat in the wrong, they digest the reproof like a thrashing, and make better intellectual blood. They stand corrected by a whisper; a word or a glance reminds them of the great eternal law. But it is not so with all. Others in conversation seek rather contact with their fellow-men than increase of knowledge or clarity of thought. The drama, not the philosophy, of life is the sphere of their intellectual activity. Even when they pursue truth, they desire as much as possible of what we may call human scenery along the road they follow. They dwell in the heart of life; the blood sounding in their ears, their eyes laying hold of what delights them with a brutal avidity that makes them blind to all besides, their interest riveted on people, living, loving, talking, tangible people. To a man of this description, the sphere of argument seems very pale and ghostly. By a strong expression, a perturbed countenance, floods of tears, an insult which his conscience obliges him to swallow, he is brought round to knowledge which no syllogism would have conveyed to him. His own experience is so vivid, he is so superlatively conscious of himself, that if, day after day, he is allowed to hector and hear nothing but approving echoes, he will lose his hold on the soberness of things and take himself in earnest for a god. Talk might be to such an one the very way of moral ruin; the school where he might learn to be at once intolerable and ridiculous.

This character is perhaps commoner than philosophers suppose. And for persons of that stamp to learn much by conversation, they must speak with their superiors, not in intellect, for that is a superiority that must be proved, but in station. If they cannot find a friend to bully them for their good, they must find either an old man, a woman, or some one so far below them in the artificial order of society, that courtesy may be particularly exercised.

The best teachers are the aged. To the old our mouths are

always partly closed; we must swallow our obvious retorts and listen. They sit above our heads, on life's raised daïs, and appeal at once to our respect and pity. A flavour of the old school, a touch of something different in their manner – which is freer and rounder, if they come of what is called a good family, and often more timid and precise if they are of the middle class – serves, in these days, to accentuate the difference of age and add a distinction to grey hairs. But their superiority is founded more deeply than by outward marks or gestures. They are before us in the march of man; they have more or less solved the irking problem; they have battled through the equinox of life; in good and evil they have held their course; and now, without open shame, they near the crown and harbour. It may be we have been struck with one of fortune's darts; we can scarce be civil, so cruelly is our spirit tossed. Yet long before we were so much as thought upon, the like calamity befell the old man or woman that now, with pleasant humour, rallies us upon our inattention, sitting composed in the holy evening of man's life, in the clear shining after rain. We grow ashamed of our distresses, new and hot and coarse, like villainous roadside brandy; we see life in aerial perspective, under the heavens of faith; and out of the worst, in the mere presence of contented elders, look forward and take patience. Fear shrinks before them 'like a thing reproved,' not the flitting and ineffectual fear of death, but the instant, dwelling terror of the responsibilities and revenges of life. Their speech, indeed, is timid; they report lions in the path; they counsel a meticulous footing; but their serene, marred faces are more eloquent and tell another story. Where they have gone, we will go also, not very greatly fearing; what they have endured unbroken, we also, God helping us, will make a shift to bear.

Not only is the presence of the aged in itself remedial, but their minds are stored with antidotes, wisdom's simples, plain considerations overlooked by youth. They have matter to communicate, be they never so stupid. Their talk is not merely literature, it is great literature; classic in virtue of the speaker's detachment, studded, like a book of travel, with things we should not otherwise have learnt. In virtue, I have said, of the speaker's detachment, – and this is why, of two old men, the one who is not your father speaks to you with the more sensible authority; for in the paternal relation the oldest have lively interests and remain still young. Thus I have known two young men great friends; each swore by the other's father; the father of each swore by the other lad; and yet each pair of parent and child were perpetually by the ears. This is typical: it reads like the germ of some kindly comedy.

The old appear in conversation in two characters: the critically silent and the garulous anecdotic. The last is perhaps what we look for; it is perhaps the more instructive. An old gentleman, well on in years, sits handsomely and naturally in the bow-window of his age, scanning experience with reverted eye; and chirping and smiling, communicates the accidents and reads the lesson of his long career. Opinions are strengthened, indeed, but they are also weeded out in the course of years. What remains steadily present to the eye of the retired veteran in his hermitage, what still ministers to his content, what still quickens his old honest heart – these are 'the real long-lived things' that Whitman tells us to prefer. Where youth agrees with age, not where they differ, wisdom lies; and it is when the young disciple finds his heart to beat in tune with his grey-bearded teacher's that a lesson may be learned. I have known one old gentleman, whom I may name, for he is now gathered to his stock – Robert Hunter, Sheriff of Dumbarton, and author of an excellent law-book still re-edited and republished. Whether he was originally big or little is more than I can guess. When I knew him he was all fallen away and fallen in; crooked and shrunken; buckled into a stiff waistcoat for support; troubled by ailments, which kept him hobbling in and out of the room; one foot gouty; a wig for decency, not for deception, on his head; close shaved, except under his chin – and for that he never failed to apologise, for it went sore against the traditions of his life. You can imagine how he would fare in a novel by Miss Mather; yet this rag of a Chelsea veteran lived to his last year in the plenitude of all that is best in man, brimming with human kindness, and staunch as a Roman soldier under his manifold infirmities. You could not say that he had lost his memory, for he would repeat Shakespeare and Webster and Jeremy Taylor and Burke by the page together; but the parchment was filled up, there was no room for fresh inscriptions, and he was capable of repeating the same anecdote on many successive visits. His voice survived in its full power, and he took a pride in using it. On his last voyage as Commissioner of Lighthouses, he hailed a ship at sea and made himself clearly audible without a speaking trumpet, ruffling the while with a proper vanity in his achievement. He had a habit of eking out his words with interrogative hems, which was puzzling and a little wearisome, suited ill with his appearance, and seemed a survival from some former stage of bodily portliness. Of yore, when he was a great pedestrian and no enemy to good claret, he may have pointed with these minute guns his allocutions to the bench. His humour was perfectly equable, set beyond the reach of fate; gout, rheumatism, stone and gravel might have combined their forces against that frail tabernacle, but when I came round on Sunday evening, he would lay aside Jeremy Taylor's *Life of Christ* and greet me with the same open brow, the same kind formality of manner. His opinions and sympathies dated the man almost to a decade. He had begun life, under his mother's influence, as an admirer of Junius, but on maturer knowledge had transferred his admiration to Burke. He cautioned me, with entire gravity, to be punctilious in writing English; never to forget that I was a Scotchman, that English was a foreign tongue, and that if I attempted the colloquial, I should certainly be shamed: the remark was apposite, I suppose, in the days of David Hume. Scott was too new for him; he had known the author – known him, too, for a Tory; and to the genuine classic a contemporary is always something of a trouble. He had the old, serious love of the play; had even, as he was proud to tell, played a certain part in the history of Shakespearian revivals, for he had successfully pressed on Murray, of the old Edinburgh Theatre, the idea of producing Shakespeare's fairy pieces with great scenic display. A moderate in religion, he was much struck in the last years of his life by a conversation with two young lads, revivalists. 'H'm,' he would say – 'new to me. I have had – h'm – no such experience.' It struck him, not with pain, rather with a solemn philosophic interest, that he, a Christian as he hoped, and a Christian of so old a standing, should hear these young fellows talking of his own subject, his own weapons that he had fought the battle of life with, – 'and – h'm – not understand.' In this wise and graceful attitude he did justice to himself and others, reposed unshaken in his old beliefs, and recognised their limits without anger or alarm. His last recorded remark, on the last night of his life, was after he had been arguing against Calvinism with his minister and was interrupted by an intolerable pang. 'After all,' he said, 'of all the 'isms, I know none so bad as rheumatism.' My own last sight of him was some time before, when we dined together at an inn; he had been on circuit, for he stuck to his duties like a chief part of his existence; and I remember it as the only occasion on which he ever soiled his lips with slang – a thing he loathed. We were both Roberts; and as we took our places at table, he addressed me with a twinkle: 'We are just what you would call two bob.' He offered me port, I remember, as the proper milk of youth; spoke of 'twenty-shilling notes;' and throughout the meal was full of old-world pleasantry and quaintness, like an ancient boy on a holiday. But what I recall chiefly was his confession that he had never read *Othello* to an end. Shakespeare was his continual study. He loved nothing better than to display his knowledge and memory by adducing parallel passages from Shakespeare, passages where the same word was employed, or the same idea differently treated. But *Othello* had beaten him. 'That noble gentleman and that noble lady – h'm – too painful for me.' The same night the hoardings were covered with posters, 'Burlesque of *Othello*,' and the contrast blazed up in my mind like a bonfire. An unforgettable look it gave me into that kind man's soul. His acquaintance was indeed a liberal and pious education. All the humanities were taught in that bare dining-room beside his gouty footstool. He was a piece of good advice; he was himself the instance that pointed and adorned his various talk. Nor could a young man have found elsewhere a place so set apart from envy, fear, discontent, or any of the passions that debase; a life so honest and composed; a soul like an ancient violin, so subdued to harmony, responding to a touch in music – as in that dining-room, with Mr Hunter chatting at the eleventh hour, under the shadow of eternity, fearless and gentle.

The second class of old people are not anecdotic; they are rather hearers than talkers, listening to the young with an amused and critical attention. To have this sort of intercourse to perfection, I think we must go to old ladies. Women are better hearers than men, to begin with; they learn, I fear in anguish, to bear with the tedious and infantile vanity of the other sex; and we will take more from a woman than even from the oldest man in the way of biting comment. Biting comment is the chief part, whether for profit or amusement, in this business. The old lady that I have in my eye is a very caustic speaker, her tongue, after years of practice, in absolute command, whether for silence or attack. If she chance to dislike you, you will be tempted to curse the malignity of age. But if you chance to please even slightly, you will be listened to with a particular laughing grace of sympathy, and from time to time chastised, as if in play, with a parasol as heavy as a pole-axe. It requires a singular art, as well as the vantage-ground of age, to deal these stunning corrections among the coxcombs of the young. The pill is disguised in sugar of wit; it is administered as a compliment – if you had not pleased, you would not have been censured; it is a personal affair – a hyphen, a *trait d'union*, between you and your censor; age's philandering, for her pleasure and your good. Incontestably the young man feels very much of a fool; but he must be a perfect Malvolio, sick with self-love, if he cannot take an open buffet and still smile. The correction of silence is what kills; when you know you have transgressed, and your friend says nothing and avoids your eye. If a man were made of gutta-percha, his heart would quail at such a moment. But when the word is out, the worst is over; and a fellow with any good-humour at all may pass through a perfect hail of witty criticism, every bare place on his soul hit to the quick with a shrewd missile, and reappear, as if after a dive, tingling with a fine moral reaction, and ready, with a shrinking readiness, one-third loath, for a repetition of the discipline.

There are few women, not well sunned and ripened, and perhaps toughened, who can thus stand apart from a man and say the true thing with a kind of genial cruelty. Still there are some – and I doubt if there be any man who can return the compliment. The class of man represented by Vernon Whitford in *The Egoist* says, indeed, the true thing, but he says it stockishly. Vernon is a noble fellow, and makes, by the way, a noble and instructive contrast to Daniel Deronda; his conduct is the conduct of a man of honour; but we agree with him, against our consciences, when he remorsefully considers 'its astonishing dryness.' He is the best of men, but the best of women manage to combine all that and something more. Their very faults assist them; they are helped even by the falseness of their position in life. They can retire into the fortified camp of the proprieties. They can touch a subject and suppress it. The most adroit employ a somewhat elaborate reserve as a means to be frank, much as they wear gloves when they shake hands. But a man has the full responsibility of his freedom, cannot evade a question, can scarce be silent without rudeness, must answer for his words upon the moment, and is not seldom left face to face with a damning choice, between the more or less dishonourable wriggling of Deronda and the downright wooden-ness of Vernon Whitford.

But the superiority of women is perpetually menaced; they do not sit throned on infirmities like the old; they are suitors as well as sovereigns; their vanity is engaged, their affections are too apt to follow; and hence much of the talk between the sexes degenerates into something unworthy of the name. The desire to please, to shine with a certain softness of lustre and to draw a fascinating picture of oneself, banishes from conversation all that is sterling and most of what is humorous. As soon as a strong current of mutual admiration begins to flow, the human interest triumphs entirely over the intellectual, and the commerce of words, consciously or not, becomes secondary to the commercing of eyes. But even where this ridiculous danger is avoided, and a man and woman converse equally and honestly, something in their nature or their education falsifies the strain. An instinct prompts them to agree; and where that is impossible, to agree to differ. Should they neglect the warning, at the first suspicion of an argument, they find themselves in different hemispheres. About any point of business or conduct, any actual affair demanding settlement, a woman will speak and listen, hear and answer arguments, not only with natural wisdom, but with candour and logical honesty. But if the subject of debate be something in the air, an abstraction, an excuse for talk, a logical Aunt Sally, then may the male debater instantly abandon hope; he may employ reason, adduce facts, be supple, be smiling, be angry, all shall avail him nothing; what the woman said first, that (unless she has forgotten it) she will repeat at the end. Hence, at the very junctures when a talk between men grows brighter and quicker and begins to promise to bear fruit, talk between the sexes is menaced with dissolution. The point of difference, the point of interest, is evaded by the brilliant woman, under a shower of irrelevant conversational rockets; it is bridged by the discreet woman with a rustle of silk, as she passes smoothly forward to the nearest point of safety. And this sort of prestidigitation, juggling the dangerous topic out of sight until it can be reintroduced with safety in an altered shape, is a piece of tactics among the true drawing-room queens.

The drawing-room is, indeed, an artificial place; it is so by our choice and for our sins. The subjection of women; the ideal imposed upon them from the cradle, and worn, like a hair-shirt, with so much constancy; their motherly, superior tenderness to man's vanity and self-importance; their managing arts – the arts of a civilised slave among good-natured barbarians – are all painful ingredients and all help to falsify relations. It is not till we get clear of that amusing artificial scene that genuine relations are founded, or ideas honestly compared. In the garden, on the road or the hillside, or *tête-à-tête* and apart from interruptions, occasions arise when we may learn much from any single woman; and nowhere more often than in married life. Marriage is one long conversation, chequered by disputes. The disputes are valueless; they but ingrain the difference; the heroic heart of woman prompting her at once to nail her colours to the mast. But in the intervals, almost unconsciously and with no desire to shine, the whole material of life is turned over and over, ideas are struck out and shared, the two persons more and more adapt their notions one to suit the other, and in process of time, without sound of trumpet, they conduct each other into new worlds of thought.

THOMAS STEVENSON,
CIVIL ENGINEER

The death of Thomas Stevenson will mean not very much to the general reader. His service to mankind took on forms of which the public knows little and understands less. He came seldom to London, and then only as a task, remaining always a stranger and a convinced provincial; putting up for years at the same hotel where his father had gone before him; faithful for long to the same restaurant, the same church, and the same theatre, chosen simply for propinquity: steadfastly refusing to dine out. He had a circle of his own, indeed, at home; few men were more beloved in Edinburgh, where he breathed an air that pleased him; and wherever he went, in railway carriages or hotel smoking-rooms, his strange, humorous vein of talk, and his transparent honesty, raised him up friends and admirers. But to the general public and the world of London, except about the parliamentary committee-rooms, he remained unknown. All the time, his lights were in every part of the world, guiding the mariner; his firm were consulting engineers to the Indian, the New Zealand, and the Japanese Lighthouse Boards, so that Edinburgh was a world centre for that branch of applied science; in Germany, he had been called 'the Nestor of lighthouse illumination;' even in France, where his claims were long denied, he was at last, on the occasion of the late Exposition, recognised and medalled. And to show by one instance the inverted nature of his reputation, comparatively small at home, yet filling the world, a friend of mine was this winter on a visit to the Spanish main, and was asked by a Peruvian if he 'knew Mr Stevenson the author, because his works were much esteemed in Peru?' My friend supposed the reference was to the writer of tales; but the Peruvian had never heard of *Dr Jekyll*; what he had in his eye, what was esteemed in Peru, were the volumes of the engineer.

Thomas Stevenson was born at Edinburgh in the year 1818, the grandson of Thomas Smith, first engineer to the Board of Northern Lights, son of Robert Stevenson, brother of Alan and David; so that his nephew, David Alan Stevenson, joined with him at the time of his death in the engineership, is the sixth of the family who has held, successively or conjointly, that office. The Bell Rock, his father's great triumph, was finished before he was born; but he served under his brother Alan in the building of Skerryvore, the noblest of all extant deep-sea lights; and, in conjunction with his brother David, he added two – the Chickens and Dhu Heartach – to that small number of man's extreme outposts in the ocean. Of shore lights, the two brothers last named erected no fewer than twenty-seven; of beacons,[1] about twenty-five. Many harbours were successfully carried out: one, the harbour of Wick, the chief disaster of my father's life, was a failure; the sea proved too strong for man's arts; and after expedients hitherto unthought of, and on a scale hyper-cyclopean, the work must be deserted, and now stands a ruin in that bleak, God-forsaken bay, ten miles from John-o'-Groat's. In the improvement of rivers the brothers were likewise in a large way of practice over both England and Scotland, nor had any British engineer anything approaching their experience.

It was about this nucleus of his professional labours that all my father's scientific inquiries and inventions centred; these proceeded from, and acted back upon, his daily business. Thus it was as a harbour engineer that he became interested in the propagation and reduction of waves; a difficult subject in regard to which he has left behind him much suggestive matter and some valuable approximate results. Storms were his sworn adversaries, and it was through the study of storms that he approached that of meteorology at large. Many who knew him not otherwise, knew – perhaps have in their gardens – his louvre-boarded screen for instruments. But the great achievement of his life was, of course, in optics as applied to lighthouse illumination. Fresnel had done much; Fresnel had settled the fixed light apparatus on a principle that still seems unimprovable; and when Thomas Stevenson stepped in and brought to a comparable perfection the revolving light, a not unnatural jealousy and much painful controversy rose in France. It had its hour; and, as I have told already, even in France it has blown by.

[1] In Dr Murray's admirable new dictionary, I have remarked a flaw *sub voce* Beacon. In its express, technical sense, a beacon may be defined as 'a founded, artificial sea-mark, not lighted.'

Had it not, it would have mattered the less, since all through his life my father continued to justify his claim by fresh advances. New apparatus for lights in new situations was continually being designed with the same unwearied search after perfection, the same nice ingenuity of means; and though the holophotal revolving light perhaps still remains his most elegant contrivance, it is difficult to give it the palm over the much later condensing system, with its thousand possible modifications. The number and the value of these improvements entitle their author to the name of one of mankind's benefactors. In all parts of the world a safer landfall awaits the mariner. Two things must be said: and, first, that Thomas Stevenson was no mathematician. Natural shrewdness, a sentiment of optical laws, and a great intensity of consideration led him to just conclusions; but to calculate the necessary formulæ for the instruments he had conceived was often beyond him, and he must fall back on the help of others, notably on that of his cousin and lifelong intimate friend, *emeritus* Professor Swan, of St Andrews, and his later friend, Professor P. G. Tait. It is a curious enough circumstance, and a great encouragement to others, that a man so ill equipped should have succeeded in one of the most abstract and arduous walks of applied science. The second remark is one that applies to the whole family, and only particularly to Thomas Stevenson from the great number and importance of his inventions: holding as the Stevensons did a Government appointment, they regarded their original work as something due already to the nation, and none of them has ever taken out a patent. It is another cause of the comparative obscurity of the name: for a patent not only brings in money, it infallibly spreads reputation; and my father's instruments enter anonymously into a hundred light-rooms, and are passed anonymously over in a hundred reports, where the least considerable patent would stand out and tell its author's story.

But the life-work of Thomas Stevenson remains; what we have lost, what we now rather try to recall, is the friend and companion. He was a man of a somewhat antique strain: with a blended sternness and softness that was wholly Scottish and at first somewhat bewildering; with a profound essential melancholy of disposition and (what often accompanies it) the most humorous geniality in company; shrewd and childish; passionately attached, passionately prejudiced; a man of many extremes, many faults of temper, and no very stable foothold for himself among life's troubles. Yet he was a wise adviser; many men, and these not inconsiderable, took counsel with him habitually. 'I sat at his feet,' writes one of these, 'when I asked his advice, and when the broad brow was set in thought and the firm mouth said his say, I always knew that no man could add to the worth of the conclusion.' He had excellent taste, though whimsical and partial; collected old furniture and delighted specially in sunflowers long before the days of Mr Wilde; took a lasting pleasure in prints and pictures; was a devout admirer of Thomson of Duddingston at a time when few shared the taste; and though he read little, was constant to his favourite books. He had never any Greek; Latin he happily re-taught himself after he had left school, where he was a mere consistent idler: happily, I say, for Lactantius, Vossius, and Cardinal Bona were his chief authors. The first he must have read for twenty years uninterruptedly, keeping it near him in his study, and carrying it in his bag on journeys. Another old theologian, Brown of Wamphray, was often in his hands. When he was indisposed, he had two books, *Guy Mannering* and *The Parent's Assistant*, of which he never wearied. He was a strong Conservative, or, as he preferred to call himself, a Tory; except in so far as his views were modified by a hot-headed chivalrous sentiment for women. He was actually in favour of a marriage law under which any woman might have a divorce for the asking, and no man on any ground whatever; and the same sentiment found another expression in a Magdalen Mission in Edinburgh, founded and largely supported by himself. This was but one of the many channels of his public generosity; his private was equally unstrained. The Church of Scotland, of which he held the doctrines (though in a sense of his own) and to which he bore a clansman's loyalty, profited often by his time and money; and though, from a morbid sense of his own unworthiness, he would never consent to be an officer-bearer, his advice was often sought, and he served the Church on many committees. What he perhaps valued highest in his work were his contributions to the defence of Christianity; one of which, in particular, was praised by Hutchinson Stirling and reprinted at the request of Professor Crawford.

His sense of his own unworthiness I have called morbid; morbid, too, were his sense of the fleetingness of life and his concern for death. He had never accepted the conditions of man's life or his own character; and his inmost thoughts were ever tinged with the Celtic melancholy. Cases of conscience were sometimes grievous to him, and that delicate employment of a scientific witness cost him many qualms. But he found respite from these troublesome humours in his work, in his lifelong study of natural science, in the society of those he loved, and in his daily walks, which now would carry him far into the country with some congenial friend, and now keep him dangling about the town from one old bookshop to another, and scraping romantic acquaintance with every dog that passed. His talk, compounded of so much sterling sense and so much freakish humour, and clothed in language so apt, droll, and emphatic, was a perpetual delight to all who knew him before the clouds began to settle on his mind. His use of language was both just and picturesque; and when at the beginning of his illness he began to feel the ebbing of this power, it was strange and painful to hear him reject one word after another as inadequate, and at length desist from the search and leave his phrase unfinished rather than finish it without propriety. It was perhaps another Celtic trait that his affections and emotions, passionate as these were, and liable to passionate ups and downs, found the most eloquent expression both in words and gestures. Love, anger, and indignation shone through him and broke forth in imagery, like what we read of Southern races. For all these emotional extremes, and in spite of the melancholy ground of his character, he had upon the whole a happy life; nor was he less fortunate in his death, which at the last came to him unaware.

A HUMBLE REMONSTRANCE

I

We have recently enjoyed a quite peculiar pleasure: hearing, in some detail, the opinions, about the art they practise, of Mr Walter Besant and Mr Henry James; two men certainly of very different calibre: Mr James so precise of outline, so cunning of fence, so scrupulous of finish, and Mr Besant so genial, so friendly, with so persuasive and humorous a vein of whim: Mr James the very type of the deliberate artist, Mr Besant the impersonation of good nature. That such doctors should differ will excite no great surprise; but one point in which they seem to agree fills me, I confess, with wonder. For they are both content to talk about the 'art of fiction;' and Mr Besant, waxing exceedingly bold, goes on to oppose this so-called 'art of fiction' to the 'art of poetry.' By the art of poetry he can mean nothing but the art of verse, an art of handicraft, and only comparable with the art of prose. For that heat and height of sane emotion which we agree to call by the name of poetry, is but a libertine and vagrant quality; present, at times, in any art, more often absent from them all; too seldom present in the prose novel, too frequently absent from the ode and epic. Fiction is in the same case; it is no substantive art, but an element which enters largely into all the arts but architecture. Homer, Wordsworth, Phidias, Hogarth, and Salvini, all deal in fiction; and yet I do not suppose that either Hogarth or Salvini, to mention but these two, entered in any degree into the scope of Mr Besant's interesting lecture or Mr James's charming essay. The art of fiction, then, regarded as a definition, is both too ample and too scanty. Let me suggest another; let me suggest that what both Mr James and Mr Besant had in view was neither more nor less than the art of narrative.

But Mr Besant is anxious to speak solely of 'the modern English novel,' the stay and bread-winner of Mr Mudie; and in the author of the most pleasing novel on that roll, *All Sorts and Conditions of*

Men, the desire is natural enough. I can conceive then, that he would hasten to propose two additions, and read thus: the art of *fictitious* narrative *in prose*.

Now the fact of the existence of the modern English novel is not to be denied; materially, with its three volumes, leaded type, and gilded lettering, it is easily distinguishable from other forms of literature; but to talk at all fruitfully of any branch of art, it is needful to build our definitions on some more fundamental ground than binding. Why, then, are we to add 'in prose'? *The Odyssey* appears to me the best of romances; *The Lady of the Lake* to stand high in the second order; and Chaucer's tales and prologues to contain more of the matter and art of the modern English novel than the whole treasury of Mr Mudie. Whether a narrative be written in blank verse or the Spenserian stanza, in the long period of Gibbon or the clipped phrase of Charles Reade, the principles of the art of narrative must be equally observed. The choice of a noble and swelling style in prose affects the problem of narration in the same way, if not to the same degree, as the choice of measured verse; for both imply a closer synthesis of events, a higher key of dialogue, and a more picked and stately strain of words. If you are to refuse *Don Juan*, it is hard to see why you should include *Zanoni* or (to bracket works of very different value) *The Scarlet Letter*; and by what discrimination are you to open your doors to *The Pilgrim's Progress* and close them on *The Faery Queen*? To bring things closer home, I will here propound to Mr Besant a conundrum. A narrative called *Paradise Lost* was written in English verse by one John Milton; what was it then? It was next translated by Chateaubriand into French prose; and what was it then? Lastly, the French translation was, by some inspired compatriot of George Gilfillan (and of mine) turned bodily into an English novel; and, in the name of clearness, what was it then?

But, once more, why should we add 'fictitious'? The reason why is obvious. The reason why not, if something more recondite, does not want for weight. The art of narrative, in fact, is the same, whether it is applied to the selection and illustration of a real series of events or of an imaginary series. Boswell's *Life of Johnson* (a work of cunning and inimitable art) owes its success to the same technical manœuvres as (let us say) *Tom Jones*: the clear conception of certain characters of man, the choice and presentation of certain incidents out of a great number that offered, and the invention (yes, invention) and preservation of a certain key in dialogue. In which these things are done with the more art – in which with the greater air of nature – readers will differently judge. Boswell's is, indeed, a very special case, and almost a generic; but it is not only in Boswell, it is in every biography with any salt of life, it is in every history where events and men, rather than ideas, are presented – in Tacitus, in Carlyle, in Michelet, in Macaulay – that the novelist will find many of his own methods most conspicuously and adroitly handled. He will find besides that he, who is free – who has the right to invent or steal a missing incident, who has the right, more precious still, of wholesale omission – is frequently defeated, and, with all his advantages, leaves a less strong impression of reality and passion. Mr James utters his mind with a becoming fervour on the sanctity of truth to the novelist; on a more careful examination truth will seem a word of very debateable propriety, not only for the labours of the novelist, but for those of the historian. No art – to use the daring phrase of Mr James – can successfully 'compete with life;' and the art that seeks to do so is condemned to perish *montibus aviis*. Life goes before us, infinite in complication; attended by the most various and surprising meteors; appealing at once to the eye, to the ear, to the mind – the seat of wonder, to the touch – so thrillingly delicate, and to the belly – so imperious when starved. It combines and employs in its manifestation the method and material, not of one art only, but of all the arts. Music is but an arbitrary trifling with a few of life's majestic chords; painting is but a shadow of its pageantry of light and colour; literature does but drily indicate that wealth of incident, of moral obligation, of virtue, vice, action, rapture and agony, with which it teems. To 'compete with life,' whose sun we cannot look upon, whose passions and diseases waste and slay us – to compete with the flavour of wine, the beauty of the dawn, the scorching of fire, the bitterness of death and separation – here is, indeed, a projected escalade of heaven; here are, indeed, labours for a Hercules in a dress coat, armed with a pen and a dictionary to depict the passions, armed with a tube of superior flake-white to paint the portrait of the insufferable sun. No art is true in this sense: none can 'compete with life:' not even history, built indeed of indisputable facts, but these facts robbed of their vivacity and sting; so that even when we read of the sack of a city or the fall of an empire, we are surprised, and justly commend the author's talent, if our pulse be quickened. And mark, for a last differentia, that this quickening of the pulse is, in almost every case, purely agreeable; that these phantom reproductions of experience, even at their most acute, convey decided pleasure; while experience itself, in the cockpit of life, can torture and slay.

What, then, is the object, what the method, of an art, and what the source of its power? The whole secret is that no art does 'compete with life.' Man's one method, whether he reasons or creates, is to half-shut his eyes against the dazzle and confusion of reality. The arts, like arithmetic and geometry, turn away their eyes from the gross, coloured and mobile nature at our feet, and regard instead a certain figmentary abstraction. Geometry will tell us of a circle, a thing never seen in nature; asked about a green circle or an iron circle, it lays its hand upon its mouth. So with the arts. Painting, ruefully comparing sunshine and flake-white, gives up truth of colour, as it had already given up relief and movement; and instead of vying with nature, arranges a scheme of harmonious tints. Literature, above all in its most typical mood, the mood of narrative, similarly flees the direct challenge and pursues instead an independent and creative aim. So far as it imitates at all, it imitates not life but speech: not the facts of human destiny, but the emphasis and the suppressions with which the human actor tells of them. The real art that dealt with life directly was that of the first men who told their stories round the savage camp-fire. Our art is occupied, and bound to be occupied, not so much in making stories true as in making them typical; not so much in capturing the lineaments of each fact, as in marshalling, all of them towards a common end. For the welter of impressions, all forcible but all discrete, which life presents, it substitutes a certain artificial series of impressions, all indeed most feebly represented, but all aiming at the same effect, all eloquent of the same idea, all chiming together like consonant notes in music or like the graduated tints in a good picture. From all its chapters, from all its pages, from all its sentences, the well-written novel echoes and re-echoes its one creative and controlling thought; to this must every incident and character contribute; the style must have been pitched in unison with this; and if there is anywhere a word that looks another way, the book would be stronger, clearer, and (I had almost said) fuller without it. Life is monstrous, infinite, illogical, abrupt and poignant; a work of art, in comparison, is neat, finite, self-contained, rational, flowing and emasculate. Life imposes by brute energy, like inarticulate thunder; art catches the ear, among the far louder noises of experience, like an air artificially made by a discreet musician. A proposition of geometry does not compete with life; and a proposition of geometry is a fair and luminous parallel for a work of art. Both are reasonable, both untrue to the crude fact; both inhere in nature, neither represents it. The novel, which is a work of art, exists, not by its resemblances to life, which are forced and material, as a shoe must still consist of leather, but by its immeasurable difference from life, which is designed and significant, and is both the method and the meaning of the work.

The life of man is not the subject of novels, but the inexhaustible magazine from which subjects are to be selected; the name of these is legion; and with each new subject – for here again I must differ by the whole width of heaven from Mr James – the true artist will vary his method and change the point of attack. That which was in one case an excellence, will become a defect in another; what was the making of one book, will in the next be impertinent or dull. First each novel, and then each class of novels, exists by and for itself. I will take, for instance, three main classes, which are fairly distinct: first, the novel of adventure, which appeals to certain almost sensual and quite illogical tendencies in man; second, the novel of character, which appeals to our intellectual appreciation of man's foibles and mingled and inconstant motives; and third, the dramatic novel, which deals with the same stuff as the serious theatre, and appeals to our emotional nature and moral judgement.

And first for the novel of adventure. Mr James refers, with singular generosity of praise, to a little book about a quest for hidden treasure; but he lets fall, by the way, some rather startling words. In this book he misses what he calls the 'immense luxury' of being able to quarrel with his author. The luxury, to most of us, is to lay by our judgement, to be submerged by the tale as by a billow, and only to awake, and begin to distinguish and find fault, when the piece is over and the volume laid aside. Still more remarkable is Mr James's reason. He cannot criticise the author, as he goes, 'because,' says he, comparing it with another work, '*I have been a child, but I have never been on a quest for buried treasure.*' Here is, indeed, a wilful paradox; for if he has never been on a quest for buried treasure, it can be demonstrated that he has never been a child. There never was a child (unless Master James) but has hunted gold, and been a pirate, and a military commander, and a bandit of the mountains; but has fought, and suffered shipwreck and prison, and imbrued its little hands in gore, and gallantly retrieved the lost battle, and triumphantly protected innocence and beauty. Elsewhere in his essay Mr James has protested with excellent reason against too narrow a conception of experience; for the born artist, he contends, the 'faintest hints of life' are converted into revelations; and it will be found true, I believe, in a majority of cases, that the artist writes with more gusto and effect of those things which he has only wished to do, than of those which he has done. Desire is a wonderful telescope, and Pisgah the best observatory. Now, while it is true that neither Mr James nor the author of the work in question has ever, in the fleshly sense, gone questing after gold, it is probable that both have ardently desired and fondly imagined the details of such a life in youthful day-dreams; and the author, counting upon that, and well aware (cunning and low-minded man!) that this class of interest, having been frequently treated, finds a readily accessible and beaten road to the sympathies of the reader, addressed himself throughout to the building up and cir-cumstantiation of this boyish dream. Character to the boy is a sealed book; for him, a pirate is a beard, a pair of wide trousers and a liberal complement of pistols. The author, for the sake of circumstantiation and because he was himself more or less grown up, admitted character, within certain limits, into his design; but only within certain limits. Had the same puppets figured in a scheme of another sort, they had been drawn to very different purpose; for in this elementary novel of adventure, the characters need to be presented with but one class of qualities – the warlike and formidable. So as they appear insidious in deceit and fatal in the combat, they have served their end. Danger is the matter with which this class of novel deals; fear, the passion with which it idly trifles; and the characters are portrayed only so far as they realise the sense of danger and provoke the sympathy of fear. To add more traits, to be too clever, to start the hare of moral or intellectual interest while we are running the fox of material interest, is not to enrich but to stultify your tale. The stupid reader will only be offended, and the clever reader lose the scent.

The novel of character has this difference from all others: that it requires no coherency of plot, and for this reason, as in the case of *Gil Blas*, it is sometimes called the novel of adventure. It turns on the humours of the persons represented; these are, to be sure, embodied in incidents, but the incidents themselves, being tributary, need not march in a progression; and the characters may be statically shown. As they enter, so they may go out; they must be consistent, but they need not grow. Here Mr James will recognise the note of much of his own work: he treats, for the most part, the statics of character, studying it at rest or only gently moved; and, with his usual delicate and just artistic instinct, he avoids those stronger passions which would deform the attitudes he loves to study, and change his sitters from the humorists of ordinary life to the brute forces and bare types of more emotional moments. In his recent *Author of Beltraffio*, so just in conception, so nimble and neat in workmanship, strong passion is indeed employed; but observe that it is not displayed. Even in the heroine the working of the passion is suppressed; and the great struggle, the true tragedy, the *scène-à-faire*, passes unseen behind the panels of a locked door. The delectable invention of the young visitor is introduced, consciously or not, to this end: that Mr James, true to his method, might avoid the scene of passion. I trust no reader will suppose me guilty of undervaluing this little masterpiece. I mean merely that it belongs to one marked class of novel, and that it would have been very differently conceived and treated had it belonged to that other marked class, of which I now proceed to speak.

I take pleasure in calling the dramatic novel by that name, because it enables me to point out by the way a strange and peculiarly English misconception. It is sometimes supposed that the drama consists of incident. It consists of passion, which gives the actor his opportunity; and that passion must progressively increase, or the actor, as the piece proceeded, would be unable to carry the audience from a lower to a higher pitch of interest and emotion. A good serious play must therefore be founded on one of the passionate *cruces* of life, where duty and inclination come nobly to the grapple; and the same is true of what I call, for that reason, the dramatic novel. I will instance a few worthy specimens, all of our own day and language; Meredith's *Rhoda Fleming*, that wonderful and painful book, long out of print,[1] and hunted for at bookstalls like an Aldine; Hardy's *Pair of Blue Eyes*; and two of Charles Reade's, *Griffith Gaunt* and *The Double Marriage*, originally called *White Lies*, and founded (by an accident quaintly favourable to my nomenclature) on a play by Maquet, the partner of the great Dumas. In this kind of novel the closed door of *The Author of Beltraffio* must be broken open; passion must appear upon the scene and utter its last word; passion is the be-all and the end-all, the plot and the solution, the

[1] Now no longer so, thank Heaven!

protagonist and the *deus ex machina* in one. The characters may come anyhow upon the stage: we do not care; the point is, that, before they leave it, they shall become transfigured and raised out of themselves by passion. It may be part of the design to draw them with detail; to depict a full-length character, and then behold it melt and change in the furnace of emotion. But there is no obligation of the sort; nice portraiture is not required; and we are content to accept mere abstract types, so they be strongly and sincerely moved. A novel of this class may be even great, and yet contain no individual figure; it may be great, because it displays the workings of the perturbed heart and the impersonal utterance of passion; and with an artist of the second class it is, indeed, even more likely to be great, when the issue has thus been narrowed and the whole force of the writer's mind directed to passion alone. Cleverness again, which has its fair field in the novel of character, is debarred all entry upon this more solemn theatre. A far-fetched motive, an ingenious evasion of the issue, a witty instead of a passionate turn, offend us like an insincerity. All should be plain, all straightforward to the end. Hence it is that, in *Rhoda Fleming*, Mrs Lovel raises such resentment in the reader; her motives are too flimsy, her ways are too equivocal, for the weight and strength of her surroundings. Hence the hot indignation of the reader when Balzac, after having begun the *Duchesse de Langeais* in terms of strong if somewhat swollen passion, cuts the knot by the derangement of the hero's clock. Such personages and incidents belong to the novel of character; they are out of place in the high society of the passions; when the passions are introduced in art at their full height, we look to see them, not baffled and impotently striving, as in life, but towering above circumstance and acting substitutes for fate.

And here I can imagine Mr James, with his lucid sense, to intervene. To much of what I have said he would apparently demur; in much he would, somewhat impatiently, acquiesce. It may be true; but it is not what he desired to say or to hear said. He spoke of the finished picture and its worth when done; I, of the brushes, the palette, and the north light. He uttered his views in the tone and for the ear of good society; I, with the emphasis and technicalities of the obtrusive student. But the point, I may reply, is not merely to amuse the public, but to offer helpful advice to the young writer. And the young writer will not so much be helped by genial pictures of what an art may aspire to at its highest, as by a true idea of what it must be on the lowest terms. The best that we can say to him is this: Let him choose a motive, whether of character or passion; carefully construct his plot so that every incident is an illustration of the motive, and every property employed shall bear to it a near relation of congruity or contrast; avoid a sub-plot, unless, as sometimes in Shakespeare, the sub-plot be a reversion or complement of the main intrigue; suffer not his style to flag below the level of the argument; pitch the key of conversation, not with any thought of how men talk in parlours, but with a single eye to the degree of passion he may be called on to express; and allow neither himself in the narrative nor any character in the course of the dialogue, to utter one sentence that is not part and parcel of the business of the story or the discussion of the problem involved. Let him not regret if this shortens his book; it will be better so; for to add irrelevant matter is not to lengthen but to bury. Let him not mind if he miss a thousand qualities, so that he keeps unflaggingly in pursuit of the one he has chosen. Let him not care particularly if he miss the tone of conversation, the pungent material detail of the day's manners, the reproduction of the atmosphere and the environment. These elements are not essential: a novel may be excellent, and yet have none of them; a passion or a character is so much the better depicted as it rises clearer from material circumstance. In this age of the particular, let him remember the ages of the abstract, the great books of the past, the brave men that lived before Shakespeare and before Balzac. And as the root of the whole matter, let him bear in mind that his novel is not a transcript of life, to be judged by its exactitude; but a simplification of some side or point of life, to stand or fall by its significant simplicity. For although, in great men, working upon great motives, what we observe and admire is often their complexity, yet underneath appearances the truth remains unchanged: that simplification was their method, and that simplicity is their excellence.

II

Since the above was written another novelist has entered repeatedly the lists of theory: one well worthy of mention, Mr W. D. Howells; and none ever couched a lance with narrower convictions. His own work and those of his pupils and masters singly occupy his mind; he is the bondslave, the zealot of his school; he dreams of an advance in art like what there is in science; he thinks of past things as radically dead; he thinks a form can be outlived: a strange immersion in his own history; a strange forgetfulness of the history of the race! Meanwhile, by a glance at his own works (could he see them with the eager eyes of his readers) much of this illusion would be dispelled. For while he holds all the poor little orthodoxies of the day – no poorer and no smaller than those of yesterday or tomorrow, poor and small, indeed, only so far as they are exclusive – the living quality of much that he has done is of a contrary, I had almost said of a heretical, complexion. A man, as I read him, of an originally strong romantic bent – a certain glow of romance still resides in many of his books, and lends them their distinction. As by accident he runs out and revels in the exceptional; and it is then, as often as not, that his reader rejoices – justly, as I contend. For in all this excessive eagerness to be centrally human, is there not one central human thing that Mr Howells is too often tempted to neglect: I mean himself? A poet, a finished artist, a man in love with the appearances of life, a cunning reader of the mind, he has other passions and aspirations than those he loves to draw. And why should he suppress himself and do such reverence to the Lemuel Barkers? The obvious is not of necessity the normal; fashion rules and deforms; the majority fall tamely into the contemporary shape, and thus attain, in the eyes of the true observer, only a higher power of insignificance; and the danger is lest, in seeking to draw the normal, a man should draw the null, and write the novel of society instead of the romance of man.

A CHAPTER ON DREAMS

The past is all of one texture – whether feigned or suffered – whether acted out in three dimensions, or only witnessed in that small theatre of the brain which we keep brightly lighted all night long, after the jets are down, and darkness and sleep reign undisturbed in the remainder of the body. There is no distinction on the face of our experiences; one is vivid indeed, and one dull, and one pleasant, and another agonising to remember; but which of them is what we call true, and which a dream, there is not one hair to prove. The past stands on a precarious footing; another straw split in the field of metaphysic, and behold us robbed of it. There is scarce a family that can count four generations but lays a claim to some dormant title or some castle and estate: a claim not prosecutable in any court of law, but flattering to the fancy and a great alleviation of idle hours. A man's claim to his own past is yet less valid. A paper might turn up (in proper story-book fashion) in the secret drawer of an old ebony secretary, and restore your family to its ancient honours, and reinstate mine in a certain West Indian islet (not far from St Kitt's, as beloved tradition hummed in my young ears) which was once ours, and is now unjustly someone else's, and for that matter (in the state of the sugar trade) is not worth anything to anybody. I do not say that these revolutions are likely; only no man can deny that they are possible; and the past, on the other hand, is lost for ever: our old days and deeds, our old selves, too, and the very world in which these scenes were acted, all brought down to the same faint residuum as a last night's dream, to some incontinuous images, and an echo in the chambers of the brain. Not an hour, not a mood, not a glance of the eye, can we revoke; it is all gone, past conjuring. And yet conceive us robbed of it, conceive that little thread of memory that we trail behind us broken at the pocket's edge; and in what naked nullity should we be left! for we only guide ourselves, and only know ourselves, by these air-painted pictures of the past.

Upon these grounds, there are some among us who claim to have lived longer and more richly than their neighbours; when they lay asleep they claim they were still active; and among the treasures of memory that all men review for their amusement, these count in no second place the harvests of their dreams. There is one of this kind whom I have in my eye, and whose case is perhaps unusual enough to be described. He was from a child an ardent and uncomfortable dreamer. When he had a touch of fever at night, and the room swelled and shrank, and his clothes, hanging on a nail, now loomed up instant to the bigness of a church, and now drew away into a horror of infinite distance and infinite littleness, the poor soul was very well aware of what must follow, and struggled hard against the approaches of that slumber which was the beginning of sorrows. But his struggles were in vain; sooner or later the night-hag would have him by the throat, and pluck him, strangling and screaming, from his sleep. His dreams were at times commonplace enough, at times very strange: at times they were almost formless, he would be haunted, for instance, by nothing more definite than a certain hue of brown, which he did not mind in the least while he was awake, but feared and loathed while he was dreaming; at times, again, they took on every detail of circumstance, as when once he supposed he must swallow the populous world, and awoke screaming with the horror of the thought. The two chief troubles of his very narrow existence – the practical and everyday trouble of school tasks and the ultimate and airy one of hell and judgement – were often confounded together into one appalling nightmare. He seemed to himself to stand before the Great White Throne; he was called on, poor little devil, to recite some form of words, on which his destiny depended; his tongue stuck, his memory was blank, hell gaped for him; and he would awake, clinging to the curtain-rod with his knees to his chin.

These were extremely poor experiences, on the whole; and at that time of life my dreamer would have very willingly parted with his power of dreams. But presently, in the course of his growth, the cries and physical contortions passed away, seemingly for ever; his visions were still for the most part miserable, but they were more constantly supported; and he would awake with no more extreme symptom than a flying heart, a freezing scalp, cold sweats, and the speechless midnight fear. His dreams, too, as befitted a mind better stocked with particulars, became more circumstantial, and had more the air and continuity of life. The look of the world beginning to take hold on his attention, scenery came to play a part in his sleeping as well as in his waking thoughts, so that he would take long, uneventful journeys and see strange towns and beautiful places as he lay in bed. And, what is more significant, an odd taste that he had for the Georgian costume and for stories laid in that period of English history, began to rule the features of his dreams; so that he masqueraded there in a three-cornered hat, and was much engaged with Jacobite conspiracy between the hour for bed and that for breakfast. About the same time, he began to read in his dreams – tales, for the most part, and for the most part after the manner of G. P. R. James, but so incredibly more vivid and moving than any printed book, that he has ever since been malcontent with literature.

And then, while he was yet a student, there came to him a dream-adventure which he has no anxiety to repeat; he began, that is to say, to dream in sequence and thus to lead a double life – one of the day, one of the night – one that he had every reason to believe was the true one, another that he had no means of proving to be false. I should have said he studied, or was by way of studying, at Edinburgh College, which (it may be supposed) was how I came to know him. Well, in his dream-life, he passed a long day in the surgical theatre, his heart in his mouth, his teeth on edge, seeing monstrous malformations and the abhorred dexterity of surgeons. In a heavy, rainy, foggy evening he came forth into the South Bridge, turned up the High Street, and entered the door of a tall *land*, at the top of which he supposed himself to lodge. All night long, in his wet clothes, he climbed the stairs, stair after stair in endless series, and at every second flight a flaring lamp with a reflector. All night long, he brushed by single persons passing downward – beggarly women of the street, great, weary, muddy labourers, poor scarecrows of men, pale parodies of women – but all drowsy and weary like himself, and all single, and all brushing against him as they passed. In the end, out of a northern window, he would see day beginning to whiten over the Firth, give up the ascent, turn to descend, and in a breath be back again upon the streets, in his wet clothes, in the wet, haggard dawn, trudging to another day of monstrosities and operations. Time went quicker in the life of dreams, some seven hours (as near as he can guess) to one; and it went, besides, more intensely, so that the gloom of these fancied experiences clouded the day, and he had not shaken off their shadow ere it was time to lie down and to renew them. I cannot tell how long it was that he endured this discipline; but it was long enough to leave a great black blot upon his memory, long enough to send him, trembling for his reason, to the doors of a certain doctor; whereupon with a simple draught he was restored to the common lot of man.

The poor gentleman has since been troubled by nothing of the sort; indeed, his nights were for some while like other men's, now blank, now chequered with dreams, and these sometimes charming, sometimes appalling, but except for an occasional vividness, of no extraordinary kind. I will just note one of these occasions, ere I pass on to what makes my dreamer truly interesting. It seemed to him that he was in the first floor of a rough hill-farm. The room showed some poor efforts at gentility, a carpet on the floor, a piano, I think, against the wall; but, for all these refinements, there was no mistaking he was in a moorland place, among hillside people, and set in miles of heather. He looked down from the window upon a bare farmyard, that seemed to have been long disused. A great, uneasy stillness lay upon the world. There was no sign of the farm-folk or of any livestock, save for an old, brown, curly dog of the retriever breed, who sat close in against the wall of the house and seemed to be dozing. Something about this dog disquieted the dreamer; it was quite a nameless feeling, for the beast looked right enough – indeed, he was so old and dull and dusty and broken-down, that he should rather have awakened pity; and yet the conviction came and grew upon the dreamer that this was no proper dog at all, but something hellish. A great many dozing summer flies hummed about the yard; and presently the dog thrust forth his paw, caught a fly in his open palm, carried it to his mouth like an ape, and looking suddenly up at the dreamer in the window, winked to him with one eye. The dream went on, it matters not how it went; it was a good dream as dreams go; but there was nothing in the sequel worthy of that devilish brown dog. And the point of interest for me lies partly in that very fact: that having found so singular an incident, my imperfect dreamer should prove unable to carry the tale to a fit end and fall back on indescribable noises and indiscriminate horrors. It would be different now; he knows his business better!

For, to approach at last the point: This honest fellow had long been in the custom of setting himself to sleep with tales, and so had his father before him; but these were irresponsible inventions, told for the teller's pleasure, with no eye to the crass public or the thwart reviewer: tales where a thread might be dropped, or one adventure quitted for another, on fancy's least suggestion. So that the little people who manage man's internal theatre had not as yet received a very rigorous training; and played upon their stage like children who should have slipped into the house and found it empty, rather than like drilled actors performing a set piece to a huge hall of faces. But presently my dreamer began to turn his former amusement of story-telling to (what is called) account; by which I mean that he began to write and sell his tales. Here was he, and here were the little people who did that part of his business, in quite new conditions. The stories must now be trimmed and pared and set upon all fours, they must run from a beginning to an end and fit (after a manner) with the laws of life; the pleasure, in one word, had become a business; and that not only for the dreamer, but for the little people of his theatre. These understood the change as well as he. When he lay down to prepare himself for sleep, he no longer sought amusement, but printable and profitable tales; and after he had dozed off in his box-seat, his little people continued their evolutions with the same mercantile designs. All other forms of dream deserted him but two: he still occasionally reads the most delightful books, he still visits at times the most delightful places; and it is perhaps worthy of note that to these same places, and to one in particular, he returns at intervals of months and years, finding new field-paths, visiting new neighbours, beholding that happy valley under new effects of noon and dawn and sunset. But all the rest of the family of visions is quite lost to him: the common, mangled version of yesterday's affairs, the raw-head-and-bloody-bones nightmare, rumoured to be the child of toasted cheese – these and their like are gone; and, for the most part, whether awake or asleep, he is simply occupied – he or his little people – in consciously making stories for the market. This dreamer (like many other persons) has encountered some trifling vicissitudes of fortune. When the bank begins to send letters and the butcher to linger at the back gate, he sets to belabouring his brains after a story, for that is his readiest money-winner; and, behold! at once the little people begin to bestir themselves in the same quest, and labour all night long, and all night long set before him truncheons of tales upon their lighted theatre. No fear of his being frightened now; the flying heart and the frozen scalp are things bygone; applause, growing applause, growing interest, growing exultation in his own cleverness (for he takes all the credit), and at last a jubilant leap to wakefulness, with the cry, 'I have it, that'll do!' upon his lips: with such and similar emotions he sits at these nocturnal dramas, with such outbreaks, like Claudius in the play, he scatters the performance in the midst. Often enough the waking is a disappointment: he has been too deep asleep, as I explain the thing; drowsiness has gained his little people, they have gone stumbling and maundering through their parts; and the play, to the awakened mind, is seen to be a tissue of absurdities. And yet how often have these sleepless Brownies done him honest service, and given him, as he sat idly taking his pleasure in the boxes, better tales than he could fashion for himself.

Here is one, exactly as it came to him. It seemed he was the son of a very rich and wicked man, the owner of broad acres and a most damnable temper. The dreamer (and that was the son) had lived much abroad, on purpose to avoid his parent; and when at length he returned to England, it was to find him married again to a young wife, who was supposed to suffer cruelly and to loathe her yoke. Because of this marriage (as the dreamer indistinctly understood) it was desirable for father and son to have a meeting; and yet both being proud and both angry, neither would condescend upon a visit. Meet they did accordingly, in a desolate, sandy country by the sea; and there they quarrelled, and the son, stung by some intolerable insult, struck down the father dead. No suspicion was aroused; the dead man was found and buried, and the dreamer succeeded to the broad estates, and found himself installed under the same roof with his father's widow, for whom no provision had been made. These two lived very much alone, as people may after a bereavement, sat down to table together, shared the long evenings, and grew daily better friends; until it seemed to him of a sudden that she was prying about dangerous matters, that she had conceived a notion of his guilt, that she watched him and tried him with questions. He drew back from her company as men draw back from a precipice suddenly discovered; and yet so strong was the attraction that he would drift again and again into the old intimacy, and again and again be startled back by some suggestive question or some inexplicable meaning in her eye. So they lived at cross purposes, a life full of broken dialogue, challenging glances, and suppressed passion; until, one day, he saw the woman slipping from the house in a veil, followed her to the station, followed her in the train to the seaside country, and out over the sandhills to the very place where the murder was done. There she began to grope among the bents, he watching her, flat upon his face; and presently she had something in her hand – I cannot remember what it was, but it was deadly evidence against the dreamer – and as she held it up to look at it, perhaps from the shock of the discovery, her foot slipped, and she hung at some peril on the brink of the tall sand-wreaths. He had no thought but to spring up and rescue her; and there they stood face to face, she with that deadly matter openly in her hand – his very presence on the spot another link of proof. It was plain she was about to speak, but this was more than he could bear – he could bear to be lost, but not to talk of it with his destroyer; and he cut her short with trivial conversation. Arm in arm, they returned together to the train, talking he knew not what, made the journey back in the same carriage, sat down to dinner, and passed the evening in the drawing-room as in the past. But suspense and fear drummed in the dreamer's bosom. 'She has not denounced me yet' – so his thoughts ran – 'when will she denounce me? Will it be tomorrow?' And it was not tomorrow, nor the next day, nor the next; and their life settled back on the old terms, only that she seemed kinder than before, and that, as for him, the burthen of his suspense and wonder grew daily more unbearable, so that he wasted away like a man with a disease. Once, indeed, he broke all bounds of decency, seized an occasion when she was abroad, ransacked her room, and at last, hidden away among her jewels, found the damning evidence. There he stood, holding this thing, which was his life, in the hollow of his hand, and marvelling at her inconsequent behaviour, that she should seek and keep, and yet not use it; and then the door opened, and behold herself. So, once more, they stood, eye to eye, with the evidence between them; and once more she raised to him a face brimming with some communication; and once more he shied away from speech and cut her off. But before he left the room, which he had turned upside down, he laid back his death-warrant where he had found it; and at that, her face lighted up. The next thing he heard, she was explaining to her maid, with some ingenious falsehood, the disorder of her things. Flesh and blood could bear the strain no longer; and I think it was the next morning (though chronology is always hazy in the theatre of the mind) that he burst from his reserve. They had been breakfasting together in one corner of a great, parqueted, sparely-furnished room of many windows; all the time of the meal she had tortured him with sly allusions; and no sooner were the servants gone, and these two protagonists alone together, than he leaped to his feet. She too sprang up, with a pale face; with a pale face, she heard him as he raved out his complaint: Why did she torture him so? she knew all, she knew he was no enemy to her; why did she not denounce him at once? what signified her whole behaviour? why did she torture him? and yet again, why did she torture him? And when he had done, she fell upon her knees, and with outstretched hands: 'Do you not understand?' she cried. 'I love you!'

Hereupon, with a pang of wonder and mercantile delight, the dreamer awoke. His mercantile delight was not of long endurance; for it soon became plain that in this spirited tale there were unmarketable elements; which is just the reason why you have it here so briefly told. But his wonder has still kept growing; and I think the reader's will also, if he consider it ripely. For now he sees why I speak of the little people as of substantive inventors and performers. To the end they had kept their secret. I will go bail for the dreamer (having excellent grounds for valuing his candour) that he had no guess whatever at the motive of the woman – the hinge of the whole well-invented plot – until the instant of that highly dramatic declaration. It was not his tale; it was the little people's! And observe: not only was the secret kept, the story was told with really guileful craftsmanship. The conduct of both actors is (in the cant phrase) psychologically correct, and the emotion aptly graduated up to the surprising climax. I am awake now, and I know this trade; and yet I cannot better it. I am awake, and I live by this business; and yet I could not outdo – could not perhaps equal – that crafty artifice (as of some old, experienced carpenter of plays, some Dennery or Sardou) by which the same situation is twice presented and the two actors twice brought face to face over the evidence, only once it is in her hand, once in his – and these in their due order, the least dramatic first. The more I think of it, the more I am moved to press upon the world my question: Who are the Little People? They are near connections of the dreamer's, beyond doubt; they share in his financial worries and have an eye to the bank-book; they share plainly in his training; they have plainly learned like him to build the scheme of a considerate story and to arrange emotion in progressive order; only I think they have more talent; and one thing is beyond doubt, they can tell him a story piece by piece, like a serial, and keep him all the while in ignorance of where they aim. Who are they, then? and who is the dreamer?

Well, as regards the dreamer, I can answer that, for he is no less a person than myself; – as I might have told you from the beginning, only that the critics murmur over my consistent egotism; – and as I am positively forced to tell you now, or I could advance but little farther with my story. And for the Little People, what shall I say they are but just my Brownies, God bless them! who do one-half my work for me while I am fast asleep, and in all human likelihood, do the rest for me as well, when I am wide awake and fondly suppose I do it for myself. That part which is done while I am sleeping is the Brownies' part beyond contention; but that which is done when I am up and about is by no means necessarily mine, since all goes to show the Brownies have a hand in it even then. Here is a doubt that much concerns my conscience. For myself – what I call I, my conscious ego, the denizen of the pineal gland unless he has changed his residence since Descartes, the man with the conscience and the variable bank-account, the man with the hat and the boots, and the privilege of voting and not carrying his candidate at the general elections – I am sometimes tempted to suppose he is no storyteller at all, but a creature as matter of fact as any cheesemonger or any cheese, and a realist bemired up to the ears in actuality; so that, by that account, the whole of my published fiction should be the single-handed product of some Brownie, some Familiar, some unseen collaborator, whom I keep locked in a back garret, while I get all the praise and he but a share (which I cannot prevent him getting) of the pudding. I am an excellent adviser, something like Molière's servant; I pull back and I cut down; and I dress the whole in the best words and sentences that I can find and make; I hold the pen, too; and I do the sitting at the table, which is about the worst of it; and when all is done, I make up the manuscript and pay for the registration; so that, on the whole, I have some claim to share, though not so largely as I do, in the profits of our common enterprise.

I can but give an instance or so of what part is done sleeping and what part awake, and leave the reader to share what laurels there are, at his own nod, between myself and my collaborators; and to do this I will first take a book that a number of persons have been polite enough to read, the *Strange Case of Dr Jekyll and Mr Hyde*. I had long been trying to write a story on this subject, to find a body, a vehicle, for that strong sense of man's double being which must at times come in upon and overwhelm the mind of every thinking creature. I had even written one, *The Travelling*

Companion, which was returned by an editor on the plea that it was a work of genius and indecent, and which I burned the other day on the ground that it was not a work of genius, and that *Jekyll* had supplanted it. Then came one of those financial fluctuations to which (with an elegant modesty) I have hitherto referred in the third person. For two days I went about racking my brains for a plot of any sort; and on the second night I dreamed the scene at the window, and a scene afterward split in two, in which Hyde, pursued for some crime, took the powder and underwent the change in the presence of his pursuers. All the rest was made awake, and consciously, although I think I can trace in much of it the manner of my Brownies. The meaning of the tale is therefore mine, and had long pre-existed in my garden of Adonis, and tried one body after another in vain; indeed, I do most of the morality, worse luck! and my Brownies have not a rudiment of what we call a conscience. Mine, too, is the setting, mine the characters. All that was given me was the matter of three scenes, and the central idea of a voluntary change becoming involuntary. Will it be thought ungenerous, after I have been so liberally ladling out praise to my unseen collaborators, if I here toss them over, bound hand and foot, into the arena of the critics? For the business of the powders, which so many have censured, is, I am relieved to say, not mine at all but the Brownies'. Of another tale, in case the reader should have glanced at it, I may say a word: the not very defensible story of *Olalla*. Here the court, the mother, the mother's niche, Olalla, Olalla's chamber, the meetings on the stair, the broken window, the ugly scene of the bite, were all given me in bulk and detail as I have tried to write them; to this I added only the external scenery (for in my dream I never was beyond the court), the portrait, the characters of Felipe and the priest, the moral, such as it is, and the last pages, such as, alas! they are. And I may even say that in this case the moral itself was given me; for it arose immediately on a comparison of the mother and the daughter, and from the hideous trick of atavism in the first. Sometimes a parabolic sense is still more undeniably present in a dream; sometimes I cannot but suppose my Brownies have been aping Bunyan, and yet in no case with what would possibly be called a moral in a tract; never with the ethical narrowness; conveying hints instead of life's larger limitations and that sort of sense which we seem to perceive in the arabesque of time and space.

For the most part, it will be seen, my Brownies are somewhat fantastic, like their stories hot and hot, full of passion and the picturesque, alive with animating incident; and they have no prejudice against the supernatural. But the other day they gave me a surprise, entertaining me with a love-story, a little April comedy, which I ought certainly to hand over to the author of *A Chance Acquaintance*, for he could write it as it should be written, and I am sure (although I mean to try) that I cannot. – But who would have supposed that a Brownie of mine should invent a tale for Mr Howells?

LETTER TO A YOUNG GENTLEMAN
WHO PROPOSES TO EMBRACE
THE CAREER OF ART

With the agreeable frankness of youth, you address me on a point of some practical importance to yourself and (it is even conceivable) of some gravity to the world: Should you or should you not become an artist? It is one which you must decide entirely for yourself; all that I can do is to bring under your notice some of the materials of that decision; and I will begin, as I shall probably conclude also, by assuring you that all depends on the vocation.

To know what you like is the beginning of wisdom and of old age. Youth is wholly experimental. The essence and charm of that unquiet and delightful epoch is ignorance of self as well as ignorance of life. These two unknowns the young man brings together again and again, now in the airiest touch, now with a bitter hug; now with exquisite pleasure, now with cutting pain; but never with indifference, to which he is a total stranger, and never with that near kinsman of indifference, contentment. If he be a youth of dainty senses or a brain easily heated, the interest of this series of experiments grows upon him out of all proportion to the pleasure he receives. It is not beauty that he loves, nor pleasure that he seeks, though he may think so; his design and his sufficient reward is to verify his own existence and taste the variety of human fate. To him, before the razor-edge of curiosity is dulled, all that is not actual living and the hot chase of experience wears a face of a disgusting dryness difficult to recall in later days; or if there be any exception – and here destiny steps in – it is in those moments when, wearied or surfeited of the primary activity of the senses, he calls up before memory the image of transacted pains and pleasures. Thus it is that such an one shies from all cut-and-dry professions, and inclines insensibly toward that career of art which consists only in the tasting and recording of experience.

This, which is not so much a vocation for art as an impatience of all other honest trades, frequently exists alone; and so existing, it will pass gently away in the course of years. Emphatically, it is not to be regarded; it is not a vocation, but a temptation; and when your father the other day so fiercely and (in my view) so properly discouraged your ambition, he was recalling not improbably some similar passage in his own experience. For the temptation is perhaps nearly as common as the vocation is rare. But again we have vocations which are imperfect; we have men whose minds are bound up, not so much in any art, as in the general *ars artium* and common base of all creative work; who will now dip into painting, and now study counterpoint, and anon will be inditing a sonnet: all these with equal interest, all often with genuine knowledge. And of this temper, when it stands alone, I find it difficult to speak; but I should counsel such an one to take to letters, for in literature (which drags with so wide a net) all his information may be found some day useful, and if he should go on as he has begun, and turn at last into the critic, he will have learned to use the necessary tools. Lastly we come to those vocations which are at once decisive and precise; to the men who are born with the love of pigments, the passion of drawing, the gift of music, or the impulse to create with words, just as other and perhaps the same men are born with the love of hunting, or the sea, or horses, or the turning-lathe. These are predestined; if a man love the labour of any trade, apart from any question of success or fame, the gods have called him. He may have the general vocation too: he may have a taste for all the arts, and I think he often has; but the mark of his calling is this laborious partiality for one, this inextinguishable zest in its technical successes, and (perhaps above all) a certain candour of mind, to take his very trifling enterprise with a gravity that would befit the cares of empire, and to think the smallest improvement worth accomplishing at any expense of time and industry. The book, the statue, the sonata, must be gone upon with the unreasoning good faith and the unflagging spirit of children at their play. *Is it worth doing?* – when it shall have occurred to any artist to ask himself that question, it is implicitly answered in the negative. It does not occur to the child as he plays at being a pirate on the dining-room sofa, nor to the hunter as he pursues his quarry; and the candour of the one and the ardour of the other should be united in the bosom of the artist.

If you recognise in yourself some such decisive taste, there is no room for hesitation: follow your bent. And observe (lest I should too much discourage you) that the disposition does not usually burn so brightly at the first, or rather not so constantly. Habit and practice sharpen gifts; the necessity of toil grows less disgusting, grows even welcome, in the course of years; a small taste (if it be only genuine) waxes with indulgence into an exclusive passion. Enough, just now, if you can look back over a fair interval, and see that your chosen art has a little more than held its own among the thronging interests of youth. Time will do the rest, if devotion help it; and soon your every thought will be engrossed in that beloved occupation.

But even with devotion, you may remind me, even with unfaltering and delighted industry, many thousand artists spend their lives, if the result be regarded, utterly in vain; a thousand artists, and never one work of art. But the vast mass of mankind are incapable of doing anything reasonably well, art among the rest. The worthless artist would not improbably have been a quite incompetent baker. And the artist, even if he does not amuse the public, amuses himself; so that there will always be one man the happier for his vigils. This is the practical side of art: its inexpugnable fortress for the true practitioner. The direct returns – the wages of the trade – are small, but the indirect – the wages of the life – are incalculably great. No other business offers a man his daily bread upon such joyful terms. The soldier and the explorer have moments of a worthier excitement, but they are purchased by cruel hardships and periods of tedium that beggar language. In the life of the artist there need be no hour without its pleasure. I take the author, with whose career I am best acquainted; and it is true he works in a rebellious material, and that the act of writing is cramped and trying both to the eyes and the temper; but remark him in his study, when matter crowds upon him and words are not wanting – in what a continual series of small successes time flows by; with what a sense of power as of one moving mountains, he marshals his petty characters; with what pleasures, both of the ear and eye, he sees his airy structure growing on the page; and how he labours in a craft to which the whole material of his life is tributary, and which opens a door to all his tastes, his loves, his hatreds, and his convictions, so that what he writes is only what he longed to utter. He may have enjoyed many things in this big, tragic playground of the world; but what shall he have enjoyed more fully than a morning of successful work? Suppose it ill paid: the wonder is it should be paid at all. Other men pay, and pay dearly, for pleasures less desirable.

Nor will the practice of art afford you pleasure only; it affords besides an admirable training. For the artist works entirely upon honour. The public knows little or nothing of those merits in the quest of which you are condemned to spend the bulk of your endeavours. Merits of design, the merit of first-hand energy, the merit of a certain cheap accomplishment which a man of the artistic temper easily acquires – these they can recognise, and these they value. But to those more exquisite refinements of proficiency and finish, which the artist so ardently desires and so keenly feels, for which (in the vigorous words of Balzac) he must toil 'like a miner buried in a landslip,' for which, day after day, he recasts and revises and rejects – the gross mass of the public must be ever blind. To those lost pains, suppose you attain the highest pitch of merit, posterity may possibly do justice; suppose, as is so probable, you fail by even a hair's breadth of the highest, rest certain they shall never be observed. Under the shadow of this cold thought, alone in his studio, the artist must preserve from day to day his constancy to the ideal. It is this which makes his life noble; it is by this that the practice of his craft strengthens and matures his character; it is for this that even the serious countenance of the great emperor was turned approvingly (if only for a moment) on the followers of Apollo, and that sternly gentle voice bade the artist cherish his art.

And here there fall two warnings to be made. First, if you are to continue to be a law to yourself, you must beware of the first signs of laziness. This idealism in honesty can only be supported by perpetual effort; the standard is easily lowered, the artist who says '*It will do*,' is on the downward path; three or four pot-boilers are enough at times (above all at wrong times) to falsify a talent, and by the practice of journalism a man runs the risk of becoming wedded to cheap finish. This is the danger on the one side; there is not less upon the other. The consciousness of how much the artist is (and must be) a law to himself, debauches the small heads. Perceiving recondite merits very hard to attain, making or swallowing artistic formulæ, or perhaps falling in love with some particular proficiency of his own, many artists forget the end of all art: to please. It is doubtless tempting to exclaim against the ignorant bourgeois; yet it should not be forgotten, it is he who is to pay us, and that (surely on the face of it) for services that he shall desire to have performed. Here also, if properly considered, there is a question of transcendental honesty. To give the public what they do not want, and yet expect to be supported: we have there a strange pretension, and yet not uncommon, above all with painters. The first duty in this world is for a man to pay his way; when that is quite accomplished, he may plunge into what eccentricity he likes; but emphatically not till then. Till then, he must pay assiduous court to the bourgeois who carries the purse. And if in the course of these capitulations he shall falsify his talent, it can never have been a strong one, and he will have preserved a better thing than talent – character. Or if he be of a mind so independent that he cannot stoop to this necessity, one course is yet open: he can desist from art, and follow some more manly way of life.

I speak of a more manly way of life, it is a point on which I must be frank. To live by a pleasure is not a high calling; it involves patronage, however veiled; it numbers the artist, however ambitious, along with dancing girls and billiard markers. The French have a romantic evasion for one employment, and call its practitioners the Daughters of Joy. The artist is of the same family, he is of the Sons of Joy, chose his trade to please himself, gains his livelihood by pleasing others, and has parted with something of the sterner dignity of man. Journals but a little while ago declaimed against the Tennyson peerage; and this Son of Joy was blamed for condescension when he followed the example of Lord Lawrence and Lord Cairns and Lord Clyde. The poet was more happily inspired; with a better modesty he accepted the honour; and anonymous journalists have not yet (if I am to believe them) recovered the vicarious disgrace to their profession. When it comes to their turn, these gentlemen can do themselves more justice; and I shall be glad to think of it; for to my barbarian eyesight, even Lord Tennyson looks somewhat out of place in that assembly. There should be no honours for the artist; he has already, in the practice of his art, more than his share of the rewards of life; the honours are pre-empted for other trades, less agreeable and perhaps more useful.

But the devil in these trades of pleasing is to fail to please. In ordinary occupations, a man offers to do a certain thing or to produce a certain article with a merely conventional accomplishment, a design in which (we may almost say) it is difficult to fail. But the artist steps forth out of the crowd and proposes to delight: an impudent design, in which it is impossible to fail without odious circumstances. The poor Daughter of Joy, carrying her smiles and finery quite unregarded through the crowd, makes a figure which it is impossible to recall without a wounding pity.

She is the type of the unsuccessful artist. The actor, the dancer, and the singer must appear like her in person, and drain publicly the cup of failure. But though the rest of us escape this crowning bitterness of the pillory, we all court in essence the same humiliation. We all profess to be able to delight. And how few of us are! We all pledge ourselves to be able to continue to delight. And the day will come to each, and even to the most admired, when the ardour shall have declined and the cunning shall be lost, and he shall sit by his deserted booth ashamed. Then shall he see himself condemned to do work for which he blushes to take payment. Then (as if his lot were not already cruel) he must lie exposed to the gibes of the wreckers of the press, who earn a little bitter bread by the condemnation of trash which they have not read, and the praise of excellence which they cannot understand.

And observe that this seems almost the necessary end at least of writers. *Les Blancs et les Bleus* (for instance) is of an order of merit very different from *Le Vicomte de Bragelonne*; and if any gentleman can bear to spy upon the nakedness of *Castle Dangerous*, his name I think is Ham: let it be enough for the rest of us to read of it (not without tears) in the pages of Lockhart. Thus in old age, when occupation and comfort are most needful, the writer must lay aside at once his pastime and his breadwinner. The painter indeed, if he succeed at all in engaging the attention of the public, gains great sums and can stand to his easel until a great age without dishonourable failure. The writer has the double misfortune to be ill-paid while he can work, and to be incapable of working when he is old. It is thus a way of life which conducts directly to a false position.

For the writer (in spite of notorious examples to the contrary) must look to be ill-paid. Tennyson and Montépin make handsome livelihoods; but we cannot all hope to be Tennyson, and we do not all perhaps desire to be Montépin. If you adopt an art to be your trade, weed your mind at the outset of all desire of money. What you may decently expect, if you have some talent and much industry, is such an income as a clerk will earn with a tenth or perhaps a twentieth of your nervous output. Nor have you the right to look for more; in the wages of the life, not in the wages of the trade, lies your reward; the work is here the wages. It will be seen I have little sympathy with the common lamentations of the artist class. Perhaps they do not remember the hire of the field labourer; or do they think no parallel will lie? Perhaps they have never observed what is the retiring allowance of a field officer; or do they suppose their contributions to the arts of pleasing more important than the services of a colonel? Perhaps they forget on how little Millet was content to live; or do they think, because they have less genius, they stand excused from the display of equal virtues? But upon one point there should be no dubiety: if a man be not frugal, he has no business in the arts. If he be not frugal, he steers directly for that last tragic scene of *le vieux saltimbanque*; if he be not frugal, he will find it hard to continue to be honest. Some day, when the butcher is knocking at the door, he may be tempted, he may be obliged, to turn out and sell a slovenly piece of work. If the obligation shall have arisen through no wantonness of his own, he is even to be commended; for words cannot describe how far more necessary it is that a man should support his family, than that he should attain to – or preserve – distinction in the arts. But if the pressure comes through his own fault, he has stolen, and stolen under trust, and stolen (which is the worst of all) in such a way that no law can reach him.

And now you may perhaps ask me, if the debutant artist is to have no thought of money, and if (as is implied) he is to expect no honours from the State, may he not at least look forward to the delights of popularity? Praise, you will tell me, is a savoury dish. And in so far as you may mean the countenance of other artists, you would put your finger on one of the most essential and enduring pleasures of the career of art. But in so far as you should have an eye to the commendations of the public or the notice of the newspapers, be sure you would but be cherishing a dream. It is true that in certain esoteric journals the author (for instance) is duly criticised, and that he is often praised a great deal more than he deserves, sometimes for qualities which he prided himself on eschewing, and sometimes by ladies and gentlemen who have denied themselves the privilege of reading his work. But if a man be sensitive to this wild praise, we must suppose him equally alive to that which often accompanies and always follows it – wild ridicule. A man may have done well for years, and then he may fail; he will hear of his failure. Or he may have done well for years, and still do well, but the critics may have tired of praising him, or there may have sprung up some new idol of the instant, some 'dust a little gilt,' to whom they now prefer to offer sacrifice. Here is the obverse and the reverse of that empty and ugly thing called popularity. Will any man suppose it worth the gaining?

MY FIRST BOOK
TREASURE ISLAND

It was far, indeed, from being my first book, for I am not a novelist alone. But I am well aware that my paymaster, the great public, regards what else I have written with indifference, if not aversion. If it call upon me at all, it calls on me in the familiar and indelible character; and when I am asked to talk of my first book, no question in the world but what is meant is my first novel.

Sooner or later, somehow, anyhow, I was bound I was to write a novel. It seems vain to ask why. Men are born with various manias: from my earliest childhood it was mine to make a plaything of imaginary series of events; and as soon as I was able to write, I became a good friend to the paper-makers. Reams upon reams must have gone to the making of *Rathillet*, the *Pentland Rising*,[1] the *King's Pardon* (otherwise *Park Whitehead*), *Edward Ferren*, *A Country Dance*, and a *Vendetta in the West*; and it is consolatory to remember that these reams are now all ashes, and have been received again into the soil. I have named but a few of my ill-fated efforts: only such, indeed, as came to a fair bulk ere they were desisted from; and even so they cover a long vista of years. *Rathillet* was attempted before fifteen, the *Vendetta* at twenty-nine, and the succession of defeats lasted unbroken till I was thirty-one. By that time I had written little books and little essays and short stories, and had got patted on the back and paid for them – though not enough to live upon. I had quite a reputation. I was the successful man. I passed my days in toil, the futility of which would sometimes make my cheek to burn, – that I should spend a man's energy upon this business, and yet could not earn a livelihood; and still there shone ahead of me an unattained

---

[1] *Ne pas confondre.* Not the slim green pamphlet with the imprint of Andrew Elliott, for which (as I see with amazement from the book-lists) the gentlemen of England are willing to pay fancy prices; but its predecessor, a bulky historical romance without a spark of merit, and now deleted from the world.

ideal. Although I had attempted the thing with rigour not less than ten or twelve times, I had not yet written a novel. All – all my pretty ones – had gone for a little, and then stopped inexorably, like a schoolboy's watch. I might be compared to a cricketer of many years' standing who should never have made a run. Anybody can write a short story – a bad one, I mean – who has industry and paper and time enough; but not everyone may hope to write even a bad novel. It is the length that kills. The accepted novelist may take his novel up and put it down, spend days upon it in vain, and write not any more than he makes haste to blot. Not so the beginner. Human nature has certain rights; instinct – the instinct of self-preservation – forbids that any man (cheered and supported by the consciousness of no previous victory) should endure the miseries of unsuccessful literary toil beyond a period to be measured in weeks. There must be something for hope to feed upon. The beginner must have a slant of wind, a lucky vein must be running, he must be in one of those hours when the words come and the phrases balance of themselves – *even to begin*. And having begun, what a dread looking forward is that until the book shall be accomplished! For so long a time the slant is to continue unchanged, the vein to keep running; for so long a time you must hold at command the same quality of style; for so long a time your puppets are to be always vital, always consistent, always vigorous. I remember I used to look, in those days, upon every three-volume novel with a sort of veneration, as a feat – not possibly of literature – but at least of physical and moral endurance and the courage of Ajax.

In the fated year I came to live with my father and mother at Kinnaird, above Pitlochry. There I walked on the red moors and by the side of the golden burn. The rude, pure air of our mountains inspirited, if it did not inspire us; and my wife and I projected a joint volume of bogie stories, for which she wrote *The Shadow on the Bed*, and I turned out *Thrawn Janet*, and a first draft of the *Merry Men*. I love my native air, but it does not love me; and the end of this delightful period was a cold, a fly blister, and a migration, by Strathairdle and Glenshee, to the Castleton of Braemar. There it blew a good deal and rained in a proportion. My native air was more unkind than man's ingratitude; and I must consent to pass a good deal of my time between four walls in a house lugubriously known as 'the late Miss M'Gregor's cottage.' And now admire the finger of predestination. There was a schoolboy in the late Miss M'Gregor's cottage, home for the holidays, and much in want of 'something craggy to break his mind upon.' He had no thought of literature; it was the art of Raphael that received his fleeting suffrages, and with the aid of pen and ink and a shilling box of water-colours, he had soon turned one of the rooms into a picture-gallery. My more immediate duty towards the gallery was to be showman; but I would sometimes unbend a little, join the artist (so to speak) at the easel, and pass the afternoon with him in a generous emulation, making coloured drawings. On one of these occasions I made the map of an island; it was elaborately and (I thought) beautifully coloured; the shape of it took my fancy beyond expression; it contained harbours that pleased me like sonnets; and with the unconsciousness of the predestined, I ticketed my performance *Treasure Island*. I am told there are people who do not care for maps, and find it hard to believe. The names, the shapes of the woodlands, the courses of the roads and rivers, the prehistoric footsteps of man still distinctly traceable up hill and down dale, the mills and the ruins, the ponds and the ferries, perhaps the *Standing Stone* or the *Druidic Circle* on the heath; here is an inexhaustible fund of interest for any man with eyes to see, or tuppenceworth of imagination to understand with. No child but must remember laying his head in the grass, staring into the infinitesimal forest, and seeing it grow populous with fairy armies. Somewhat in this way, as I pored upon my map of *Treasure Island*, the future characters of the book began to appear there visibly among imaginary woods; and their brown faces and bright weapons peeped out upon me from unexpected quarters, as they passed to and fro, fighting and hunting treasure, on these few square inches of a flat projection. The next thing I knew, I had some paper before me and was writing out a list of chapters. How often have I done so, and the thing gone no farther! But there seemed elements of success about this enterprise. It was to be a story for boys; no need of psychology or fine writing; and I had a boy at hand to be a touchstone. Women were excluded. I was unable to handle a brig (which the *Hispaniola* should have been), but I thought I could make shift to sail her as a schooner without public shame. And then I had an idea for John Silver from which I promised myself funds of entertainment: to take an admired friend of mine (whom the reader very likely knows and admires as much as I do), to deprive him of all his finer qualities and higher graces of temperament, to leave him with nothing but his strength, his courage, his quickness, and his magnificent geniality, and to try to express these in terms of the culture of a raw tarpaulin. Such psychical surgery is, I think, a common way of 'making character'; perhaps it is, indeed, the only way. We can put in the quaint figure that spoke a hundred words with us yesterday by the wayside; but do we know him? Our friend, with his infinite variety and flexibility, we know – but can we put him in? Upon the first we must engraft secondary and imaginary qualities, possibly all wrong; from the second, knife in hand, we must cut away and deduct the needless arborescence of his nature; but the trunk and the few branches that remain we may at least be fairly sure of.

On a chill September morning, by the cheek of a brisk fire, and the rain drumming on the window, I began *The Sea Cook*, for that was the original title. I have begun (and finished) a number of other books, but I cannot remember to have sat down to one of them with more complacency. It is not to be wondered at, for stolen waters are proverbially sweet. I am now upon a painful chapter. No doubt the parrot once belonged to Robinson Crusoe. No doubt the skeleton is conveyed from Poe. I think little of these, they are trifles and details: and no man can hope to have a monopoly of skeletons or make a corner in talking birds. The stockade, I am told, is from *Masterman Ready*. It may be, I care not a jot. These useful writers had fulfilled the poet's saying: departing, they had left behind them

> Footprints on the sands of time;
> Footprints that perhaps another –

and I was the other! It is my debt to Washington Irving that exercises my conscience, and justly so, for I believe plagiarism was rarely carried farther. I chanced to pick up the *Tales of a Traveller* some years ago, with a view to an anthology of prose narrative, and the book flew up and struck me; Billy Bones, his chest, the company in the parlour, the whole inner spirit and a good deal of the material detail of my first chapters – all were there, all were the property of Washington Irving. But I had no guess of it then as I sat writing by the fireside, in what seemed the springtide of a somewhat pedestrian inspiration; nor yet day by day, after lunch, as I read aloud my morning's work to the family. It seemed to me original as sin; it seemed to belong to me like my right eye. I had counted on one boy; I found I had two in my audience. My father caught fire at once with all the romance and childishness of his original nature. His own stories, that every night of his life he put himself to sleep with, dealt perpetually with ships, roadside inns, robbers, old sailors, and commercial travellers before the era of steam. He never finished one of these romances: the lucky man did not require to! But in *Treasure Island* he recognised something kindred to his own imagination; it was *his* kind of picturesque; and he not only heard with delight the daily chapter, but set himself actively to collaborate. When the time came for Billy Bones's chest to be ransacked, he must have passed the better part of a day preparing, on the back of a legal envelope, an inventory of its contents, which I exactly followed; and the name of 'Flint's old ship,' the *Walrus*, was given at his particular request. And now, who should come dropping in, *ex machina*, but Doctor Japp, like the disguised prince who is to bring down the curtain upon peace and happiness in the last act, for he carried in his pocket, not a horn or a talisman, but a publisher; had, in fact, been charged by my old friend, Mr Henderson, to unearth new writers for *Young Folks*. Even the ruthlessness of a united family recoiled before the extreme measure of inflicting on our guest the mutilated members of *The Sea Cook*; at the same time we would by no means stop our readings, and accordingly the tale was begun again at the beginning, and solemnly redelivered for the benefit of Doctor Japp. From that moment on I have thought highly of his critical faculty; for when he left us, he carried away the manuscript in his portmanteau.

Here, then, was everything to keep me up – sympathy, help, and now a positive engagement. I had chosen besides a very easy style. Compare it with the almost contemporary *Merry Men*; one would prefer the one style, one the other – 'tis an affair of character, perhaps of mood; but no expert can fail to see that the one is much more difficult, and the other much easier, to maintain. It seems as though a full-grown, experienced man of letters might engage to turn out *Treasure Island* at so many pages a day, and keep his pipe alight. But alas! this was not my case. Fifteen days I stuck to it, and turned out fifteen chapters; and then, in the early paragraphs of the sixteenth, ignominiously lost hold. My mouth was empty; there was not one word more of *Treasure Island* in my bosom; and here were the proofs of the beginning already waiting me at the *Hand and Spear*! There I corrected them, living for the most part alone, walking on the heath at Weybridge on dewy autumn mornings, a good deal pleased with what I had done, and more appalled than I can depict to you in words at what remained for me to do. I was thirty-one; I was the head of a family; I had lost my health; I had never yet paid my way, had never yet made two hundred pounds a year; my father had quite recently bought back and cancelled a book that was judged a failure; was this to be another and last fiasco? I was indeed very close on despair; but I shut my mouth hard, and during the journey to Davos, where I was to pass the winter, had the resolution to think of other things, and bury myself in the novels of M. du Boisgobey. Arrived at my destination, down I sat one morning to the unfinished tale, and behold! it flowed from me like small talk; and in a second tide of delighted industry, and again at the rate of a chapter a day, I finished *Treasure Island*. It had to be transacted almost secretly. My wife was ill, the school-boy remained alone of the faithful, and John Addington Symonds (to whom I timidly mentioned what I was engaged on) looked on me askance. He was at that time very eager I should write on the *Characters* of Theophrastus, so far out may be judgements of the wisest men. But Symonds (to be sure) was scarce the confidant to go to for sympathy in a boy's story. He was large-minded; 'a full man,' if there ever was one; but the very name of my enterprise would suggest to him only capitulations of sincerity and sole-cisms of style. Well, he was not far wrong.

Treasure Island – it was Mr Henderson who deleted the first title, *The Sea Cook* – appeared duly in the story paper, where it figured in the ignoble midst without woodcuts and attracted not the least attention. I did not care. I liked the tale myself, for much the same reason as my father liked the beginning: it was my kind of picturesque. I was not a little proud of John Silver also, and to this day rather admire that smooth and formidable adventurer. What was infinitely more exhilarating, I had passed a landmark; I had finished a tale, and written 'The End' upon my manuscript, as I had not done since the *Pentland Rising*, when I was a boy of sixteen, not yet at college. In truth it was so by a set of lucky accidents: had not Doctor Japp come on his visit, had not the tale flowed from me with singular ease, it must have been laid aside like its predecessors, and found a circuitous and unlamented way to the fire. Purists may suggest it would have been better so. I am not of that mind. The tale seems to have given much pleasure, and it brought (or was the means of bringing) fire and food and wine to a deserving family in which I took an interest. I need scarce say I mean my own.

But the adventures of *Treasure Island* are not yet quite at an end. I had written it up to the map. The map was the chief part of my plot. For instance, I had called an islet *Skeleton Island*, not knowing what I meant, seeking only for the immediate picturesque; and it was to justify this name that I broke into the gallery of Mr Poe and stole Flint's pointer. And in the same way, it was because I had made two harbours that the *Hispaniola* was sent on her wanderings with Israel Hands. The time came when it was decided to republish, and I sent in my manuscript and the map along with it to Messrs Cassell. The proofs came, they were corrected, but I heard nothing of the map. I wrote and asked; was told it had never been received, and sat aghast. It is one thing to draw a map at random, set a scale in one corner of it at a venture, and write up a story to the measurements. It is quite another to have to examine a whole book, make an inventory of all the allusions contained in it, and with a pair of compasses painfully design a map to suit the data. I did it, and the map was drawn again in my father's office, with embellishments of blowing whales and sailing ships; and my father himself brought into service a knack he had of various writing, and elaborately *forged* the signature of Captain Flint and the sailing directions of Billy Bones. But somehow it was never *Treasure Island* to me.

I have said it was the most of the plot. I might almost say it was the whole. A few reminiscences of Poe, Defoe, and Washington Irving, a copy of Johnson's *Buccaneers*, the name of the Dead Man's Chest from Kingsley's *At Last*, some recollections of canoeing on the high seas, a cruise in a fifteen-ton schooner yacht, and the map itself with its infinite, eloquent suggestion, made up the whole of my materials. It is perhaps not often that a map figures so largely in a tale; yet it is always important. The author must know his countryside whether real or imaginary, like his hand; the distances, the points of the compass, the place of the sun's rising, the behaviour of the moon, should all be beyond cavil. And how troublesome the moon is! I have come to grief over the moon in *Prince Otto*; and, so soon as that was pointed out to me, adopted a precaution which I recommend to other men – I never write now without an almanac. With an almanac, and the map of the country and the plan of every house, either actually plotted on paper or clearly and immediately apprehended in the mind, a man may hope to avoid some of the grossest possible blunders. With the map before him, he will scarce allow the sun to set in the east, as it does in the *Antiquary*. With the almanac at hand, he will scarce allow two horsemen, journeying on the most urgent affair, to employ six days, from three of the Monday morning till late in the Saturday night, upon a journey of, say, ninety or a hundred miles; and before the week is out, and still on the same nags, to cover fifty in one day, as he may read at length in the inimitable novel of *Rob Roy*. And it is certainly well, though far from necessary, to avoid such *croppers*. But it is my contention – my superstition, if you like – that he who is faithful to his map, and consults it, and draws from it his inspiration, daily and hourly, gains positive support, and not mere negative immunity from accident. The tale has a root there: it grows in that soil; it has a spine of its own behind the words. Better if the country be real, and he has walked every foot of it and knows every milestone. But, even with imaginary places, he will do well in the beginning to provide a map. As he studies it, relations will appear that he had not thought upon. He will discover obvious though unsuspected short cuts and footpaths for his messengers; and even when a map is not all the plot, as it was in *Treasure Island*, it will be found to be a mine of suggestion.

THE GENESIS OF
'THE MASTER OF BALLANTRAE'

I was walking one night in the verandah of a small house in which I lived, outside the hamlet of Saranac. It was winter; the night was very dark; the air extraordinary clear and cold, and sweet with the purity of forests. From a good way below, the river was to be heard contending with ice and boulders: a few lights appeared, scattered unevenly among the darkness, but so far away as not to lessen the sense of isolation. For the making of a story here were fine conditions. I was besides moved with the spirit of emulation, for I had just finished my third or fourth perusal of *The Phantom Ship*. 'Come,' said I to my engine, 'let us make a tale, a story of many years and countries, of the sea and the land, savagery and civilisation; a story that shall have the same large features, and may be treated in the same summary elliptic method as the book you have been reading and admiring.' I was here brought up with a reflection exceedingly just in itself, but which, as the sequel shows, I failed to profit by. I saw that Marryat, not less than Homer, Milton and Virgil, profited by the choice of a familiar and legendary subject; so that he prepared his readers on the very title-page; and this set me cudgelling my brains, if by any chance I could hit upon some similar belief to be the centre-piece of my own meditated fiction. In the course of this vain search there cropped up in my memory a singular case of a buried and resuscitated fakir, which I had been often told by an uncle of mine, then lately dead, Inspector-General John Balfour.

On such a fine frosty night, with no wind and the thermometer below zero, the brain works with much vivacity; and the next moment I had seen the circumstance transplanted from India and the tropics to the Adirondack wilderness and the stringent cold of the Canadian border. Here then, almost before I had begun my story, I had two countries, two of the ends of the earth involved: and thus though the notion of the resuscitated man failed entirely on the score of general acceptation, or even (as I have since found) acceptability, it fitted at once with my design of a tale of many lands; and this decided me to consider further of its possibilities. The man who should thus be buried was the first question: a good man, whose return to life would be hailed by the reader and the other characters with gladness? This trenched upon the Christian picture, and was dismissed. If the idea, then, was to be of any use at all for me, I had to create a kind of evil genius to his friends and family, take him through many disappearances, and make this final restoration from the pit of death, in the icy American wilderness, the last and the grimmest of the series. I need not tell my brothers of the craft that I was now in the most interesting moment of an author's life; the hours that followed that night upon the balcony, and the following nights and days, whether walking abroad or lying wakeful in my bed, were hours of unadulterated joy. My mother, who was then living with me alone, perhaps had less enjoyment; for, in the absence of my wife, who is my usual helper in these times of parturition, I must spur her up at all seasons to hear me relate and try to clarify my unformed fancies.

And while I was groping for the fable and the character required, behold I found them lying ready and nine years old in my memory. Pease porridge hot, pease porridge cold, pease porridge in the pot, nine years old. Was there ever a more complete justification of the rule of Horace? Here, thinking of quite other things, I had stumbled on the solution, or perhaps I should rather say (in stagewright phrase) the Curtain or final Tableau of a story conceived long before on the moors between Pitlochry and Strathardle, conceived in Highland rain, in the blend of the smell of heather and bog-plants, and with a mind full of the Athole correspondence and the memories of the dumlicide Justice. So long ago, so far away it was, that I had first evoked the faces and the mutual tragic situation of the men of Durrisdeer.

My story was now world-wide enough: Scotland, India, and America being all obligatory scenes. But of these India was strange to me except in books; I had never known any living Indian save a Parsee, a member of my club in London, equally civilised, and (to all seeing) equally occidental with myself. It was plain, thus far, that I should have to get into India and out of it again upon a foot of fairy lightness; and I believe this first suggested to me the idea of the Chevalier Burke for a narrator. It was at first intended that he should be Scottish, and I was then filled with fears that he might prove only the degraded shadow of my own Alan Breck. Presently, however, it began to occur to me it would be like my Master to curry favour with the Prince's Irishmen; and then an Irish refugee would have a particular reason to find himself in India with his countryman, the unfortunate Lally. Irish, therefore, I decided he should be, and then, all of a sudden, I was aware of a tall shadow across my path, the shadow of Barry Lyndon. No man (in Lord Foppington's phrase) of a nice morality could go very deep with my Master: in the original idea of this story conceived in Scotland, this companion had been besides intended to be worse than the bad elder son with whom (as it was then meant) he was to visit Scotland; if I took an Irishman, and a very bad Irishman, in the midst of the eighteenth century, how was I to evade Barry Lyndon? The wretch besieged me, offering his services; he gave me excellent references; he proved that he was highly fitted for the work I had to do; he, or my own evil heart, suggested it was easy to disguise his ancient livery with a little lace and a few frogs and buttons, so that Thackeray himself should hardly recognise him. And then of a sudden there came to me memories of a young Irishman, with whom I was once intimate, and had spent long nights walking and talking with, upon a very desolate coast in a bleak autumn: I recalled him as a youth of an extraordinary moral simplicity – almost vacancy; plastic to any influence, the creature of his admirations: and putting such a youth in fancy into the career of a soldier of fortune, it occurred to me that he would serve my turn as well as Mr Lyndon, and in place of entering into competition with the Master, would afford a slight though a distinct relief. I know not if I have done him well, though his moral dissertations always highly entertained me: but I own I have been surprised to find that he reminded some critics of Barry Lyndon after all . . .

POEMS

Bed in Summer

In winter I get up at night
And dress by yellow candle-light.
In summer, quite the other way,
I have to go to bed by day.

I have to go to bed and see
The birds still hopping on the tree,
Or hear the grown-up people's feet
Still going past me in the street.

And does it not seem hard to you,
When all the sky is clear and blue,
And I should like so much to play,
To have to go to bed by day?

The Land of Counterpane

When I was sick and lay a-bed,
I had two pillows at my head,
And all my toys beside me lay
To keep me happy all the day.

And sometimes for an hour or so
I watched my leaden soldiers go,
With different uniforms and drills,
Among the bed-clothes, through the hills;

And sometimes sent my ships in fleets
All up and down among the sheets;
Or brought my trees and houses out,
And planted cities all about.

I was the giant great and still
That sits upon the pillow-hill,
And sees before him, dale and plain,
The pleasant land of counterpane.

The Land of Nod

From breakfast on through all the day
At home among my friends I stay,
But every night I go abroad
Afar into the land of Nod.

All by myself I have to go,
With none to tell me what to do –
All alone beside the streams
And up the mountain-sides of dreams.

The strangest things are there for me,
Both things to eat and things to see,
And many frightening sights abroad
Till morning in the land of Nod.

Try as I like to find the way,
I never can get back by day,
Nor can remember plain and clear
The curious music that I hear.

My Shadow

I have a little shadow that goes in and out with me,
And what can be the use of him is more than I can see.
He is very, very like me from the heels up to the head;
And I see him jump before me, when I jump into my bed.

The funniest thing about him is the way he likes to grow —
Not at all like proper children, which is always very slow;
For he sometimes shoots up taller like an india-rubber ball,
And he sometimes gets so little that there 's none of him at all.

He has n't got a notion of how children ought to play,
And can only make a fool of me in every sort of way.
He stays so close beside me, he 's a coward you can see;
I 'd think shame to stick to nursie as that shadow sticks to me!

One morning, very early, before the sun was up,
I rose and found the shining dew on every buttercup;
But my lazy little shadow, like an arrant sleepy-head,
Had stayed at home behind me and was fast asleep in bed.

System

Every night my prayers I say,
And get my dinner every day;
And every day that I 've been good,
I get an orange after food.

The child that is not clean and neat,
With lots of toys and things to eat,
He is a naughty child, I 'm sure —
Or else his dear papa is poor.

The Lamplighter

My tea is nearly ready and the sun has left the sky;
It's time to take the window to see Leerie going by;
For every night at teatime and before you take your seat,
With lantern and with ladder he comes posting up the street.

Now Tom would be a driver and Maria go to sea,
And my papa's a banker and as rich as he can be;
But I, when I am stronger and can choose what I'm to do,
O Leerie, I'll go round at night and light the lamps with you!

For we are very lucky, with a lamp before the door,
And Leerie stops to light it as he lights so many more;
And O! before you hurry by with ladder and with light,
O Leerie, see a little child and nod to him to-night!

From a Railway Carriage

Faster than fairies, faster than witches,
Bridges and houses, hedges and ditches;
And charging along like troops in a battle,
All through the meadows the horses and cattle:
All of the sights of the hill and the plain
Fly as thick as driving rain;
And ever again, in the wink of an eye,
Painted stations whistle by.

Here is a child who clambers and scrambles,
All by himself and gathering brambles;
Here is a tramp who stands and gazes;
And there is the green for stringing the daisies!
Here is a cart run away in the road
Lumping along with man and load;
And here is a mill and there is a river:
Each a glimpse and gone for ever!

The Unseen Playmate

When children are playing alone on the green
In comes the playmate that never was seen.
When children are happy and lonely and good,
The Friend of the Children comes out of the wood.

Nobody heard him and nobody saw,
His is a picture you never could draw,
But he 's sure to be present, abroad or at home,
When children are happy and playing alone.

He lies in the laurels, he runs on the grass,
He sings when you tinkle the musical glass;
Whene'er you are happy and cannot tell why,
The Friend of the Children is sure to be by!

He loves to be little, he hates to be big,
'Tis he that inhabits the caves that you dig;
'Tis he when you play with your soldiers of tin
That sides with the Frenchmen and never can win.

'Tis he, when at night you go off to your bed,
Bids you go to your sleep and not trouble your head;
For wherever they 're lying, in cupboard or shelf,
'Tis he will take care of your playthings himself!

To *any reader*

As from the house your mother sees
You playing round the garden trees,
So you may see, if you will look
Through the windows of this book,
Another child, far, far away,
And in another garden, play.
But do not think you can at all,
By knocking on the window, call
That child to hear you. He intent
Is all on his play-business bent.
He does not hear; he will not look,
Nor yet be lured out of this book.
For, long ago, the truth to say,
He has grown up and gone away,
And it is but a child of air
That lingers in the garden there.

To Mrs Will H. Low

Even in the bluest noonday of July,
There could not run the smallest breath of wind
But all the quarter sounded like a wood;
And in the chequered silence and above
The hum of city cabs that sought the Bois,
Suburban ashes shivered into song.
A patter and a chatter and a chirp
And a long dying hiss – it was as though
Starched old brocaded dames through all the house
Had trailed a strident skirt, or the whole sky
Even in a wink had over-brimmed in rain.
Hark, in these shady parlours, how it talks
Of the near autumn, how the smitten ash
Trembles and augurs floods! O not too long
In these inconstant latitudes delay,
O not too late from the unbeloved north
Trim your escape! For soon shall this low roof
Resound indeed with rain, soon shall your eyes
Search the foul garden, search the darkened rooms,
Nor find one jewel but the blazing log.

12 RUE VERNIER, PARIS.

Henry James

Who comes to-night? We ope the doors in vain.
Who comes? My bursting walls, can you contain
The presences that now together throng
Your narrow entry, as with flowers and song,
As with the air of life, the breath of talk?
Lo, how these fair immaculate women walk
Behind their jocund maker; and we see
Slighted *De Mauves*, and that far different she,
Gressie, the trivial sphynx; and to our feast
Daisy and *Barb* and *Chancellor* (she not least!)
With all their silken, all their airy kin,
Do like unbidden angels enter in.
But he, attended by these shining names,
Comes (best of all) himself – our welcome James.

The Mirror Speaks

Where the bells peal far at sea
Cunning fingers fashioned me.
There on palace walls I hung
While that Consuelo sung;
But I heard, though I listened well,
Never a note, never a trill,
Never a beat of the chiming bell.
There I hung and looked, and there
In my grey face, faces fair
Shone from under shining hair.
Well I saw the poising head,
But the lips moved and nothing said;
And when lights were in the hall,
Silent moved the dancers all.

So awhile I glowed, and then
Fell on dusty days and men;
Long I slumbered packed in straw,
Long I none but dealers saw;
Till before my silent eye
One that sees came passing by.
Now with an outlandish grace,
To the sparkling fire I face
In the blue room at Skerryvore;
Where I wait until the door
Open, and the Prince of Men,
Henry James, shall come again.

Requiem

Under the wide and starry sky,
   Dig the grave and let me lie.
Glad did I live and gladly die,
   And I laid me down with a will.

This be the verse you grave for me:
Here he lies where he longed to be;
Home is the sailor, home from sea,
   And the hunter home from the hill.

The Celestial Surgeon

If I have faltered more or less
In my great task of happiness;
If I have moved among my race
And shown no glorious morning face;
If beams from happy human eyes
Have moved me not; if morning skies,
Books, and my food, and summer rain
Knocked on my sullen heart in vain: —
Lord, thy most pointed pleasure take
And stab my spirit broad awake;
Or, Lord, if too obdurate I,
Choose thou, before that spirit die,
A piercing pain, a killing sin,
And to my dead heart run them in!

To *my father*

Peace and her huge invasion to these shores
Puts daily home; innumerable sails
Dawn on the far horizon and draw near;
Innumerable loves, uncounted hopes
To our wild coasts, not darkling now, approach:
Not now obscure, since thou and thine are there,
And bright on the lone isle, the foundered reef,
The long, resounding foreland, Pharos stands.

These are thy works, O father, these thy crown;
Whether on high the air be pure, they shine
Along the yellowing sunset, and all night
Among the unnumbered stars of God they shine;
Or whether fogs arise and far and wide
The low sea-level drown — each finds a tongue
And all night long the tolling bell resounds:
So shine, so toll, till night be overpast,
Till the stars vanish, till the sun return,
And in the haven rides the fleet secure.

In the first hour, the seaman in his skiff
Moves through the unmoving bay, to where the town
Its earliest smoke into the air upbreathes
And the rough hazels climb along the beach.
To the tugg'd oar the distant echo speaks.
The ship lies resting, where by reef and roost
Thou and thy lights have led her like a child.

This hast thou done, and I — can I be base?
I must arise, O father, and to port
Some lost, complaining seaman pilot home.

The Maker to Posterity

Far 'yont amang the years to be
When a' we think, an' a' we see,
An' a' we luve, 's been dung ajee
        By time's rouch shouther,
An' what was richt and wrang for me
        Lies mangled throu'ther,

It 's possible – it' s hardly mair –
That some ane, ripin' after lear –
Some auld professor or young heir,
        If still there' s either –
May find an' read me, an' be sair
        Perplexed, puir brither!

'What tongue does your auld bookie speak?'
He' ll spier; an' I, his mou to steik:
'No bein' fit to write in Greek,
        I wrote in Lallan,
Dear to my heart as the peat reek,
        Auld as Tantallon.

'Few spak it then, an' noo there' s nane.
My puir auld sangs lie a' their lane,
Their sense, that aince was braw an' plain,
        Tint a'thegether,
Like runes upon a standin' stane
        Amang the heather.

'But think not you the brae to speel;
You, tae, maun chow the bitter peel;
For a' your lear, for a' your skeel,
        Ye' re nane sae lucky;
An' things are mebbe waur than weel
        For you, my buckie.

'The hale concern (baith hens an' eggs,
Baith books an' writers, stars an' clegs)
Noo stachers upon lowsent legs,
        An' wears awa';
The tack o' mankind, near the dregs,
        Rins unco law.

'Your book, that in some braw new tongue,
Ye wrote or prentit, preached or sung,
Will still be just a bairn, an' young
 In fame an' years,
Whan the hale planet's guts are dung
 About your ears;

'An' you, sair gruppin' to a spar
Or whammled wi' some bleezin' star,
Cryin' to ken whaur deil ye are,
 Hame, France, or Flanders –
Whang sindry like a railway car
 An' flie in danders.'

Ille Terrarum

Frae nirly, nippin', Eas'lan' breeze,
Frae Norlan' snaw, an' haar o' seas,
Weel happit in your gairden trees,
          A bonny bit,
Atween the muckle Pentland's knees,
          Secure ye sit.

Beeches an' aiks entwine their theek,
An' firs, a stench, auld-farrant clique.
A' simmer day, your chimleys reek,
          Couthy and bien;
An' here an' there your windies keek
          Amang the green.

A pickle plats an' paths an' posies,
A wheen auld gillyflowers an' roses:
A ring o' wa's the hale encloses
          Frae sheep or men;
An' there the auld housie beeks an' doses,
          A' by her lane.

The gairdner crooks his weary back
A' day in the pitaty-track,
Or mebbe stops awhile to crack
          Wi' Jane the cook,
Or at some buss, worm-eaten black,
          To gie a look.

Frae the high hills the curlew ca's;
The sheep gang baaing by the wa's;
Or whiles a clan o' roosty craws.
          Cangle thegether;
The wild bees seek the gairden raws,
          Weariet wi' heather.

Or in the gloamin' douce an' grey
The sweet-throat mavis tunes her lay;
The herd comes linkin' doun the brae;
          An' by degrees
The muckle siller müne maks way
          Amang the trees.

Here aft hae I, wi' sober heart,
For meditation sat apairt,
When orra loves or kittle art
      Perplexed my mind;
Here socht a balm for ilka smart
      O' humankind.

Here aft, weel neukit by my lane,
Wi' Horace, or perhaps Montaigne,
The mornin' hours hae come an' gane
      Abüne my heid –
I wadnae gi'en a chucky-stane
      For a' I 'd read.

But noo the auld city, street by street,
An' winter fu' o' snaw an' sleet,
Awhile shut in my gangrel feet
      An' goavin' mettle;
Noo is the soopit ingle sweet,
      An' liltin' kettle.

An' noo the winter winds complain;
Cauld lies the glaur in ilka lane;
On draigled hizzie, tautit wean
      An' drucken lads,
In the mirk nicht, the winter rain
      Dribbles an' blads.

Whan bugles frae the Castle rock,
An' beaten drums wi' dowie shock,
Wauken, at cauld-rife sax o'clock,
      My chitterin' frame,
I mind me on the kintry cock,
      The kintry hame.

I mind me on yon bonny bield;
An' Fancy traivels far afield
To gaither a' that gairdens yield
      O' sun an Simmer:
To hearten up a dowie chield,
      Fancy 's the limmer!

'When aince Aprile has fairly come . . . '

When aince Aprile has fairly come,
An' birds may bigg in winter's lum,
An' pleisure's spreid for a' and some
      O' whatna state,
Love, wi' her auld recruitin' drum,
      Than taks the gate.

The heart plays dunt wi' main an' micht;
The lasses' een are a' sae bricht,
Their dresses are sae braw an' ticht,
      The bonny birdies! –
Puir winter virtue at the sicht
      Gangs heels ower hurdies.

An' aye as love frae land to land
Tirls the drum wi' eident hand,
A' men collect at her command,
      Toun-bred or land'art,
An' follow in a denty band
      Her gaucy standart.

An' I, wha sang o' rain an' snaw,
An' weary winter weel awa',
Noo busk me in a jacket braw,
      An' tak my place
I' the ram-stam, harum-scarum raw,
      Wi' smilin' face.

from
SONGS OF TRAVEL

The Vagabond

(To an air of Schubert)

Give to me the life I love,
  Let the lave go by me,
Give the jolly heaven above
  And the byway nigh me.
Bed in the bush with stars to see,
  Bread I dip in the river –
There 's the life for a man like me,
  There 's the life for ever.

Let the blow fall soon or late,
  Let what will be o'er me;
Give the face of earth around,
  And the road before me.
Wealth I seek not, hope nor love,
  Nor a friend to know me;
All I seek the heaven above
  And the road below me.

Or let autumn fall on me
  Where afield I linger,
Silencing the bird on tree,
  Biting the blue finger:
White as meal the frosty field –
  Warm the fireside haven –
Not to autumn will I yield,
  Not to winter even!

Let the blow fall soon or late,
  Let what will be o'er me;

Give the face of earth around,
   And the road before me.
Wealth I ask not, hope nor love,
   Nor a friend to know me.
All I ask the heaven above,
   And the road below me.

'I will make you brooches . . .'

I will make you brooches and toys for your delight
Of bird-song at morning and star-shine at night.
I will make a palace fit for you and me
Of green days in forests and blue days at sea.

I will make my kitchen, and you shall keep your room,
Where white flows the river and bright blows the broom,
And you shall wash your linen and keep your body white
In rainfall at morning and dewfall at night.

And this shall be for music when no one else is near,
The fine song for singing, the rare song to hear!
That only I remember, that only you admire,
Of the broad road that stretches and the roadside fire.

Wandering Willie

Home no more home to me, whither must I wander?
　Hunger my driver, I go where I must.
Cold blows the winter wind over hill and heather;
　Thick drives the rain, and my roof is in the dust.
Loved of wise men was the shade of my roof-tree.
　The true word of welcome was spoken in the door –
Dear days of old, with the faces in the firelight,
　Kind folks of old, you come again no more.

Home was home then, my dear, full of kindly faces,
　Home was home then, my dear, happy for the child.
Fire and the windows bright glittered on the moorland;
　Song, tuneful song, built a palace in the wild.
Now, when day dawns on the brow of the moorland,
　Lone stands the house, and the chimney-stone is cold.
Lone let it stand, now the friends are all departed,
　The kind hearts, the true hearts, that loved the place of old.

Spring shall come, come again, calling up the moorfowl,
　Spring shall bring the sun and rain, bring the bees and flowers;
Red shall the heather bloom over hill and valley,
　Soft flow the stream through the even-flowing hours;

Fair the day shine as it shone on my childhood –
　Fair shine the day on the house with open door;
Birds come and cry there and twitter in the chimney –
　But I go forever and come again no more.

If this were faith

God, if this were enough,
That I see things bare to the buff
And up to the buttocks in mire;
That I ask nor hope nor hire,
Nut in the husk,
Nor dawn beyond the dusk,
Nor life beyond death:
God, if this were faith?

Having felt thy wind in my face
Spit sorrow and disgrace,
Having seen thine evil doom
In Golgotha and Khartoum,
And the brutes, the work of thine hands,
Fill with injustice lands
And stain with blood the sea:
If still in my veins the glee
Of the black night and the sun
And the lost battle, run:
If, an adept,
The iniquitous lists I still accept
With joy, and joy to endure and be withstood,
And still to battle and perish for a dream of good:
God, if that were enough?

If to feel, in the ink of the slough,
And the sink of the mire,
Veins of glory and fire
Run through and transpierce and transpire,
And a secret purpose of glory in every part,
And the answering glory of battle fill my heart;
To thrill with the joy of girded men
To go on for ever and fail and go on again,
And be mauled to the earth and arise,
And contend for the shade of a word and a thing not
        seen with the eyes:
With the half of a broken hope for a pillow at night
That somehow the right is the right
And the smooth shall bloom from the rough:
Lord, if that were enough?

My *wife*

Trusty, dusky, vivid, true,
With eyes of gold and bramble-dew,
    Steel-true and blade-straight,
The great artificer
    Made my mate.

Honour, anger, valour, fire;
A love that life could never tire,
    Death quench or evil stir,
The mighty master
    Gave to her.

Teacher, tender, comrade, wife,
A fellow-farer true through life,
    Heart-whole and soul-free
The august father
    Gave to me.

Winter

In rigorous hours, when down the iron lane
The redbreast looks in vain
    For hips and haws
Lo, shining flowers upon my window-pane
    The silver pencil of the winter draws.

When all the snowy hill
And the bare woods are still;
When snipes are silent in the frozen bogs,
    And all the garden garth is whelmed in mire,
Lo, by the hearth, the laughter of the logs –
    More fair than roses, lo, the flowers of fire!

SARANAC LAKE.

'The Tropics vanish . . .'

The tropics vanish, and meseems that I,
From Halkerside, from topmost Allermuir,
Or steep Caerketton, dreaming gaze again.
Far set in fields and woods, the town I see
Spring gallant from the shallows of her smoke,
Cragged, spired, and turreted, her virgin fort
Beflagged. About, on seaward-drooping hills,
New folds of city glitter. Last, the Forth
Wheels ample waters set with sacred isles,
And populous Fife smokes with a score of towns.

There, on the sunny frontage of a hill,
Hard by the house of kings, repose the dead,
My dead, the ready and the strong of word.
Their works, the salt-encrusted, still survive;
The sea bombards their founded towers; the night
Thrills pierced with their strong lamps. The artificers,
One after one, here in this grated cell,
Where the rain erases and the rust consumes,
Fell upon lasting silence. Continents
And continental oceans intervene;

A sea uncharted, on a lampless isle,
Environs and confines their wandering child
In vain. The voice of generations dead
Summons me, sitting distant, to arise,
My numerous footsteps nimbly to retrace,
And all mutation over, stretch me down
In that denoted city of the dead.

APEMAMA.

To S. C.

I heard the pulse of the besieging sea
Throb far away all night. I heard the wind
Fly crying and convulse tumultuous palms.
I rose and strolled. The isle was all bright sand,
And flailing fans and shadows of the palm;
The heaven all moon and wind and the blind vault;
The keenest planet slain, for Venus slept.

    The king, my neighbour, with his host of wives,
Slept in the precinct of the palisade;
Where single, in the wind, under the moon,
Among the slumbering cabins, blazed a fire,
Sole street-lamp and the only sentinel.

    To other lands and nights my fancy turned –
To London first, and chiefly to your house,
The many-pillared and the well-beloved.
There yearning fancy lighted; there again
In the upper room I lay, and heard far off
The unsleeping city murmur like a shell;
The muffled tramp of the Museum guard
Once more went by me; I beheld again
Lamps vainly brighten the dispeopled street;
Again I longed for the returning morn,
The awaking traffic, the bestirring birds,
The consentaneous trill of tiny song
That weaves round monumental cornices
A passing charm of beauty. Most of all,
For your light foot I wearied, and your knock
That was the glad réveillé of my day.

    Lo, now, when to your task in the great house
At morning through the portico you pass,
One moment glance, where by the pillared wall
Far-voyaging island gods, begrimed with smoke,
Sit now unworshipped, the rude monument
Of faiths forgot and races undivined:
Sit now disconsolate, remembering well
The priest, the victim, and the songful crowd,
The blaze of the blue noon, and that huge voice

Incessant, of the breakers on the shore.
As far as these from their ancestral shrine,
So far, so foreign, your divided friends
Wander, estranged in body, not in mind.

APEMAMA.

An End of Travel

Let now your soul in this substantial world
Some anchor strike. Be here the body moored:
This spectacle immutably from now
The picture in your eye; and when time strikes,
And the green scene goes on the instant blind,
The ultimate helpers, where your horse to-day
Conveyed you dreaming, bear your body dead.

VAILIMA.

'We uncommiserate pass into the night . . .'

We uncommiserate pass into the night
From the loud banquet, and departing leave
A tremor in men's memories, faint and sweet
And frail as music. Features of our face,
The tones of the voice, the touch of the loved hand,
Perish and vanish, one by one, from earth:
Meanwhile, in the hall of song, the multitude
Applauds the new performer. One, perchance,
One ultimate survivor lingers on,
And smiles, and to his ancient heart recalls
The long forgotten. Ere the morrow die,
He too, returning, through the curtain comes,
And the new age forgets us and goes on.

The Last Sight

Once more I saw him. In the lofty room,
Where oft with lights and company his tongue
Was trump to honest laughter, sate attired
A something in his likeness. – 'Look!' said one,
Unkindly kind, 'look up, it is your boy!'
And the dread changeling gazed on me in vain.

'Sing me a song of a lad that is gone . . .'

Sing me a song of a lad that is gone,
　　Say, could that lad be I?
Merry of soul he sailed on a day
　　Over the sea to Skye.

Mull was astern, Rum on the port,
　　Egg on the starboard bow;
Glory of youth glowed in his soul:
　　Where is that glory now?

Sing me a song of a lad that is gone,
　　Say, could that lad be I?
Merry of soul he sailed on a day
　　Over the sea to Skye.

Give me again all that was there,
　　Give me the sun that shone!
Give me the eyes, give me the soul,
　　Give me the lad that 's gone!

Sing me a song of a lad that is gone,
　　Say, could that lad be I?
Merry of soul he sailed on a day
　　Over the sea to Skye.

Billow and breeze, islands and seas,
　　Mountains of rain and sun,
All that was good, all that was fair,
　　All that was me is gone.

To S. R. Crockett

(In Reply to a Dedication)

Blows the wind to-day, and the sun and the rain are flying,
    Blows the wind on the moors to-day and now,
Where about the graves of the martyrs the whaups are
       crying,
    My heart remembers how!

Grey recumbent tombs of the dead in desert places,
    Standing stones on the vacant wine-red moor,
Hills of sheep, and the homes of the silent vanished races,
    And winds, austere and pure:

Be it granted me to behold you again in dying,
    Hills of home! and to hear again the call;
Hear about the graves of the martyrs the peewees crying,
    And hear no more at all.

VAILIMA.

from
BALLADS

Ticonderoga

A LEGEND OF THE WEST HIGHLANDS

This is the tale of the man
    Who heard a word in the night
In the land of the heathery hills,
    In the days of the feud and the fight.
By the sides of the rainy sea,
    Where never a stranger came,
On the awful lips of the dead,
    He heard the outlandish name.
It sang in his sleeping ears,
    It hummed in his waking head:
The name – Ticonderoga,
    The utterance of the dead.

I. THE SAYING OF THE NAME

On the loch-sides of Appin,
    When the mist blew from the sea,
A Stewart stood with a Cameron:
    An angry man was he.
The blood beat in his ears,
    The blood ran hot to his head,
The mist blew from the sea,
    And there was the Cameron dead.
'Oh, what have I done to my friend,
    O, what have I done to mysel',
That he should be cold and dead,
    And I in the danger of all?
Nothing but danger about me,
    Danger behind and before,
Death at wait in the heather
    In Appin and Mamore,

Hate at all of the ferries
   And death at each of the fords,
Camerons priming gunlocks
   And Camerons sharpening swords.'

But this was a man of counsel,
   This was a man of a score,
There dwelt no pawkier Stewart
   In Appin or Mamore.
He looked on the blowing mist,
   He looked on the awful dead,
And there came a smile on his face
   And there slipped a thought in his head.

Out over cairn and moss,
   Out over scrog and scaur,
He ran as runs the clansman
   That bears the cross of war.
His heart beat in his body,
   His hair clove to his face,
When he came at last in the gloaming
   To the dead man's brother's place.
The east was white with the moon,
   The west with the sun was red,
And there, in the house-doorway,
   Stood the brother of the dead.

'I have slain a man to my danger,
   I have slain a man to my death.
I put my soul in your hands,'
   The panting Stewart saith.
'I lay it bare in your hands,
   For I know your hands are leal;
And be you my targe and bulwark
   From the bullet and the steel.'

Then up and spoke the Cameron,
   And gave him his hand again:
'There shall never a man in Scotland
   Set faith in me in vain;
And whatever man you have slaughtered,
   Of whatever name or line,
By my sword and yonder mountain,
   I make your quarrel mine.[1]
I bid you in to my fireside,
   I share with you house and hall;
It stands upon my honour
   To see you safe from all.'

It fell in the time of midnight,
  When the fox barked in the den
And the plaids were over the faces
  In all the houses of men,
That as the living Cameron
  Lay sleepless on his bed,
Out of the night and the other world,
  Came in to him the dead.

'My blood is on the heather,
  My bones are on the hill;
There is joy in the home of ravens
  That the young shall eat their fill.
My blood is poured in the dust,
  My soul is spilled in the air;
And the man that has undone me
  Sleeps in my brother's care.'
'I'm wae for your death, my brother,
  But if all of my house were dead,
I couldnae withdraw the plighted hand,
  Nor break the word once said.'

'O, what shall I say to our father,
  In the place to which I fare?
O, what shall I say to our mother,
  Who greets to see me there?
And to all the kindly Camerons
  That have lived and died long-syne –
Is this the word you send them,
  Fause-hearted brother mine?'

'It's neither fear nor duty,
  It's neither quick nor dead
Shall gar me withdraw the plighted hand,
  Or break the word once said.'
Thrice in the time of midnight,
  When the fox barked in the den,
And the plaids were over the faces
  In all the houses of men,
Thrice as the living Cameron
  Lay sleepless on his bed,
Out of the night and the other world
  Came in to him the dead,
And cried to him for vengeance
  On the man that laid him low;
And thrice the living Cameron
  Told the dead Cameron, no.

'Thrice have you see me, brother,
  But now shall see me no more,
Till you meet your angry fathers
  Upon the farther shore.
Thrice have I spoken, and now,
  Before the cock be heard,
I take my leave forever
  With the naming of a word.
It shall sing in your sleeping ears,
  It shall hum in your waking head,
The name – Ticonderoga,
  And the warning of the dead.'

Now when the night was over
  And the time of people's fears,
The Cameron walked abroad,
  And the word was in his ears.
'Many a name I know,
  But never a name like this;
O, where shall I find a skilly man
  Shall tell me what it is?'

With many a man he counselled
  Of high and low degree,
With the herdsmen on the mountains
  And the fishers of the sea.
And he came and went unweary,
  And read the books of yore,
And the runes that were written of old
  On the stones upon the moor.
And many a name he was told,
  But never the name of his fears –
Never, in east or west,
  The name that rang in his ears:
Names of men and of clans,
  Names for the grass and the tree,
For the smallest tarn in the mountains,
  The smallest reef in the sea:
Names for the high and low,
  The names of the craig and the flat;
But in all the land of Scotland,
  Never a name like that.

II. THE SEEKING OF THE NAME

And now there was speech in the south,
   And a man of the south that was wise,
A periwig'd lord of London,[2]
   Called on the clans to rise.
And the riders rode, and the summons
   Came to the western shore,
To the land of the sea and the heather,
   To Appin and Mamore.
It called on all to gather
   From every scrog and scaur,
That loved their father's tartan
   And the ancient game of war.
And down the watery valley
   And up the windy hill,
Once more, as in the olden,
   The pipes were sounding shrill;
Again in highland sunshine
   The naked steel was bright;
And the lads, once more in tartan,
   Went forth again to fight.

'O, why should I dwell here
   With a weird upon my life,
When the clansmen shout for battle
   And the war-swords clash in strife?
I cannae joy at feast,
   I cannae sleep in bed,
For the wonder of the word
   And the warning of the dead.
It sings in my sleeping ears,
   It hums in my waking head,
The name – Ticonderoga,
   The utterance of the dead.
Then up, and with the fighting men
   To march away from here,
Till the cry of the great war-pipe
   Shall drown it in my ear!'

Where flew King George's ensign
   The plaided soldiers went:
They drew the sword in Germany,
   In Flanders pitched the tent.
The bells of foreign cities
   Rang far across the plain:

They passed the happy Rhine,
  They drank the rapid Main.
Through Asiatic jungles
  The Tartans filed their way,
And the neighing of the war-pipes
  Struck terror in Cathay.[3]
'Many a name have I heard,' he thought,
  'In all the tongues of men,'
Full many a name both here and there,
  Full many both now and then.
When I was at home in my father's house
  In the land of the naked knee,
Between the eagles that fly in the lift
  And the herrings that swim in the sea,
And now that I am a captain-man
  With a braw cockade in my hat –
Many a name have I heard,' he thought,
  'But never a name like that.'

III. THE PLACE OF THE NAME

There fell a war in a woody place,
  Lay far across the sea,
A war of the march in the mirk midnight
  And the shot from behind the tree,
The shaven head and the painted face,
  The silent foot in the wood,
In a land of a strange, outlandish tongue
  That was hard to be understood.

It fell about the gloaming
  The general stood with his staff,
He stood and he looked east and west
  With little mind to laugh.
'Far have I been and much have I seen,
  And kent both gain and loss,
But here we have woods on every hand
  And a kittle water to cross.
Far have I been and much have I seen,
  But never the beat of this:
And there's one must go down to that waterside
  To see how deep it is.'

It fell in the dusk of the night
  When unco things betide,
The skilly captain, the Cameron,
  Went down to that waterside.

Canny and soft the captain went;
   And a man of the woody land,
With the shaven head and the painted face,
   Went down at his right hand.
It fell in the quiet night,
   There was never a sound to ken;
But all of the woods to the right and the left
   Lay filled with the painted men.

'Far have I been and much have I seen,
   Both as a man and boy,
But never have I set forth a foot
   On so perilous an employ.'

It fell in the dusk of the night
   When unco things betide,
That he was aware of a captain-man
   Drew near to the waterside.
He was aware of his coming
   Down in the gloaming alone;
And he looked in the face of the man
   And lo! the face was his own.

'This is my weird,' he said,
   'And now I ken the worst;
For many shall fall the morn,
   But I shall fall with the first.
O, you of the outland tongue,
   You of the painted face,
This is the place of my death;
   Can you tell me the name of the place?'

'Since the Frenchmen have been here
   They have called it Sault-Marie;
But that is a name for priests,
   And not for you and me.
It went by another word,'
   Quoth he of the shaven head:
'It was called Ticonderoga
   In the days of the great dead.'

And it fell on the morrow's morning,
   In the fiercest of the fight,
That the Cameron bit the dust
   As he foretold at night;
And far from the hills of heather,
   Far from the isles of the sea,
He sleeps in the place of the name
   As it was doomed to be.

NOTES TO TICONDEROGA

Introduction. I first heard this legend of my own country from that friend of men of letters, Mr Alfred Nutt, 'there in roaring London's central stream'; and since the ballad first saw the light of day in *Scribner's Magazine*, Mr Nutt and Lord Archibald Campbell have been in public controversy on the facts. Two clans, the Camerons and the Campbells, lay claim to this bracing story; and they do well: the man who preferred his plighted troth to the commands and menaces of the dead is an ancestor worth disputing. But the Campbells must rest content: they have the broad lands and the broad page of history; this appanage must be denied them; for between the name of *Cameron* and that of *Campbell*, the muse will never hesitate.

Note 1, verse 67. Mr Nutt reminds me it was 'by my sword and Ben Cruachan' the Cameron swore.
Note 2, verse 159. '*A periwig'd lord of London.*' The first Pitt.
Note 3, verse 204. '*Cathay.*' There must be some omission in General Stewart's charming 'History of the Highland Regiments', a book that might well be republished and continued; or it scarce appears how our friend could have got to China.

PRAYERS

WRITTEN AT VAILIMA

PRAYERS

For Success

Lord, behold our family here assembled. We thank Thee for this place in which we dwell; for the love that unites us; for the peace accorded us this day; for the hope with which we expect the morrow; for the health, the work, the food, and the bright skies, that make our lives delightful; for our friends in all parts of the earth, and our friendly helpers in this foreign isle. Let peace abound in our small company. Purge out of every heart the lurking grudge. Give us grace and strength to forbear and to persevere. Offenders, give us the grace to accept and to forgive offenders. Forgetful ourselves, help us to bear cheerfully the forgetfulness of others. Give us courage and gaiety and the quiet mind. Spare to us our friends, soften to us our enemies. Bless us, if it may be, in all our innocent endeavours. If it may not, give us the strength to encounter that which is to come, that we be brave in peril, constant in tribulation, temperate in wrath, and in all changes of fortune, and, down to the gates of death, loyal and loving one to another. As the clay to the potter, as the windmill to the wind, as children of their sire, we beseech of Thee this help and mercy for Christ's sake.

For Grace

Grant that we here before Thee may be set free from the fear of vicissitude and the fear of death, may finish what remains before us of our course without dishonour to ourselves or hurt to others, and, when the day comes, may die in peace. Deliver us from fear and favour: from mean hopes and cheap pleasures. Have mercy on each in his deficiency; let him be not cast down; support the stumbling on the way, and give at last rest to the weary.

At Morning

The day returns and brings us to the petty round of irritating concerns and duties. Help us to play the man, help us to perform them with laughter and kind faces, let cheerfulness abound with industry. Give us to go blithely on our business all this day, bring us to our resting beds weary and content and undishonoured, and grant us in the end the gift of sleep.

Evening

We come before Thee, O Lord, in the end of thy day with thanksgiving.

Our beloved in the far parts of the earth, those who are now beginning the labours of the day what time we end them, and those with whom the sun now stands at the point of noon, bless, help, console, and prosper them.

Our guard is relieved, the service of the day is over, and the hour come to rest. We resign into thy hands our sleeping bodies, our cold hearths, and open doors. Give us to awake with smiles, give us to labour smiling. As the sun returns in the east, so let our patience be renewed with dawn; as the sun lightens the world, so let our loving-kindness make bright this house of our habitation.

Another for Evening

Lord, receive our supplications for this house, family, and country. Protect the innocent, restrain the greedy and the treacherous, lead us out of our tribulation into a quiet land.

Look down upon ourselves and upon our absent dear ones. Help us and them; prolong our days in peace and honour. Give us health, food, bright weather, and light hearts. In what we meditate of evil, frustrate our will; in what of good, further our endeavours. Cause injuries to be forgot and benefits to be remembered.

Let us lie down without fear and awake and arise with exultation. For his sake, in whose words we now conclude.

In Time of Rain

We thank Thee, Lord, for the glory of the late days and the

excellent face of thy sun. We thank Thee for good news received. We thank Thee for the pleasures we have enjoyed and for those we have been able to confer. And now, when the clouds gather and the rain impends over the forest and our house, permit us not to be cast down; let us not lose the savour of past mercies and past pleasures; but, like the voice of a bird singing in the rain, let grateful memory survive in the hour of darkness. If there be in front of us any painful duty, strengthen us with the grace of courage; if any act of mercy, teach us tenderness and patience.

Another in Time of Rain

Lord, Thou sendest down rain upon the uncounted millions of the forest, and givest the trees to drink exceedingly. We are here upon this isle a few handfuls of men, and how many myriads upon myriads of stalwart trees! Teach us the lesson of the trees. The sea around us, which this rain recruits, teems with the race of fish; teach us, Lord, the meaning of the fishes. Let us see ourselves for what we are, one out of the countless number of the clans of thy handiwork. When we would despair, let us remember that these also please and serve Thee.

Before a Temporary Separation

To-day we go forth separate, some of us to pleasure, some of us to worship, some upon duty. Go with us, our guide and angel; hold Thou before us in our divided paths the mark of our low calling, still to be true to what small best we can attain to. Help us in that, our maker, the dispenser of events – Thou, of the vast designs, in which we blindly labour, suffer us to be so far constant to ourselves and our beloved.

For Friends

For our absent loved ones we implore thy loving-kindness. Keep them in life, keep them in growing honour; and for us, grant that we remain worthy of their love. For Christ's sake, let not our beloved blush for us, nor we for them. Grant us but that, and grant us courage to endure lesser ills unshaken, and to accept death, loss, and disappointment as it were straws upon the tide of life.

For the Family

Aid us, if it be thy will, in our concerns. Have mercy on this land and innocent people. Help them who this day contend in disappointment with their frailties. Bless our family, bless our forest house, bless our island helpers. Thou who hast made for us this place of ease and hope, accept and inflame our gratitude; help us to repay, in service one to another, the debt of thine unmerited benefits and mercies, so that, when the period of our stewardship draws to a conclusion, when the windows begin to be darkened, when the bond of the family is to be loosed, there shall be no bitterness of remorse in our farewells.

Help us to look back on the long way that Thou hast brought us, on the long days in which we have been served, not according to our deserts, but our desires; on the pit and the miry clay, the blackness of despair, the horror of misconduct, from which our feet have been plucked out. For our sins forgiven or prevented, for our shame unpublished, we bless and thank Thee, O God. Help us yet again and ever. So order events, so strengthen our frailty, as that day by day we shall come before Thee with this song of gratitude, and in the end we be dismissed with honour. In their weakness and their fear, the vessels of thy handiwork so pray to Thee, so praise Thee. Amen.

Sunday

We beseech Thee, Lord, to behold us with favour, folk of many families and nations gathered together in the peace of this roof, weak men and women subsisting under the covert of thy patience. Be patient still; suffer us yet awhile longer; — with our broken purposes of good, with our idle endeavours against evil, suffer us awhile longer to endure, and (if it may be) help us to do better. Bless to us our extraordinary mercies; if the day come when these must be taken, brace us to play the man under affliction. Be with our friends, be with ourselves. Go with each of us to rest; if any awake, temper to them the dark hours of watching; and when the day returns, return to us, our sun and comforter, and call us up with morning faces and with morning hearts – eager to labour – eager to be happy, if happiness shall be our portion – and if the day be marked for sorrow, strong to endure it.

We thank Thee and praise Thee; and in the words of him to whom this day is sacred, close our oblation.

For Self-blame

Lord, enlighten us to see the beam that is in our own eye, and blind us to the mote that is in our brother's. Let us feel our offences with our hands, make them great and bright before us like the sun, make us eat them and drink them for our diet. Blind us to the offences of our beloved, cleanse them from our memories, take them out of our mouths for ever. Let all here before Thee carry and measure with the false balances of love, and be in their own eyes and in all conjunctures the most guilty. Help us at the same time with the grace of courage, that we be none of us cast down when we sit lamenting amid the ruins of our happiness or our integrity; touch us with fire from the altar, that we may be up and doing to rebuild our city: in the name and by the method of him in whose words of prayer we now conclude.

For Self-forgetfulness

Lord, the creatures of thy hand, thy disinherited children, come before Thee with their incoherent wishes and regrets: Children we are, children we shall be, till our mother the earth hath fed upon our bones. Accept us, correct us, guide us, thy guilty innocents. Dry our vain tears, wipe out our vain resentments, help our yet vainer efforts. If there be any here, sulking as children will, deal with and enlighten him. Make it day about that person, so that he shall see himself and be ashamed. Make it heaven about him, Lord, by the only way to heaven, forgetfulness of self, and make it day about his neighbours, so that they shall help, not hinder him.

For Renewal of Joy

We are evil, O God, and help us to see it and amend. We are good, and help us to be better. Look down upon thy servants with a

patient eye, even as Thou sendest sun and rain; look down, call
upon the dry bones, quicken, enliven; recreate in us the soul of
service, the spirit of peace; renew in us the sense of joy.